PEACE TIME

PEACE TIME

Cease-Fire Agreements and the Durability of Peace

Virginia Page Fortna

PRINCETON UNIVERSITY PRESS

PRINCETON AND OXFORD

Copyright © 2004 by Princeton University Press
Published by Princeton University Press, 41 William Street, Princeton,
New Jersey 08540
In the United Kingdom: Princeton University Press, 3 Market Place,
Woodstock, Oxfordshire OX20 1SY

ISBN: 0-691-11511-7 (cl.)
ISBN: 0-691-11512-5 (paper)

British Library Cataloging-in-Publication Data is available

This book has been composed in Sabon and American Gothic

Printed on acid-free paper. ∞

pup.princeton.edu

Printed in the United States of America

10 9 8 7 6 5 4 3 2

ISBN-13: 978-0-691-11512-2 (pbk.)

To my parents, Robert and Evelyn Fortna

PEACE

CONTENTS

FIGURES AND MAPS

FIGURES

MAPS

TABLES

ACKNOWLEDGMENTS

I STARTED THIS PROJECT when the subject of wars between states seemed almost passé. Despite the Gulf War a few years earlier, much of the focus of the study of war and peace was turning to civil wars, which had become much more prevalent than interstate wars. Unfortunately, however, the issue of maintaining peace between sovereign states has not faded. As I write these acknowledgments the United States is attacking Iraq. Peace has failed again, as it has between so many deadly foes.

Working on this project over the years, and even before embarking on it, I incurred many debts of gratitude, to more people than I can mention here. Long before this book was conceived, my undergraduate mentor at Wesleyan, Martha Crenshaw, steered me from a vague interest in studying peace toward rigorous political science and graduate study in international relations. Bill Durch at the Henry L. Stimson Center encouraged me, not least by setting a fine example of policy-relevant empirical research.

This project began as a dissertation and was ably guided by my advisors at Harvard, Lisa Martin, Celeste Wallander, Chris Gelpi, and especially by Bob Keohane. Bob read countless iterations of this work, from its earliest stages as a seminar paper to the final book manuscript, offering invaluable advice and intellectual inspiration throughout. As many others who have worked with him know, Bob sets the standard high for what a mentor should be—consistently challenging yet unfailingly supportive.

Others who encouraged me through graduate school and who helped me learn how to do research and, more important, how to think, include Jim Alt, Jorge Domínguez, Brian Hehir, Stanley Hoffmann, Gary King, Jack Levy, Andy Moravcsik, Ken Oye, Bob Putnam, and Steve Rosen. In addition to that stellar cast of characters, I was fortunate to be in Cambridge with an extremely talented group: William Aceves, Chris Afendulis, Gary Bass, Erik Bleich, Brian Burgoon, Dan Byman, Allan Castle, Dan Drezner, Wendy Franz, Claudine Gay, Hein Goemans, Amy Gurowitz, Jeff Lewis (without whom I would probably not be a political scientist, and certainly not one capable of learning duration analysis), Amy Lucky, Pauline Jones Luong, Daryl Press, Dani Reiter, Curt Signorino, and Barb Walter. Some were only passing through for a year at Olin or the Center for International Affairs, but all gave support and advice and shared ideas that vastly improved the quality of this research, not to mention the quality of my life in graduate school.

I spent two years at Stanford's Center for International Security and Cooperation (CISAC), where Scott Sagan and Lynn Eden created a wonderfully supportive and vibrant intellectual environment. There I was fortunate to have the feedback and friendship of Ade Adebajo, Nora Bensahel, Nisha Fazal (whom I'm thrilled to have again as a colleague), Doug Gibler, Hugh Gusterson, Lise Morjé Howard, Bruce Jones, Beth Kier, Risa Brooks, fellow night owl Erika Weinthal, and Joelle Zahar. Allison MacFarlane shared a map-making program with me and made sure I got out to enjoy the natural wonders of northern California. I also had the pleasure at CISAC of working with Steve Stedman and especially with Don Rothchild, who has known me since I was a baby. Jim Fearon gave me invaluable comments on the project as I turned the dissertation into a book.

At Columbia, I have found another wonderful intellectual community in the Institute of War and Peace Studies. Ingrid Gerstmann makes all that we do at IWPS infinitely easier. The collegiality of David Baldwin, Andrea Bartoli, Dick Betts, Erik Gartzke, Helen Milner, and Ken Waltz has made Columbia a wonderful place to teach and to learn. Bob Jervis and Jack Snyder deserve special mention for going beyond the call of collegial duty with advice and encouragement. Both of them read the entire manuscript, giving me detailed comments that have vastly improved the final product.

Allan Stam and Scott Bennett helped me use their powerful EUGene software to generate some of the data used in this book. Al also provided data from his study on victory and defeat. Roy Licklider, Zeev Maoz, and Suzanne Werner shared data and coding advice with me. I thank Carol St. Louis and Megan Gilroy for able research assistance. Chapter 4 of this book is much improved after the comments I received on it from the Program on International Politics, Economics and Security (PIPES) seminar at the University of Chicago.

This book would not have been possible without generous financial support from the Mellon Foundation, the Eisenhower Institute, the Mac-Arthur Harvard-MIT Program on Transnational Security, the Olin Institute for Strategic Studies, CISAC's Hamburg Fellowship, the Carnegie Corporation of New York, and the Visiting Scholars program at the American Academy of Arts and Sciences. These foundations and centers have given me the gift of time, for which I am deeply grateful. Nor would the book have been possible without the able guidance of Chuck Myers at Princeton University Press. As many people told me he would be, he has been a wonderful editor to work with.

Special thanks to my brothers, Ben and Ned, for unstinting support and encouragement, and to Pete, who has filled my life with laughter and love, and who, by the time this book goes to press, I will have the unbelievable fortune to have as my husband.

My greatest thanks go to my parents, Robert and Evelyn, for bringing me up in a house full of books, for taking me and my brothers all over the world, including some of the war-torn places that are the focus of this book, for working for peace in the world, and of course for their love and support. This book is dedicated to them.

PEACE TIME

INTRODUCTION

THIS BOOK IS ABOUT making peace last in the least likely places. It is about cease-fires, why they sometimes hold and sometimes fail, and what, if anything, can be done to make them more likely to last. It is a study of how even deadly enemies can maintain peace.

In mid-July 1948, in the midst of the first Arab-Israeli war in Palestine, the United Nations Security Council ordered Israel and the Arab states to cease fire. They did so. The cease-fire lasted three months before fighting resumed with an Israeli offensive in mid-October. After a few more months of fighting, the war ended in 1949 with armistice agreements between Israel and each of its Arab neighbors. This second cease-fire fared much better but ultimately faltered, in 1956 in the Sinai, and in 1967 when Israel fought with Syria and Jordan as well as Egypt.

The Korean War also ended with an armistice agreement, in 1953. But despite the deep enmity and mistrust on the Korean peninsula, there has been no "Second Korean War." True peace has eluded Korea, but the cease-fire has so far held.

Almost half of the international wars since World War II have been followed by renewed fighting between at least one pair of belligerents. Peace is notoriously hard to maintain among deadly enemies, but in some cases it succeeds and in others it fails. Why do some cease-fires fall apart within days or months, while others last for years, and still others last indefinitely? Why did that first cease-fire in 1948 in the Middle East fail so quickly? Why did the next last longer, and why did it ultimately fail? Why has the armistice in Korea held? Why did Honduras and El Salvador skirmish again seven years after the Football War, and how did they avoid full-scale hostilities? How did Ethiopia and Somalia manage to avert resumption of their 1978 war over the Ogaden? And why, in the mid-1980s, were Vietnam and China unable to avoid another round of their earlier border fighting? What would we need to know to predict whether the cease-fire reached in June 2000 between Ethiopia and Eritrea will hold?

In short, what determines whether peace lasts or war resumes? And perhaps more important, what if anything can the belligerents themselves or the international community do to improve the chances of durable peace? These are the questions that motivate this book. The field of international relations provides surprisingly little guidance on why cease-fires fail or on what helps make peace last. There is a growing scholarly interest in the termination of both civil and international wars, but very little work has examined the durability of peace once belligerents have stopped firing at each other.[1] How to maintain peace in the aftermath of war is arguably one of the most important questions of the post–Cold War era, and one of the least explored issues in the study of war and peace.

This book explores two sets of factors to help explain why peace sometimes fails quickly and sometimes lasts longer. One set consists of situational or structural factors, characteristics of the situation over which the belligerents have little or no control. These include features of the war just fought, such as the military outcome, the cost of the war, and how many states were involved in it. They also include material conditions such as geography and the relative power of the states involved, as well as features of the belligerents' relationship such as their prior history of conflict and the stakes over which they fought. These "preexisting conditions" at the time of the cease-fire establish the baseline prospects for peace. Situational factors also include shifts over time that affect the likelihood of war, such as changes in military capability or in regime type.

The second set consists of deliberate attempts to enhance the durability of peace. These include measures such as the separation of troops and the creation of demilitarized zones (DMZs), monitoring by international observers, guarantees by third parties, confidence-building measures, and dispute resolution procedures, among others. These measures are often incorporated into cease-fire agreements by belligerents with the intent of helping to enforce the agreement. But do these measures work?

This book examines the role of such agreements in shaping the chances for durable peace after interstate wars. Diplomats and international lawyers might contend that a well-crafted agreement is critical in establishing lasting peace. But many scholars of international relations would argue that like all international agreements, cease-fires agreements are merely scraps of paper; they are not binding in an anarchical system, and they can do little to constrain international behavior. Others might argue that agreements represent purposeful attempts by states to overcome or mitigate the obstacles to cooperation. This debate, between realists and institutionalists, over the prospects for cooperation is well worn, and the purpose of this book is not to defend or attack either side.[2] But the

---

[1] Examples of the war termination literature include Fox 1970; Goemans 2000; Iklé 1991; Kecskemeti 1964, 1970; Klingberg 1966; Pillar 1983; Randle 1973; Walter 1997; and Zartman 1989. Holsti 1991 surveys the great multilateral peace conferences after major wars since 1648, focusing on grand efforts to establish a stable international order, rather than attempts to create lasting peace between particular pairs of belligerents. Kacowicz et al. 2000 consider the conditions for "stable peace" in which war is not even considered. By their typology this book is a study of "precarious peace."

[2] On the debate over prospects for cooperation, see Baldwin 1993. On strategies for making cooperation easier see, for example, Oye 1986a.

disagreement between the two camps does provide a number of competing hypotheses that illuminate the practical question why some cease-fires fall apart quickly while others last, and what if anything can be done to promote stable peace.[3] Despite the inherent importance of the question, surprisingly little theoretical or empirical work has explored how to maintain peace in the aftermath of war, and no systematic studies have tested whether cease-fire agreements matter in the construction of lasting peace. Are cease-fire agreements merely scraps of paper that have no effect on stability? Or can the content of agreements improve the chances of a lasting peace?

Maintaining peace in the aftermath of war requires cooperation. This book develops and tests cooperation theory to explain how the content of agreements influences the duration of peace. In brief, war is extremely costly and both sides would be better off if they could avoid a resumption of hostilities. But both sides may have strong incentives to break the cease-fire, and both have good reason to fear the other—they are, after all, deadly enemies who have just fought a war. Moreover, in the atmosphere of mistrust just after a war, accidents and skirmishes can easily spark renewed conflict. Cease-fires are by their nature reciprocal; it is the prospect of return fire that deters attack. But for reciprocity and deterrence to keep peace, several things must be true. The cost of renewed warfare must outweigh the incentives to attack; both sides must be reassured about the other's actions and intentions; and accidents must be kept from spiraling back into war. I argue that belligerents can draft cease-fire agreements that foster peace by altering the incentives to attack, by reducing uncertainty about intentions, and by preventing and controlling accidents. This study distinguishes between and examines armistice agreements that aim to stop the fighting but do not purport to settle the conflict, and peace agreements that address the political dispute underlying the conflict.[4]

Specific mechanisms incorporated into cease-fire agreements, such as demilitarized zones, can make defection more costly by imposing physical constraints. Belligerents might also alter incentives by involving third parties in the enforcement of a cease-fire. They can reduce uncertainty

---

[3] Realism and institutionalism are certainly not the only relevant theories of international relations. Constructivists might argue that agreements affect the durability of peace in part by changing actors' understandings of their relationship. This study is not necessarily incompatible with a constructivist approach; it pays attention to variables, such as the history of conflict between belligerents, that reflect social interaction and its effects. However, the construction of interests is not "problematized" in this study. A constructivist approach might be particularly useful in a separate study focusing on the difference between cases in which war is avoided but relations remain chilly, and those that involve greater reconciliation.

[4] I treat political settlement as a variable distinct from the "strength" of mechanisms within a cease-fire agreement (see chap. 1).

by defining compliance in specific terms, and the international community can provide neutral peacekeepers to monitor a cease-fire. Mechanisms such as dispute resolution procedures, confidence-building measures, and measures to control potential rogue groups opposed to peace might help prevent and manage unintended violations, while willingness to invoke cost can provide a credible signal to alleviate fears about enemy intentions.

This study tests the relationship between cease-fire agreements and the duration of peace after interstate wars. Do stronger agreements, those that incorporate more of these measures, fare better than weaker ones? Do demilitarized zones actually help prevent war? Are more specific agreements more likely to maintain peace? Are agreements with dispute resolution provisions more successful? Does peacekeeping keep peace? This project is a systematic study of what works and what does not work to maintain peace. Cooperation theory is thus developed and tested to answer the practical questions whether and how we can foster durable peace in conflicts around the globe.

Whether the measures studied here matter in the construction of durable peace cannot be answered in isolation, however. The counterargument to the notion that cease-fire agreements foster peace is that they merely reflect other factors that determine the duration of peace. According to this argument, when cooperation is relatively easy because relations are fairly good, parties will be able to draft strong agreements incorporating many of the mechanisms examined in this study. But these are the very cases in which peace will last in any case. Conversely, when cooperation is difficult and the chances that peace will fall apart are high for other reasons, belligerents will be unable to conclude agreements that do more than paper over differences. Any apparent relationship between the strength of agreements and the duration of peace may therefore be spurious.

On the other hand, an argument can be made for just the opposite logic. If mechanisms within cease-fire agreements help belligerents keep peace, the greater the obstacles to peace, the greater the need for these mechanisms. When peace is most fragile, states will have greater incentive to invest in measures to prevent its demise. This argument suggests that the strongest agreements will be put in place in the most dangerous situations, not the easiest ones. Peacekeepers, for example may be most likely sent to assist the most precarious cease-fires; they are not needed in more secure situations. Likewise, belligerents are more likely to insist on buffer zones when they least trust the other side to comply. If either argument is right, ignoring the situational factors or the "preexisting conditions" that influence the underlying prospects for peace will skew our findings about the causal relationship between agreements and the duration of peace.

This project thus addresses three central questions: First, what factors or situational variables affect the baseline prospects for peace? How, for example, do factors such as the decisiveness of military victory, geography, the actors' relative capabilities, their history of conflict before the war, their form of government, the stakes of the war, or its cost affect whether peace lasts or falls apart?

Second, how do these situational factors affect the content of cease-fire agreements? Are belligerents and the international community likely to implement measures to try to maintain peace only in the easy cases when peace would last in any case? Or are they more likely to invest in these measures when peace would otherwise be most precarious?

And third, given the baseline prospects for peace, how does the content of cease-fire agreements affect the durability of peace empirically? Do stronger agreements improve the chances for durable peace? Do measures such as demilitarized zones or military transparency measures help maintain peace? Does peace last longer when peacekeepers or monitors are present? Or when a third party offers a guarantee of the peace? Is peace more stable if the belligerents sign a formal agreement, or is a tacit understanding just as effective?

This study is set up to provide a hard test for the notion that states can improve the chances for peace. Studies of international cooperation have mostly focused on interactions between relatively friendly states, usually in economic or environmental issues. Cooperation is generally thought to be more difficult in matters of security and war than in economics, however. According to Jervis, security issues tend to be marked by greater competition, with interests more inherently conflictual; the security dilemma, in which one's own attempt to protect oneself threatens others, operates most severely in military matters; and the stakes tend to be higher in the security field than in economics.[5]

More important, on any issue, cooperation is more difficult for deadly enemies than for friendly nations.[6] Enemies cannot rely on previously established reputations for complying with their commitments. Indeed, enemies are more likely to be concerned with their reputations for toughness than with demonstrating their cooperativeness. In the absence of any

---

[5] Jervis 1983, 174–75. Jervis is analyzing the prospects for security regimes, but his argument applies to cooperation more generally. See also Jervis 1978. The difference between prospects for cooperation in security and economic affairs does not apply across the board. The United States and Japan, for example, can cooperate much more easily in military affairs than in economic matters in which they are competitors.

[6] The important difference between relations among friends and among enemies is a key insight of constructivist approaches to international relations. Wendt 1992, 397, notes the difference for the United States between British and Soviet nuclear forces, for example. The same capabilities in the hands of a friend or a foe have very different meanings.

good will, cooperative gestures are likely to be interpreted as signs of weakness, and therefore to be avoided. Concern with relative gains also makes relations among adversaries more difficult. Deadly enemies have good reason to worry that their opponent might use any comparative advantage against them down the line.[7] And yet, despite all this, cooperation is possible. By examining success and failure where cooperation is most difficult, this study contributes to the theoretical and empirical debate over the prospects for cooperation. It draws on this debate to develop competing hypotheses about the effectiveness of measures to improve the prospects for peace, and then tests these hypotheses empirically.

This testing involves three complementary research methods: quantitative analysis, in-depth case studies, and what for lack of a better term I will call "large-N qualitative" comparison. The statistical analysis employs a duration model designed for studies of longevity (medical studies of life expectancy, for example, or in this case the durability of peace), and a data set created for this project. It covers all cease-fires in wars between sovereign states from 1946 through 1997. The data include information on the cease-fires and how long they lasted, on the situational variables that shape the underlying prospects for peace (the belligerents' history of conflict, the decisiveness of military victory, etc.), and any mechanisms put in place to help foster the chances for peace.

The in-depth case-study research focuses on India and Pakistan, and Israel and Syria. These particular cases were chosen for two reasons. First, they provide a hard test of the cooperation theory presented here. All of the cases in this study consist of enemies who have just fought a war, but these cases involve enemies more intransigent than most. Both the India-Pakistan conflict and the Israel-Syria conflict are marked by deep hostility in which animosity began at or before independence and was only exacerbated over time. Second, because in each case there have been several wars over time, and therefore several cease-fires, they provide multiple observations and variation within the two cases. Indeed the primary comparisons in this part of the analysis are within-case comparisons, not between the two cases. This allows me to hold relatively constant particularities of culture, geography, and so on.

The third research method falls somewhere between the quantitative analysis and the in-depth case studies, and draws on the strengths of both. Because the universe of cases of interstate cease-fires in the post–World War II era is relatively small (48 bilateral cease-fires in 25 wars), it is possible to examine them all qualitatively. This "systematic eyeballing" of minicases or "large-N qualitative" method allows one to see patterns

---

[7] On the debate over relative and absolute gains, see Grieco 1988; Snidal 1991; and Powell 1991.

in the data that get lost both in the condensation of complex cases into numerical data and in case studies of only a few cases. These three techniques dovetail so that each compensates for the limitations of the others.

• • •

In a world characterized by anarchy, international agreements are fundamentally unenforceable. Without a world government, states are not subject to a higher authority that will guarantee their contracts. There is nothing to stop states from breaching their commitments if it is in their interests to do so.[8] And yet, most agreements are honored most of the time. In general, international agreements appear to be more than mere scraps of paper, ignored whenever they become inconvenient.[9] This is a study of whether and how agreements affect outcomes after they are signed, of how states "enforce" their own agreements.

Related to the issue of whether and how agreements bind actors is the impact of international institutions on political outcomes. Institutionalist theory rests on the claim that the existence and form of institutions affect international relations by making cooperation easier to achieve. Critics of institutionalism claim, on the contrary, that such arrangements are epiphenomenal—they are created reflecting the interests of major powers, and they fade away when these interests shift, but they exert no independent influence on international outcomes.[10] Cease-fire agreements are not necessarily institutions,[11] but because they perform similar functions—providing information, setting standards of legitimate behavior, and making the gains from cooperation later contingent on cooperation now[12]—scholarship on institutions is relevant to the study of peacemaking. An empirical analysis of the impact of cease-fire agreements, particularly one that takes seriously the charge of spuriousness, sheds light on whether and how institutions matter in international relations.

This is also a study of "enduring rivalries" and protracted conflicts. The enduring rivalries literature focuses on pairs of states that are repeatedly in conflict with each other: "The concept of enduring rivalries is a way to understand how previous conflict interactions between states af-

---

[8] For examples of the growing literature at the intersection of international politics and international law, see Slaughter 1995; Setear 1996; Abbott et al. 2000; and Koremenos 2001.

[9] See Chayes and Chayes 1995.

[10] See, for example, Mearsheimer 1994–95.

[11] Institutions are often defined as "persistent and connected sets of rules (formal and informal) that prescribe behavioral roles, constrain activity, and shape expectations." Keohane 1989, 3. Cease-fire agreements are ad hoc rather than persistent.

[12] Keohane 1984.

fect their future propensity for conflict or cooperation."[13] But the literature has not yet answered this question directly because most studies examine only cases where there is future conflict. It has not addressed what distinguishes conflicts that set off enduring rivalries from those that are not repeated.[14] By studying both cases in which armed conflict resumes and those in which a pair of states fights only once, research on the durability of peace helps fill this gap. This book thus contributes to our understanding both of how rivalries form, and of how established rivals can maintain peace, and thereby, perhaps, end their cycle of conflict.

Last but not least, this study is a "how to" of sorts for would-be peacemakers. Studies have been done on some of the particular peace-maintaining mechanisms examined here. But this literature tends to be descriptive rather than analytic and rarely involves systematic tests of the effectiveness of these measures. Studies of peacekeeping, for example, tend to examine only cases where peacekeepers were deployed with no comparison to nonpeacekeeping cases, so that it is difficult to judge empirically what difference peacekeeping makes. This project thus aims to contribute both to important theoretical and empirical questions in international relations, and to the practical issue of how to create peace that lasts.

The following chapter develops cooperation theory to explain why agreements might be expected to affect the durability of peace. It also discusses the counterargument that agreements are merely epiphenomenal. Chapter 2 describes the evidentiary issues involved in studying why peace lasts or war resumes. It describes the three research methods used in the book: the econometric model and the data set created for the quantitative analysis, the "large-N qualitative" comparisons used to flesh out the study, and the case selection and research methods employed in the in-depth case studies of war and peace between Israel and Syria and between India and Pakistan, as well as a brief overview of these conflicts.

In the rest of the book the hypotheses generated in chapter 1 are put to empirical test. Chapter 3 is a study of the baseline prospects for peace. It examines the relationship between a number of situational variables and the durability of peace, testing, for example, whether peace lasts longer after decisive victories, whether costly wars lead to a more or a less stable peace, and so on. Five variables turn out to be particularly important: the decisiveness of military victory, the cost of war, belligerents' history before the war, the stakes of conflict, and whether the fighting states are contiguous. Other factors, relative power, the number of states in the war,

---

[13] Goertz and Diehl 1992, 153. See Goertz and Diehl 1993 for evaluations of various definitions of the concept. On protracted conflicts, see Brecher 1984; and Brecher and Wilkenfeld 1989.

[14] In the jargon, most of the literature "selects on the dependent variable." One notable exception is Stinnett and Diehl 2001.

whether the conflict is over territory, measures of states' "expected utility" for war, and changes in regime type, for example, are less helpful for understanding whether peace will last.

Chapter 4 addresses the counterargument that agreements are epiphenomenal or spurious. Despite empirical tests that are biased in favor of the counterargument, there is surprisingly little evidence that belligerents reach strong agreements only when the prospects for peace are good in any case. If anything, just the opposite is true: parties tend to invest more in keeping peace when it would otherwise be precarious.

Chapters 5 and 6 then turn to the practical question of whether and how these mechanisms work. Chapter 5 tests the central hypothesis of the book—that stronger cease-fire agreements yield more stable peace. Taking the baseline prospects for peace into account, I show that the content of agreements does indeed matter in the construction of durable peace. All else equal, peace lasts longer when stronger agreements are in place. Chapter 6 focuses on specific measures and their empirical effectiveness in maintaining peace. This chapter shows that some measures are more important than others. Demilitarized zones are particularly effective, for example, but arms control measures are not. Explicit guarantees of peace by outsiders help. Peacekeeping and monitoring by the international community can be very effective, but once a peacekeeping mission is discredited by the outbreak of another war (as in South Asia, for example) it becomes completely ineffectual. Joint commissions set up to resolve disputes as they arise also help belligerents maintain peace. The conclusion recaps the argument and findings, drawing out implications for international relations theory and for the practice of maintaining peace.

In this study peace is defined as merely the absence of war. I do not distinguish between relations that become very friendly and those that remain acrimonious despite the absence of violence. Under this definition, North and South Korea have been at "peace" for over forty years. While I do examine the role of political settlements, agreements on the underlying issues of the conflict, this is not a study of how former adversaries reconcile and become friends. It is a study of how even deadly enemies can prevent shooting wars. Nor do I address whether the peace achieved in the cases studied is just. This is not to imply that all varieties of peace are equally desirable or moral. Some wars, wars of liberation and anticolonial wars, for example, may make the world a better place; stability does not necessarily coincide with social justice. But most wars cause poverty, disease, and dislocation, and all entail the large-scale loss of human life. Repeated conflict only exacerbates these tragedies. This study is inspired by a normative concern for victims of repeated warfare and instability. By studying both durable cease-fires and those that have proved failures, and by focusing on deliberate efforts to maintain peace, I hope to contribute to practical efforts to restore lasting peace to regions torn apart by war.

CHAPTER ONE

A THEORY OF AGREEMENTS AND THE DURABILITY OF PEACE

WHEN BELLIGERENTS CEASE FIRING, what determines whether peace lasts or war resumes, and what, if anything, can be done to make peace more durable? Maintaining peace in the aftermath of war requires cooperation. Cease-fire agreements can facilitate cooperation in several ways: by making it more costly to attack, by reducing uncertainty about the other side's actions and intentions, and by preventing misunderstandings and accidents from spiraling back into war. The first part of this chapter outlines the obstacles to maintaining peace and the ways in which specific mechanisms within cease-fire agreements can help overcome these obstacles.

I argue that the content of agreements affects the durability of peace. Critics might contend that belligerents will draft strong agreements only when peace is likely to last in any case, so that the relationship between agreements and durable peace is spurious. The rebuttal to this counterargument is that just the opposite is true. Belligerents will institute measures to overcome the obstacles to peace when these are most necessary, that is, when peace is most precarious. These competing hypotheses are outlined in the second part of the chapter. Whichever argument is correct, it is important to assess the baseline prospects of peace in order to evaluate accurately the effect of agreements on whether peace lasts or falls apart. The final section of the chapter therefore discusses briefly a number of "situational variables" that might be expected to shape the baseline prospects for peace.

I. COOPERATION THEORY AND PEACE AGREEMENTS

War is costly, giving even bitter enemies a shared incentive to avoid renewed hostilities. But this common interest does not automatically lead to peace. Recent belligerents are likely to have deeply conflicting preferences and strong incentives to try to take advantage of each other. They also have good reason to fear and mistrust each other. This combination of common and conflicting interests defines the problem of cooperation.

My argument is based on three assumptions: (1) that states are rationally led; (2) that war is costly, that it is not desired for its own sake; and

(3) that recent combatants have incentives to take advantage of each other, and/or good reason to fear and mistrust each other.

First, by rationally led, I mean that leaders make decisions purposefully and that they use the information at their disposal to consider the expected costs and benefits of their actions. Their rationality may be bounded; the world is a complex place and leaders are not omniscient. But I assume that leaders do not act randomly, nor will they take action that they expect will be contrary to their own interests. I do not assume that states are unitary actors, however. Leaders are subject to domestic political pressures. And they may not exercise effective control over all of those in whose name they lead.

Second, to say that actors prefer peace to war is not to say, naively, that they prefer peace to the possibility of winning a war and dictating terms. If this were true, states would never choose to fight. Rather I mean that, if it were possible, states would prefer to reach the outcome of war without the cost of fighting it. War is costly in terms of lives and money, and it is risky—there is always the chance of losing rather than winning. Unless fighting is preferred for its own sake, even the worst enemies want to settle their disputes without resorting to war if they can. The fact that war is costly means bargains exist that all sides would prefer to renewed fighting.[1]

For deadly enemies, however, the inefficiency and cost of war do not necessarily result in peace. Among many, perhaps most, states in the international system, peace is more or less automatic. The United States and Canada do not have to concern themselves with the prospect of war between them. For friendly states, maintaining peace does not necessarily require cooperation; if both sides pursue their unilaterally preferred outcomes, peace will result. Nor does peace require cooperation between minor powers who are far apart and have little to do with each other. Belize and Mozambique have little reason to fight, for example.[2]

The third assumption, however, is that relations between enemies are marked by seriously conflicting interests and deep mistrust. This study concerns cases in which a deadly conflict has just been fought. It is unlikely that the war settled the conflict to both parties' satisfaction; indeed the war may have caused new issues of conflict, and it is sure to have caused greater mistrust. Conflicting interests and mistrust make main-

---

[1] As Fearon 1995 explains, war is ex post inefficient. In some periods of history, war may well have been seen as a good, as a vehicle for personal glory: Louis XIV viewed war as sport, for example. Holsti 1991, 10–11. In the modern period, however, war is seen as a means to a political end, and a costly one at that. See Mueller 1989. In some civil wars, some belligerents may prefer fighting for its own sake if they are able to profit financially from the ensuing instability. King 2001.

[2] For this reason, some recent quantitative work on the study of war restricts cases to "politically relevant" dyads, including only contiguous states and dyads involving a major power. See Maoz and Russett 1993.

taining peace problematic. Whatever the dispute at issue, belligerents have an incentive to take what they want by force. And both parties have good reason to fear that their enemy would like to do the same.

Cooperation can be distinguished from both a situation of harmony, in which parties pursuing their own most preferred objectives would necessarily result in peace, and a situation of deadlock in which both sides prefer war to peace.[3] The second assumption, that war is costly, distinguishes cease-fires from deadlock. It means that there are bargains both sides prefer to war. This is true even for the most bitter enemies. Consider Israel and Syria; there is little the two agree on, and neither likes the status quo very much, but both prefer it to full-scale war. The third assumption, that belligerents differ in their preferred outcomes, distinguishes cease-fires from harmony. North and South Korea have very different ideas about how best to settle their conflict, and India and Pakistan prefer very different outcomes in Kashmir. Maintaining peace requires that both sides refrain from trying to impose their preferred outcome unilaterally, by force.

These assumptions are particularly appropriate for a study of the durability of peace. The fact that belligerents have reached a cease-fire in the first place suggests that they do not prefer fighting for its own sake. The fact that they have fought once already makes it a good bet that they have conflicting interests. Taken together, these conditions mean that peace is possible, but precarious. It requires cooperation.

Theories of cooperation seek to explain why it is problematic in international relations, as well as how actors might surmount the difficulties inherent in cooperating under anarchy.[4] Since peace is preferred to war, states would be better off if they could simply agree not to fight. But with no world government or higher authority to enforce their agreements, nothing prevents them from reneging on such an agreement and attacking to gain unilateral advantage. Their conflicting interests make it hard for enemies credibly to commit to maintaining peace. Even if neither side really wants to take advantage of the other, the other cannot know this for sure. The fear of complying while the other side defects can prevent cooperation. And in the atmosphere of mistrust generated by the war, accidents can easily spiral back into war.

[3] On these distinctions, see Keohane 1984. See also Oye 1986b.
[4] Seminal works on the topic include Axelrod 1984; Grieco 1988; Keohane 1984; Oye 1986b; Waltz 1979; and the collection of essays in Baldwin 1993. To oversimplify the main debate in international relations scholarship over the prospects for cooperation: neorealists, particularly offensive realists, emphasize that cooperation is extremely difficult in an anarchic world, while institutionalists argue that states can and do devise strategies to overcome obstacles to cooperation. (Defensive realists fall somewhere in between, less pessimistic than offensive realists but more so than institutionalists.) While the theoretical debate is by now well worn, its competing perspectives help illuminate the substantive issue of interest here.

And yet, more often than not, peace lasts. Given the obstacles, how do deadly enemies ever achieve durable peace? Peace is the result of reciprocity and mutual deterrence. Each side stops fighting in exchange for the other side's doing the same, and if either breaks the cease-fire, the other will respond in kind. It is the prospect of the other side fighting back that deters attack. This is so central to the notion of a cease-fire that it seems quite obvious. Cease-fire arrangements are by their very nature reciprocal, so even though each side might desire to march in and take what it wants, it is hard to imagine the other side acquiescing in such a move. An attempt to settle the dispute unilaterally will lead back to war.[5] It is the cost of war that makes peace possible.

For reciprocity and deterrence to work, however, several things have to be true: the cost of reinitiating conflict must outweigh the incentives to attack; it must be possible to distinguish compliance from noncompliance and to respond with force if necessary; if a first strike is militarily advantageous, both sides must be reassured about the other side's actions and intentions; and accidents or unintended violations of the cease-fire must be prevented from escalating. These requisites point both to potential obstacles to peace, and to strategies for ameliorating them. If states have already reached a cease-fire, why might they go back to war?[6] Peace might break down through deliberate aggression, through fear and preemption, by accident, or most likely some combination of these paths.

Obstacles to Peace

INCENTIVES TO ATTACK

Both sides are likely to have strong incentives to cheat on a cease-fire; rarely do wars settle disputes to both sides' satisfaction. The cease-fire marks a decision to stop fighting, but this does not mean that both sides now prefer peace to victory, only that they have calculated peace to be preferable to the ongoing costs of war, perhaps only temporarily. There is nothing to guarantee that belligerents are not biding their time, waiting for a better opportunity to resume battle.

My argument draws on this debate to explain both the obstacles to maintaining peace, and mechanisms that can be used to overcome these barriers.

[5] This can be modeled as an iterated Prisoner's Dilemma. Both sides prefer peace to war, but each side would most like to attack unopposed to settle the issue with a military fait accompli. However, unless one side can be immediately and completely eliminated in an attack (see below), the victim of such an attack will fight back, leading to war. The folk theorem shows that in an iterated game, cooperation can emerge and be maintained if the players employ a reciprocal strategy, such as Tit-for-Tat, so that cooperation later depends on cooperation now, and defection is met with defection. See Axelrod 1984.

[6] Werner 1999.

One reason states fight in the first place is their inability to find a bargain acceptable to both sides. Because war is costly, such bargains exist, but because much information about military capabilities and resolve is private (i.e., one side knows, but the other does not) and because there are incentives for both sides to misrepresent their strength and what they would be willing to settle for (that is, to bluff), these bargains can be impossible to find.[7] Fighting presumably reveals information about capabilities and resolve, allowing states to cease fire and return to the negotiating table (either literally or figuratively). But this does not guarantee that a settlement can now be found. Wars rarely reveal information fully. Negotiations in the aftermath of fighting often fail to settle the issue over which war was waged. India and Pakistan, for example, reached a truce in 1949 and spent the next decade in good-faith negotiations over Kashmir but were unable to reach a solution. Pakistan eventually provoked another war to try to settle the issue by force.

Reaching an acceptable settlement even after war might be particularly difficult if fighting ended in part because of international demands. Diplomatic pressure can sometimes produce a cease-fire, but may have more difficulty inducing major concessions at the bargaining table. Israel and the Arab states agreed to a cease-fire in 1948 under significant pressure from the United States and Britain, and the threat of United Nations (UN) sanctions. But warnings from the United States and others that breaking the cease-fire might lead to UN enforcement action were disregarded by Israel. When several months of mediation failed to produce an acceptable settlement, Israel launched an attack to take militarily what it could not get at the bargaining table.[8]

Even if fighting provides enough information about bargaining positions and fighting abilities to allow at least a de facto settlement, this certainty can fade quickly, as forces are demobilized or built up, as changes take place in domestic politics, or as the interests of potential allies shift. If one side comes to believe that it can do better in war than at the negotiating table, it will attack. A state will be particularly likely to go back to war if it thinks it can inflict enough damage in a first strike to hamper the other side's ability to retaliate.[9]

Similarly, if one side thinks it can get away with cheating on a cease-fire agreement without provoking retaliation, it may try to alter the status quo. Relative to many international agreements, it is fairly easy to detect

---

[7] Fearon 1995.

[8] David Ben-Gurion noted that the threat of sanctions did not matter: "what counts is what we do here." Quoted in Bailey 1990, 46. As Israel had suspected, the Security Council reaction was mild. Bailey 1990, 36–46; Khouri 1985, 81–88.

[9] The deterrence literature has focused on the problem of a first strike undermining the second-strike capability necessary for reciprocal deterrent strategies such as mutually as-

gross violations of a cease-fire; it is hard to hide an attack for long. But states may try "salami tactics," slicing off a small piece of territory by pushing their forces forward slightly, for example, in the hopes that a small move will not provoke a war.[10]

In short, deadly enemies have strong incentives to attempt to force a more favorable settlement. For reciprocity and mutual deterrence to keep the peace, these incentives must be outweighed by the expected cost of war.

FEAR OF ATTACK

Even when the cost of war outweighs the incentives to attack, uncertainty about the opponent's intentions can undermine cooperation. The security dilemma, in which one state's attempt to ensure its own security threatens its opponents, means that even states with only defensive motives may end up at war.[11] If being the victim of aggression is extremely costly, then any uncertainty about the other side's intentions leads to great anxiety.[12] States must worry about the possibility of complete defeat and elimination in war.[13] If there is a military advantage to striking first (or a disadvantage to being struck first), then war can occur even when neither side has aggressive designs. In this situation cooperation would be easy to maintain with full information. But if one side might break the cease-fire, the other side is better off defecting as well.[14]

Actors can never know each other's intentions for certain.[15] Nor can they be sure that their opponents' intentions will stay the same over time.

---

sured destruction (MAD). Examples of the vast literature on deterrence include Morgan 1977; Schelling 1966; and George and Smoke 1974.

[10] Schelling 1966, 66, 77.

[11] Jervis 1978.

[12] This situation is often modeled as a Stag Hunt, in which both sides prefer cooperation even to unilateral defection, but cooperating while the other defects is the worst possible outcome.

[13] See Powell 1991 for an explanation of why reciprocal strategies do not work if one side can be completely eliminated. This is probably more of a concern for parties in a civil war where it is more common for one side to be completely annihilated. The complete elimination of a state in war is quite rare in recent history. The Republic of Vietnam is the only state to have been eliminated in war since World War II. Even the elimination of governments is relatively infrequent: there are only three cases in the period examined here (the Soviet Union removed Nagy from Hungary, Vietnam overthrew Pol Pot in Cambodia, and Tanzania ousted Idi Amin in Uganda). For an account and explanation of state death, see Fazal 2001.

[14] The fear of cheating can cause "market failure," in which states break cooperative agreements because they fear that complying with them while their partner cheats will leave them worse off than if they had acted unilaterally in the first place.

[15] Domestic politics may affect states' ability to gauge each other's intentions. Some have argued that policymaking is more transparent in democracies. See, for example, Fearon 1994. However, democratic leaders may also have electoral incentives to engage in inflammatory rhetoric, making it harder for their opponents to distinguish true policy statements from crowd-pleasing bravado.

If states could simply communicate their preference for peace, all would be well. Unfortunately, this communication is not credible. Those who would prefer to attack have an incentive to misrepresent their true intentions so that the opponent will cooperate and be "suckered."[16] So communication alone may not distinguish those with benign intentions from those who intend harm.[17]

For reciprocity to function, it must be possible to distinguish compliance from noncompliance. It is also important that both sides know they will not be retaliated against unless they cheat. For if there is a good chance that one will be unjustly blamed for aggression and bear the brunt of retaliation, one might as well defect to gain the payoff that results.[18] Reciprocal systems thus require that it be clear what constitutes compliance, that noncompliance will be detected, and that it is possible to determine who defected first.

At the most basic level, the rules of a cease-fire are relatively clear: do not attack. But does it constitute defection if one side moves its forces forward, or rearms them? Is an "act of war" such as closing an international waterway, as Egypt did in 1967, a violation of a cease-fire? Particularly in the atmosphere of mistrust in the immediate aftermath of fighting, it may be controversial what maintaining the cease-fire entails.

Deadly enemies are particularly likely to misperceive intentions and to assume the worst.[19] War leaves a legacy of deep mistrust, often exaggerated by tough posturing on the part of leaders. And states often break off normal diplomatic channels during warfare. In this atmosphere leaders are likely to take any accident or irregularity as a signal of aggressive intentions.[20] At best, fear that the other side intends to attack will lead to military preparations that are likely, through a security dilemma dynamic,

---

[16] States sometimes have incentives to overrepresent their willingness to fight, that is, to bluff, and sometimes have reason to underrepresent their willingness to attack to lull an opponent into a false sense of security.

[17] Akerlof 1970 illustrates this problem with the example of used-car markets. Buyers cannot tell "lemons" (bad cars) from "creampuffs" (good cars) and cannot trust owners honestly to represent the nature of the car. As Wallander 1999, 25–26, explains, in the context of security in international relations a "lemon" is a state that enters cooperative arrangements with the intention of defecting and exploiting its partner. The harder it is to tell "lemons" from "creampuffs," the more severe will be the security dilemma. For example, if it is hard to distinguish offensive technologies or maneuvers from defensive ones, it will be particularly difficult for states to gauge each other's intentions. Jervis 1978.

[18] Downs and Rocke 1995; Schelling and Halperin 1961, 94–95.

[19] For examples of this attribution bias between the superpowers during the Cold War, see Garthoff 1994.

[20] According to the informational perspective presented by Fearon 1995 and Goemans 2000, among others, wars reveal information about intentions and capabilities, so that misperception should be least likely immediately after a war. But while states may be less prone to underestimating their opponents' willingness to fight over an issue, they may be more

to themselves be interpreted as a signal of impending attack. At worst such fears can lead to preemptive war.

Reiter argues that "preemptive wars almost never happen."[21] But they are more likely to happen among enemies who have already fought, who are likely already mobilized against each other, and who mistrust each other deeply. In both of the cases examined in detail in this book, war has started or escalated significantly through preemptive attack. Israel launched a preemptive strike against its neighbors in 1967, starting the Six-Day War. In response to Indian intervention, and fearing worse to come, Pakistan attacked Indian airfields preemptively in December 1971.[22] Moreover, that preemptive war is rare does not mean it is not a potential problem. One of the reasons it does not occur more often, according to Reiter, is that states worry about it and try to guard against it.

In sum, recent belligerents have good reason to fear and mistrust each other. This fear makes bargaining and cooperation more difficult. If there is a first-strike advantage, this fear can lead to unwanted war. Offensive and defensive realists debate whether the problem of war is mostly the result of aggression or of fear.[23] In the cases examined here, involving enemies who have just fought a war, both problems are likely to apply. In all likelihood, both sides would like to take advantage of each other if possible, and both fear that the enemy feels the same way.

ACCIDENTS AND INVOLUNTARY DEFECTION

When fighting stops, opposing militaries are often left in very close proximity, facing each other across a cease-fire line. When the second Kashmir war ended in 1965, for example, Indian and Pakistani forces were in some places less than thirty yards apart.[24] When enemy soldiers are left "eyeball to eyeball," shooting incidents and accidents are very likely. Reciprocal strategies are often vulnerable to accidents and misunderstandings. If troops stray over the cease-fire line, or fire accidentally, the other side will likely respond in kind, and a vicious cycle of retaliation can quickly spin back into full-out war.[25]

Cease-fires generally freeze troop locations, giving both sides an incentive to push their positions forward before the cease-fire solidifies. It may be

---

likely to overestimate aggressive intentions, that is, less likely to believe the enemy is bluffing when it is not, but more likely to believe the enemy is aggressive when it is not.

[21] Reiter 1995.

[22] Note that Reiter does not code the latter as a preemptive war because India had already decided to intervene.

[23] On this issue see, for example, Schweller 1996; Kydd 1997; and Jervis 1999.

[24] UN document S/6719/Add. 1, 1965, 2.

[25] For an organizational culture argument about what kinds of accidents are likely, and which are likely to spiral to war, see Legro 1995.

very difficult to distinguish accidental skirmishes from such deliberate attempts to gain territory. The analytical distinction between accidents and deliberate action is also blurry. Deliberate moves to push the issue (to take control of a small slice of contested territory, for example) can lead to unwanted war if one side misjudges the other's reaction and pushes too far.

Similarly, the existence of factions on either side that might disrupt the peace also pose an obstacle to cooperation. Even if the leadership negotiates in good faith, it may not be able to control all of its military forces or civilians. Rogue groups of irregular forces, local commanders, or even individuals may violate the cease-fire. Such "involuntary defection" can easily upset a fragile cease-fire. Furthermore, states have an incentive to blame deliberate attempts to encroach across the cease-fire line on accidents or the action of rogue groups.[26] While wars rarely start purely by accident, escalating clashes at least partially the result of accident or unauthorized moves contributed to the breakdown of peace between India and Pakistan in 1965 and in 1999, and between China and Vietnam in 1987, as well as to serious fighting short of war between El Salvador and Honduras in 1976.

Accidents, actions by rogue groups opposed to peace, and misunderstandings are particularly dangerous in the atmosphere of mistrust immediately after a war. Both sides have good reason to fear attack and to assume the worst about each other's intentions. While reliable communication between leaders could keep accidents or rogue violations from dragging states back to war, normal diplomatic channels are usually severed in war. International relations theory has focused on issues of credibility in communication, and rightly so, but a prior issue, the simple physical ability to talk, should not be taken for granted among deadly enemies.

DISTRIBUTION AND RELATIVE GAINS

Neorealist critics have charged that in focusing on cheating, institutionalist theories of cooperation have ignored still another obstacle to cooperation. States wrangle over who gets what from any deal, and particularly how these gains will be used. Inability to agree on a way to divvy up the gains from cooperation can obstruct agreement. And states worry not just about how to slice the pie (distribution), but also about the implications of the other side's gains for their future security (relative gains). Relative gains matter because if your partner gains more than you do from cooperation, it might use this advantage against you in the future.[27] This means

---

[26] Martin 1992. Two-level game analysis indicates that negotiators may play up their inability to control domestic groups so as to get concessions at the bargaining table, thus exacerbating this uncertainty. Putnam 1988.

[27] According to Grieco 1988, "states worry that today's friend may be tomorrow's enemy in war, and fear that achievements of joint gains that advantage a friend in the present might

that states will avoid cooperative arrangements that make both parties better off if the gains will be uneven. Concerns about relative gains also make fear of cheating even worse. Not only do states have to worry about getting hurt if an opponent defects, they also have to worry that the adversary will use relative gains from cheating now against them in the future. In the aftermath of violent conflict, we can assume that concerns over relative gains will be quite high.[28]

Most of the debate over relative gains has centered on their effect on the prospects for reaching cooperation in the first place. Distributional issues and relative gains concerns sometimes make it hard for belligerents to implement measures that might help them maintain peace.[29] But it is important to distinguish this from the effect of these issues on maintaining cooperation. Once fighting has ceased, concerns about distributional and relative gains will affect the prospects for durable peace if one party comes to believe that peace is favoring its opponent. Consolidation of control over territory or uneven rearmament may make one side perceive that it is "losing the peace."[30] Continuing to maintain the cease-fire will leave this actor less secure in the future, giving it an incentive to reinitiate the fight now rather than wait as it loses relative power.[31] In other words, concern with relative gains can give states an extra incentive to break the cease-fire. And, as mentioned above, concerns over relative gains make fear of cheating worse. Distributional concerns over the location of the cease-fire line can also make it more likely that states will overreact to accidental violations or to small skirmishes along the line. Concerns over distribution and relative gains therefore exacerbate the other obstacles to maintaining peace: the incentives to attack, fear of cheating, and the risk of accidents.

• • •

In sum, with no higher authority to enforce agreements, and with no way of knowing each other's intentions, it is difficult for former belligerents to maintain peace. Both sides are likely to have strong incentives to take advantage of each other, and both sides must fear such defection from the

---

produce a more dangerous *potential* foe in the future." In the context of war termination, cooperation partners are not even friends to begin with.

[28] Snidal 1991 argues that at high levels of concern with relative gains, more benign games such as Stag Hunt are transformed into Prisoner's Dilemma games in which cooperation is more difficult. See also Powell 1991.

[29] Severe relative gains concerns were at play in the difficult negotiations over disengagement between Israel and Syria in the Golan Heights (see chap. 4).

[30] Both sides, for example, worried that a temporary cease-fire in 1948 during the first Arab-Israeli war was working to the military advantage of the other.

[31] On preventive war, see Levy 1987.

opponent. Simply agreeing to cooperate cannot overcome these obstacles because such commitment is not by itself credible, even though peace would make both sides better off. Moreover, incidents along the cease-fire line, even if accidental or the result of rogue forces, may reignite hostilities. Peace is precarious.

To put the problem in more concrete terms, imagine two states that have just fought a war over a piece of territory (Israel and Syria in 1973, perhaps, or El Salvador and Honduras after the 1969 Football War). They reached a cease-fire leaving each of them with some portion of the disputed territory. The war was costly and they would prefer not to fight again, but they would each like more of the disputed land. Both believe they have a right to it, and their populations see occupation of any part of it by the enemy as a travesty. The side that lost territory in the war has an incentive to try to win it back, and the side that gained may think it can now claim more. So both sides have incentives to try to encroach on the other, or even to make a dramatic advance, to push the cease-fire line farther toward the other side.

Moreover, both have good reason to fear encroachment or attack from the other side. These fears may be exacerbated by leaders' inflammatory remarks for domestic consumption. Both sides will be particularly wary of military maneuvers, resupply efforts, or anything that might be a precursor to a new attack. When the fighting stopped, soldiers were left in close proximity to their enemies, facing each other across the cease-fire line. The likelihood of troops firing across the line or of skirmishes as each side tries to improve its position is quite high. If irregular troops were involved in the fighting, or if command and control is somewhat loose, there may be incidents of unauthorized attacks or advances. And in a tense atmosphere of mistrust, with normal diplomatic channels severed, any small clash or velitation can spur escalation back to full-scale war. Whether through deliberate action, spirals of fear and preemption, or accident, the probability of war erupting anew is high.

Strategies for Improving the Prospects for Peace

Belligerents are not doomed to fight again, however. One of the insights of cooperation theory is that actors anticipate the obstacles to cooperation and may be able to write agreements that guard against opportunism.[32] Cease-fire agreements can help belligerents maintain peace by raising the cost of an attack, by reducing uncertainty about actions and intentions, and by preventing or controlling accidents.

---

[32] See Axelrod 1984; Coase 1988; Keohane 1989; Martin 1993; North 1990; and Williamson 1985, for a discussion of how actors can create self-enforcing, credible agreements.

RAISING THE COST OF ATTACK

Peace will break down if the incentives to attack outweigh the cost of war. However, there are things belligerents and the international community can do to tip the scales, to increase the cost of attack so that maintaining peace is a relatively more attractive option. Anything that increases the cost of defection helps make a cease-fire agreement self-enforcing. Combatants can tie their hands with physical or political constraints that raise the price of aggression. The most straightforward method of hand-tying is to make it physically harder for either side to attack. Withdrawal of troops away from the front lines, demilitarized buffer zones, and disarmament or limits on forces near the cease-fire line make attack more difficult and costly.[33] Commitment by a third party to guarantee the peace can also serve as a deterrent, increasing the cost of noncompliance. Even if physical constraints cannot deter aggression altogether, they may make launching a successful surprise attack much more difficult by providing opportunities for timely warning.

The very act of agreeing formally and publicly to peace can alter incentives. By committing publicly to a formal cease-fire agreement, actors stake their international reputations on compliance. By signing a formal agreement, states bind themselves under international law. Of course, with no higher authority to enforce it, international law is not binding in the way that domestic law is, and actors may care more about their reputations for toughness than for compliance.[34] International agreements can be broken. However, breaking them brings international opprobrium and legitimizes retaliation by the other side. Diplomacy becomes more difficult for the defector, and the transgression may cause aid to be withheld and increase international support for the other side. When states do break formal cease-fires, they often go to great lengths to make it look as if they were provoked so as to minimize the international costs. For example, Israel waited for an Arab provocation to launch its offensive to seize the Negev, thus ending the 1948 cease-fire in the first Arab-Israeli war. Despite learning of the impending Arab attack in 1973 hours beforehand, Israel waited and took the first blow so that it would be clear it was not the aggressor.[35] International diplomatic costs

---

[33] One-sided demilitarization is a strategy often used by victors to ensure the continued acquiescence of the vanquished. Enforcing this strategy often requires renewed resort to force, however. For a comprehensive review of the effectiveness of "enforced disarmament" see Towle 1997.

[34] Keohane 1994.

[35] Similarly, Germany waited in 1914 so that the world would know Russia had struck first. Thanks to Bob Jervis for suggesting this example.

are a form of "audience costs."[36] By declaring to an audience (the international community, especially aid donors and military sponsors) their commitment to peace, states invoke costs to breaking this commitment. The cost of the international reaction to aggression alters the incentives, at least at the margins, of reneging on a cease-fire.

Breaking an explicit agreement makes it harder for leaders to portray their side as the victim, making it harder to rally domestic, as well as international, support. If peace is popular, the domestic audience can also help hold leaders to a formal cease-fire commitment. If there are domestic pressures for aggressive action, the process of building political support at home for a formal international agreement may make it politically difficult for a government to reverse policy.[37]

REDUCING UNCERTAINTY ABOUT ACTIONS AND INTENTIONS

Physical constraints, audience costs, and the involvement of outsiders alter incentives for peace and for war, but they also serve as important signaling devices. Talk alone may not allay fears and mistrust, however, costly signals of benign intent can make commitments credible. By paying costs to invest in peace, states provide a gauge of intent. Willingness to sign on to measures that make fighting more difficult is a particularly credible signal of the absence of aggressive designs. Only actors who are not contemplating war will accept measures that make an attack considerably more costly. Physical constraints thus serve as credible signals of commitment, as does willingness to make peace despite significant domestic opposition.[38]

Cease-fire agreements can also help reduce uncertainty by marking the exact location of a cease-fire line. This provides a focal point and helps prevent salami tactics to push the line to either side's advantage. Specifying the rules of the cease-fire—what actions are permissible near the cease-fire line, for example—helps define compliance and noncompliance to prevent misunderstandings and avoid unnecessary tension. The more specific the agreement, the less uncertainty there will be about what constitutes compliance.

Monitoring mechanisms can alleviate worries about detecting aggressive moves by the opponent in time to retaliate. States are likely to rely

---

[36] Note that the term *audience costs* often refers to the cost of backing down from a threat rather than from breaking a promise to cooperate, as I use it here.

[37] Martin 1993, 415. The importance of a public commitment may be greater for inducing domestic audience costs in democracies than in other types of regimes. Fearon 1994. However, with an issue as salient as war and peace, all leaders must worry about domestic politics. The relevant audience for nondemocratic leaders may be the military or the party rather than the wider public.

[38] Domestic costs can be extreme; both Anwar Sadat and Itzhak Rabin paid, tragically, with their lives for their commitment to peace.

for the most part on their own intelligence rather than verification mechanisms set up as part of an agreement. Monitoring may therefore be less important for cease-fires than for other kinds of international agreements. However, *neutral* referees can play an important role in fostering durable peace. Because of the costs associated with being seen as the aggressor, an actor that defects will try to blame the other side for starting hostilities.[39] Without neutral observers, claims of being the victim are therefore not credible and there are bound to be disputes over "who started it."[40] Monitors to investigate incidents and give credible information on compliance are therefore important for distinguishing unprovoked aggression from legitimate retaliation. Neutral monitoring therefore works in conjunction with the audience costs discussed above. The international diplomatic costs of breaking a cease-fire depend heavily on the distinction between aggression and justified retaliation.

PREVENTING AND CONTROLLING ACCIDENTS

Cease-fire agreements often include mechanisms to help prevent accidents or to keep them from triggering renewed fighting when they do occur. Ongoing negotiations and dispute resolution procedures can provide a forum for discussion and the airing of differences before a spiral of retaliation is triggered. Without such communication it will be difficult for states to signal benign intent. The dangers of misperception and miscommunication are alleviated, though certainly not removed entirely, by direct communication. Neutral outsiders can also play an important role in the day-to-day managing of tense cease-fire lines. International monitors and peacekeepers serve as on-the-spot mediators, helping to resolve small incidents, restore local cease-fires when clashes occur, and keeping communication lines open even between enemies who politically cannot afford to deal directly with each other.

Withdrawal of forces, buffer zones, and arms regulations can help prevent accidents and misunderstandings from occurring in the first place by putting some distance between troops and restricting potentially provocative military activities.[41] Confidence-building measures to regulate and

[39] The international community condemned India in 1965 for crossing the cease-fire line, not realizing that Pakistan had incited aggression by Azad Kashmir raiders. India seems to have learned from this that sponsoring irregular forces was a relatively cheap way, politically, to undertake aggression—a strategy it used in 1971.

[40] On the politics of blaming, and a cautionary word on the role of outside audiences, see Groseclose and McCarty 2001.

[41] After the Yom Kippur War, DMZs were set up on both the Syrian and Egyptian fronts, with arms restricted in additional swaths of territory on either side. In Cyprus most of the incidents between Turks and Greeks occurred at the narrowest parts of the DMZ, and were reduced when the zones were widened. UN 1996, 166.

make transparent behavior (such as military exercises) that is likely to cause tension can also prevent misunderstandings and alleviate suspicions. Cease-fire agreements often hold each side responsible for violations coming from its own territory to prevent their being used as an excuse for intentional defection.[42] Agreements may also include concrete measures for internal control to prevent "involuntary defection." The cease-fire arrangement reached after the Football War between El Salvador and Honduras included disarming irregular forces, for example, while the United Nations Emergency Force was given responsibility for pursuing *fedayeen* fighters in the Sinai after 1956 to deal with just this sort of problem.

• • •

While these three strategies (raising the cost of attack, reducing uncertainty, and controlling accidents) are presented separately, their functions are intimately connected. Neutral monitoring helps ensure that aggressors will be identified, and this also raises the political cost of attack. Physical constraints such as buffer zones make it harder to attack but also reduce the likelihood of accidents. States are less likely to fear attack if the costs of aggression are higher. And as has been mentioned, willingness to implement measures that tie belligerents' hands (i.e., anything that raises costs) serves as a credible signal of intention. The strategies used for overcoming obstacles to cooperation may be analytically distinct, but they run together in practice.[43]

Peace Mechanisms

This discussion of strategies suggests a general hypothesis: all else equal, the more cease-fire agreements raise the cost of aggression, the more they provide credible information about actions and intentions, and the more is done to prevent and control accidents, the longer peace will last. Unfortunately, these strategies cannot be observed directly. We cannot measure the costs of attack, the credibility of information, or the danger of accidents. We can, however, observe concrete measures taken to raise costs, signal intent, prevent accidents, and so on. Below, I outline a number of specific observable mechanisms that, if my argument is correct, should help foster durable peace, ceteris paribus. As noted above, many of these mecha-

---

[42] In a related vein, Fearon and Laitin 1996 show how leaders can reach stable agreements to punish defectors from their own side to prevent interethnic conflict.

[43] Note, however, that sometimes these measures can work at cross-purposes. Pegging states' reputations to whether they initiate conflict can make them more likely to support irregular forces as proxies, making the problem of internal control harder to deal with.

nisms serve several functions at once. Measures are grouped into three categories: those that constrain belligerents physically, those that are provided by outsiders, and those that entail communication and signaling.

Moving troops back from the cease-fire line makes it physically harder for them to attack each other; it thus raises the cost of attack and alleviates fear. Possession being "nine-tenths of the law," troop withdrawals can have important territorial implications. States will be particularly reluctant to give up ground that was hard won on the battlefield, so willingness to withdraw troops also serves as a costly, and therefore credible, signal of benign intent. The UN has attempted to make withdrawal to the status quo antebellum the norm by generally refusing to recognize territorial gains through war. To the extent that this norm holds, it reduces the possible gains of military attack. Withdrawal of forces also prevents accidents and skirmishes along the cease-fire line by separating troops.

HYPOTHESIS. *Withdrawal of forces from the cease-fire line yields more durable peace.*

If they are wide enough, demilitarized zones can serve as a physical constraint, making attack, particularly surprise attack, more difficult. Buffer zones can provide early warning of an offensive thus reassuring recent combatants. By putting some space between forces, demilitarized zones can also alleviate the dangers of accidental and involuntary defection and the skirmishes they create.[44]

HYPOTHESIS. *Peace lasts longer when demilitarized zones are set up.*

Restrictions on armaments, particularly those allowed near the cease-fire line, make mobilization for an attack more difficult. Arms control measures can also prevent misunderstandings and military accidents that might provoke retaliation by regulating military activities near the cease-fire line.[45]

HYPOTHESIS. *Arms control measures increase the durability of peace.*

---

[44] DMZs might also cause problems by preventing strategic depth for defense, possibly undermining deterrence and making war more likely rather than less. Thanks to Jack Snyder for pointing this out.

[45] Much of the literature on arms control has focused on nuclear weapons, but the logic of limiting war-fighting capacity, and regulating destabilizing military activity applies

Cease-fire agreements that hold each side responsible for all acts coming from its own territory provide an incentive for belligerents to control irregular forces or potential rogue groups that might otherwise drag them back into war. Concrete provisions to disarm or deter groups that might upset a cease-fire can physically prevent "involuntary defection" by rogue parties. After the first Kashmir war, for example, Pakistan withdrew the Pathan (Pashtun) fighters who had started the war and stationed its own troops in front of Azad Kashmir irregular forces to minimize the risk of problems.

HYPOTHESIS. *Measures to prevent involuntary defection make peace more stable.*

THE ROLE OF OUTSIDERS: PEACEKEEPING AND THIRD-PARTY GUARANTEES

International peacekeepers interposed between belligerents can act as a physical constraint against attack.[46] However, because peacekeeping operates with the consent of the belligerents themselves, its deterrent value is limited. Peacekeeping troops cannot stop a determined aggressor, but their presence can make attack more costly than it would be in their absence, in large part because of the international reaction. The presence of international troops between hostile forces can also provide a buffer to prevent accidents and clashes along a cease-fire line, and can prevent a power vacuum between militaries.[47]

Whether they are armed forces or unarmed observers ("blue helmets" or "blue berets" in the UN lingo), peacekeepers also serve a monitoring function, investigating alleged violations and publicizing violations as well as serving as an early warning system. Monitoring helps ensure that noncompliance will be detected and that belligerents will not be falsely charged with violating the cease-fire. Monitors' main function is to act as referee, adjudicating "who started it" when clashes occur. In practice, monitors and armed peacekeepers often serve an important dispute resolution function, mediating small quarrels and clashes on the spot. Peacekeeping or monitoring by the United Nations or a regional organization also serves as a signal of the international community's commitment to peace in a particular conflict.

---

equally to conventional armaments. See especially Schelling and Halperin 1961. On arms control at the conclusion of conflicts, see Croft 1996, 40–44.

[46] Peacekeeping is defined here as the practice of sending neutral observers or soldiers to monitor a cease-fire or to position themselves between opposing forces. Peacekeeping can be undertaken by international organizations such as the United Nations or the Organization of American States, or by an ad hoc group of states. It takes place with the consent of the states on whose territory peacekeepers are deployed.

[47] On the theory and practice of peacekeeping, see especially Rikhye 1984, and also Ryan 1998; Diehl 1993; and Fetherston 1994. Examples of peacekeeping case studies include

HYPOTHESIS. *Peace is more likely to last if international peace-keepers are present.*

At a minimum, the explicit involvement of a powerful third state in maintaining peace invokes international audience costs to violating the agreement. Breaking the cease-fire can have international repercussions if a great power is interested in keeping peace. At a maximum, outsiders can guarantee peace by threatening reprisals against an aggressor.[48] Barbara Walter has argued that external security guarantees are crucial for the stability of peace in the aftermath of civil wars.[49] Because states maintain their own security forces after interstate war, the commitment problem Walter identifies is not as dire for states. Nonetheless, guarantees by more powerful states should help maintain peace after interstate war as well.

HYPOTHESIS. *Third-party guarantees make peace more durable.*

COMMUNICATION AND SIGNALING

The term *confidence-building measures* (CBMs) generally refers to mechanisms that regulate and increase the transparency of military activities prone to produce friction among adversaries. These measures include advance notification of troop rotations or of military exercises and joint inspection of military facilities. Direct communication links or "hot lines" are often also labeled CBMs.[50] Confidence-building measures may reduce the fear of attack and provide a credible signal of benign intent. By regulating and providing notification of activities likely to cause tension, CBMs may also reduce the chances of misunderstandings and overreactions; they can thus help alleviate the security dilemma.

HYPOTHESIS. *Peace is more durable when confidence-building measures are implemented.*

Rational models of war tend to assume that communication is unproblematic, but diplomatic relations are often severed during war, and even sending basic messages can be difficult without a forum for discussion or

---

Dawson 1994; Doyle 1995; and the collections in Durch 1993 and 1996. For a good example of comparative work on peacekeeping success, see Howard 2001.

[48] External backing for one side, as opposed to the cease-fire itself (for example, support of one side by a superpower patron) can have mixed repercussions—the supported side will be more likely to act aggressively but will be protected from threats to its survival that might otherwise make cooperation more difficult.

[49] Walter 1997.

[50] For an overview of confidence-building measures, see Krepon et al. 1993. See also Holst and Melander 1977 and Krepon and Sevak 1995.

a mediator to serve as go-between. Ongoing negotiations and mediation, or better yet, a joint commission made up of representatives of the belligerents, can provide a communication channel and forum for discussion of problems as they occur during the implementation of a cease-fire agreement. Such dispute resolution mechanisms help keep accidental violations or defection by rogue groups from spiraling out of control in a vicious cycle of retaliation. Continued willingness to work out problems as they arise also serves as an ongoing signal of the intention to keep peace.

HYPOTHESIS. *Dispute resolution procedures make peace last longer.*

Specific agreements reduce uncertainty about what constitutes compliance. The more the exact terms of an agreement are spelled out explicitly, the less possibility there is for misunderstandings by the parties themselves or by international actors reacting to perceived violations.[51] Specification and demarcation of the cease-fire line's location can help prevent small land grabs or salami tactics that can spark renewed conflict.

HYPOTHESIS. *More specific cease-fire agreements are more likely to hold.*

Publicly and formally signing a cease-fire agreement induces audience costs to breaking the commitment to peace and invokes international law. The potential cost of a damaged reputation and the prospect of an adverse international reaction that will affect military and economic aid alters the payoffs of reinitiating conflict. Especially if there is domestic opposition to the compromises of a cease-fire, a formal and public commitment can serve as a credible signal of intentions.[52]

---

[51] An opposing hypothesis would suggest that overly specific or rigid agreements can make violations more likely. For a related discussion of built-in flexibility in international agreements, see Koremenos 2001 and Koremenos, Lipson, and Snidal 2001. Interestingly, cease-fire agreements rarely if ever include formal provisions for renegotiation. This is less surprising when one considers that few of these agreements purport to settle the political issues of the conflict.

[52] On the pros and cons of formal versus informal agreements, see Lipson 1991. Formalism is equivalent to what Abbott et al. 2000 refer to as "obligation," the extent to which parties are legally bound by a rule. This is one of three dimensions of their concept of legalization. A second, "precision," is equivalent to specificity, discussed above. The third is "delegation." Third-party guarantees and dispute resolution procedures may operate in ways similar to their concept of delegation, but cease-fire agreements tend to have extremely low levels of delegation. (One exception was the eventual use of the International Court of Justice to settle the El Salvador–Honduras conflict.) Abbott and Snidal 2000 discuss the pros and cons of legalization, arguing that "hard law" increases the cost of reneging and makes commitments more credible. They also note that delegation tends to be low in security affairs (440).

HYPOTHESIS. *Formal agreements lead to more durable peace than tacit agreements.*

The foregoing discussion of obstacles to peace, strategies for overcoming these obstacles, and specific observable mechanisms thus leads to a set of testable hypotheses (which have been listed above). All else equal, each of these measures individually should be expected to lead to more stable peace. In general, peace should last longer the more (or more extensive) the measures implemented to raise costs, reduce uncertainty, and prevent accidents. I refer to the number and extent of the individual mechanisms as the strength of a cease-fire agreement.[53] If the theory outlined here is correct we should expect the following general hypothesis to hold:

HYPOTHESIS. *All else equal, the stronger the agreement implemented, the longer peace lasts.*

Individually and together, mechanisms within cease-fire agreements should affect the durability of peace.

POLITICAL SETTLEMENT

A further aspect of peace agreements that should affect stability is whether they purport to settle the political issues over which the war was fought, or whether they are simply agreements to stop hostilities. If disputants could have reached a political settlement over the issues that divided them before the war, they could have avoided combat in the first place. Wars are fought when diplomacy fails. As noted above, one of the "rationalist" explanations for war is that private information about capability and resolve can lead both sides to believe they will prevail in armed conflict. Actually fighting the war publicizes this information, and can therefore make political settlement possible. But in the period studied here, settlement is the exception rather than the rule; most wars end without resolving key political issues. Cases such as the Korean Armistice of 1953, leaving the fundamental issues of the war unsettled, are much more the norm than are political settlements such as the Israeli-Egyptian Peace Agreement in 1979. Indeed, war has been a very ineffective way to resolve conflict in the last half century. Nevertheless, in the few cases in which political settlement is reached we would expect peace to be more stable than in cases where the main political issues are still in dispute.

---

[53] By "strong" agreements I mean not that they are effective—that is the empirical question addressed in later chapters—but that they include the various mechanisms intended to maintain peace: withdrawal of forces, demilitarized zones, peacekeeping, formal agreement, confidence-building measures, etc. Cease-fires range from having no agreement at all,

Political settlement is unlike the other mechanisms and strategies discussed above. While the others involve measures to manage conflict, negotiating a political solution deals with its root causes. Finding a political solution represents an attempt to alter the relationship from one of deep enmity, to, if not friendship, at least coexistence. The ability to reach a settlement in which both sides can live with the other's claims is an indicator that the conflict is not completely intractable. Information revealed by the war or through negotiations has enabled the belligerents to find an acceptable solution. Political settlements face the same enforcement and commitment issues as do agreements merely to maintain a military cease-fire; states can agree to peace and then renege. But the political costs involved in renouncing claims, especially claims over which war has been fought, and reaching a compromise make these agreements particularly sticky. Political agreements can also serve as focal points. Distributional conflicts over the terms of substantive agreement on the core issues are sure to be severe, but once states have settled on a particular outcome, and have abandoned other claims publicly, that outcome becomes more difficult to challenge. That political settlements are so rare after war testifies to the fact that states do not enter into them lightly.

HYPOTHESIS. *Peace agreements that settle political issues lead to more durable peace than military armistice or cease-fire agreements.*[54]

A study of the effects of agreements on the durability of peace cannot ignore the issue of political settlement, but because political agreements are so rare, and because I am most interested in how adversaries can maintain peace despite deeply conflicting interests, I focus in particular on measures to alter incentives, reduce uncertainty about actions and intentions, and control accidents from spiraling out of control. I do not consider political settlement part of the strength of an agreement, but rather test its effects separately. Independent of political settlement, then, I expect the content of cease-fire agreements to matter. Stronger agreements should last longer than weaker ones, ceteris paribus. Chapters 5 and 6 test these hypotheses empirically. However, ceteris is not necessarily paribus, and that leads to a potential counterargument that must be addressed first.

---

through weak agreements with few or only weakly specified measures, to stronger agreements that implement more extensive measures to attempt to maintain peace.

[54] While I use the term *peace* to mean simply the absence of violent conflict, synonymous with cease-fire, I use the terms *peace agreement* or *peace settlement* to distinguish agreements that settle political issues from military cease-fire agreements and armistices that do not.

II. Agreements and the Baseline Prospects for Peace: A Counterargument and Rebuttal

The counterargument to the thesis that agreements have an independent effect on the durability of peace is that agreements are themselves determined by the situation at the time of the cease-fire, and it is this situation, not the agreements, that determines whether peace lasts. If strong agreements are only achievable when peace is likely to last anyway, then any apparent relationship between agreements and peace is spurious. Intuitively, we might expect that belligerents will be more likely to be able to reach strong agreements when relations are relatively good. By this logic, when cooperation is comparatively easy, parties will be able to draft strong agreements, and these agreements last. Conversely, when peace is more difficult to maintain, agreements will tend to be vague arrangements with no substance, meant to paper over deep differences, and these compacts will not last for long.[55] If this is true, we might observe a positive relationship between strength of agreement and durability of peace, but we should not infer that this relationship is causal. The counterargument is thus akin to the realist claim that international institutions are epiphenomenal.[56]

This line of reasoning seems quite plausible, but an argument can also be made that the relationship between the baseline prospects for peace and the strength of agreements is just the opposite. When cooperation is more difficult, combatants may have greater incentive to draft a strong agreement to help them maintain peace. Cease-fire agreements are deliberate attempts by belligerents to overcome obstacles to peace. According to this reasoning, the greater the obstacles to peace, the greater the need for mechanisms to alter incentives, reduce uncertainty, and prevent accidents. If these mechanisms are effective but costly, belligerents and the international community will only want to invest in them if they are truly necessary, that is, when the probability of war resuming is otherwise quite high. Moreover, combatants will be more likely to insist on strong measures to keep peace when they most expect the other side to renege.[57]

---

[55] Gray 1992 makes a similar argument about arms control: when it is possible because relations are good, it is irrelevant; when it is needed because relations are bad, it is impossible to achieve.

[56] Mearsheimer 1994–95. This argument is put most forcefully by offensive realists. Defensive realists would agree with some aspects of the rebuttal I present below, particularly that agreements can serve as important tools of statecraft. Jervis 1999.

[57] Gartzke 1999 has argued that anything that we can measure to know whether war is likely can be measured by state leaders as well. Predictable wars are avoidable wars; "war is in the error term." If this is true, then we should observe states attempting to mitigate the risk of war when the dangers are predictably high. That is, we should see them implementing peace-maintaining mechanisms such as those studied here when peace is most precarious,

If this is true, and if we look at the relationship between agreements and the durability of peace without controlling for the underlying probability of war, we would see no effect (if stronger agreements simply cancel out the greater propensity for war) or possibly even a negative relationship, because strong agreements will be put in place when peace is most precarious. We may observe that conflict is more likely to resume when peacekeepers are present, for example, not because peacekeepers stir up trouble, but because they are more likely to be in the places where war is most likely. Similarly, belligerents might be most likely to demand monitoring mechanisms when they have most reason to fear their opponent will cheat. Police and crime rates provide a good analogy. If we looked at the number of police assigned to different neighborhoods and at crime rates, we would probably find that crime rates are higher where there are more police on the streets. We would not necessarily conclude that police cause crime or even that they are ineffective because of this, but perhaps that police are sent where they are most needed.[58]

Both of these arguments, the counterargument and the rebuttal, suggest that agreements are endogenous: that is, one set of independent variables (agreement strength) may be caused by, rather than independent of, another set (situational variables). But the arguments posit opposing directions for the endogenous relationship. The first argument focuses on actors' ability to implement strong agreements. Agreement on mechanisms to facilitate cooperation itself requires cooperation, so the supply of these measures will be lower when cooperation is more difficult. The second is a functionalist argument focusing on need.[59] Actors need measures to ease cooperation more when cooperation is most difficult. The counterargument that agreements are epiphenomenal and the functionalist response thus provide opposing hypotheses about how the baseline prospects for peace are related to the content of agreements.[60] The former suggests that we should find the strongest agreements when the underlying prospects for peace are best. Only when cooperation is relatively easy (the very situations in which peace is most likely to last in any case) will

---

as the rebuttal to the counterargument holds. This book is in a sense a study of how states avoid avoidable wars.

[58] For other similar examples, see Jervis 1997, esp. 81–87.

[59] Because these competing hypotheses parallel debates between realists and institutionalists over whether international institutions are epiphenomenal or exert independent effects, I use the labels *realist* and *institutionalist* or *functionalist* as shorthand to identify them. As noted earlier, this debate is well worn and it is not my intent to test or "prove" or "disprove" realist or institutionalist approaches to international relations, only to use these approaches to shed light on the issue of agreements and the durability of peace.

[60] More specific hypotheses about the relationship between particular aspects of the situation between belligerents and the strength of agreements, as well as direct tests of these hypotheses, are presented in chapter 4.

actors be able to agree to ambitious agreements that include strong provisions for maintaining peace.

HYPOTHESIS. *Strong agreements are concluded when the baseline prospects for peace are relatively good.*

Agreements are therefore epiphenomenal. Any apparent positive relationship between the strength of agreements and the duration of peace is spurious; both agreements and durability are driven by the situation between the belligerents.

The logic of the functionalist argument suggests just the opposite. The content of agreements is affected by the situation between the belligerents, but the strongest agreements will be put in place not when peace is easiest to maintain, but when it is hardest. If strong cease-fire agreements help to maintain peace, there will be greater need for them when peace is less likely to last. Belligerents will craft strong agreements when the situation between them would otherwise make peace most fragile. They will be unwilling to cease fire unless mechanisms to ensure the cease-fire are in place. Moreover, both the parties to the conflict and the international community will only invest in measures to maintain peace when they are truly necessary.

HYPOTHESIS. *Strong agreements are concluded when the baseline prospects for peace are relatively dim.*

Whether the counterargument or the rebuttal is correct, the effect of measures within agreements on the durability of peace cannot be examined in isolation. This study must take into consideration the baseline prospects for peace. The following section suggests a number of variables that might be expected to shape these baseline prospects.

Proponents of the counterargument might contend that measuring these factors is insufficient—that it is not measurable variables such as the decisiveness of victory or the cost of the war that matter, but the actors' intentions, sometimes referred to as the "political will" of the parties. If strong mechanisms are put in place and peace lasts, it is relatively easy to argue that the mechanisms per se did not do the work—that only because the belligerents intended to keep peace anyway were they willing to implement the mechanisms. This argument is unfalsifiable, as we have no way to measure states' intentions—if intentions were knowable, diplomacy itself would not exist and perhaps neither would war.[61] But this argument

---

[61] On the difficulty of gauging intentions as a key cause of war, see Fearon 1995. Like arguments that conflicts end when they are "ripe for resolution," arguments about political will risk tautology.

also misses the point. I do not mean to argue that states' intentions are not important determinants of war or peace, nor that their intentions are unrelated to the kinds of agreements they reach. I would argue, rather, that willingness to undertake costly measures such as withdrawing troops or publicly signing an agreement with the enemy is precisely how states signal their intentions to each other.

The mechanisms discussed in this volume do not work mechanistically; they are political tools used by states to achieve their ends. That they are used intentionally does not make them irrelevant. The debate over whether tools or intentions matter is akin to the gun control debate over whether guns kill people or people kill people. The difference is that we know that firing a gun at someone can kill, but we do not yet know whether sending monitors to observe a cease-fire or setting up dispute resolution procedures will help keep peace. And so it is worth studying the effectiveness of these tools.[62]

It is possible in the abstract to distinguish between two arguments about the effects of peace mechanisms. There are two distinct causal pathways: one in which agreement mechanisms influence peace directly by constraining states or providing information about compliance or preventing accidents, and another in which they simply signal intentions by providing a measure of states' disposition to live in peace. However, the two are not so easily distinguished in reality. As the literature on signaling and "cheap talk" suggests, if there are incentives to misrepresent intentions, as there surely are among deadly enemies, signals are only credible if they are costly.[63] Specifically, signals are credible to the extent that they represent costs that those with benign intentions are willing to pay, but those with aggressive intentions are not, so that they separate between these two types. If constraining one's ability to wage war, or opening oneself up to verification, is costly in a way that is too "expensive" for those intending to attack, but not for those willing to abide by a cease-fire, these measures will serve as credible signals. The indirect signaling function depends in large part on the more direct effects of agreement mechanisms, that they raise the cost of attack or provide early warning.[64] So while these causal

[62] To exaggerate the point, saying that cease-fire agreements or international institutions have no independent effect if they only do what states want them to do is a bit like saying nuclear weapons have no independent effect on international relations because they only do things (deter attack or blow up cities) that states want them to do. The question is whether agreements allow states to do something (avoid war) that they want to do but otherwise could not.

[63] See, for example, Farrell and Rabin 1996; and Morrow 1999.

[64] Some of the mechanisms examined here signal by "tying hands," creating costs only if 11a state reneges on its commitment. This is true of the reputational costs invoked by a formal agreement, for example. Others "sink costs" by requiring payment ex ante, for example withdrawing from territory. Others, such as verification measures, may do both. On this distinction, see Fearon 1997.

arguments are analytically distinct, they will be very difficult to distinguish in practice. However, to say that agreements do part of their "work" by signaling intentions does not mean that they have no independent effect or are epiphenomenal, only that they are instrumental.

III. The Baseline Prospects for Peace: Situational Variables

Cooperation is harder in some cases than in others, and we would expect—the agreement aside—peace to last longer in some situations than in others. The discussion of obstacles to peace in the first part of this chapter suggests a number of variables that should make peace harder to maintain. We might expect states to have an easier time reaching a bargain and avoiding another war after a decisive victory that has cleared up uncertainty about military resolve and capabilities than after a war that ends in a stalemate. If the cost of war is the primary deterrent to attack, then we should expect peace to last longer after more costly fights, on the theory that the cost of the last fight provides a good predictor of future costs. Peace should be particularly difficult to maintain in conflicts that threaten the existence of one side because an eliminated state cannot retaliate. Misunderstandings and accidents might be more likely between contiguous states, or between those with a long history of conflict before the war.

Chapter 3 explores in detail these and other hypotheses about variables that might be expected to shape the baseline prospects for peace. I use the term *situational variables* to refer to characteristics of the situation between the belligerents, over which those who would make peace have little or no control. Some of these are "preexisting conditions," that is, conditions at the time of the cease-fire. These include characteristics of the war just fought (its military outcome, the cost of war, and the number of belligerents); material and physical conditions (geography and relative military capabilities); and the nature of the belligerents' relationship (their history of conflict and the stakes at issue). Changes after a cease-fire is in place might also affect its prospects. Shifts in relative capabilities might upset the peace, for example. Studies of regime type and war suggest that democratizing states might be more likely to fight, but that if both belligerents become democracies, peace will hold. Bueno de Mesquita and Lalman's measure of "expected utility" for war might also help us predict the baseline prospects for peace.

These situational variables are drawn from a variety of theoretical perspectives and empirical approaches to the study of war and peace. Realists might expect the decisiveness of victory and relative capabilities to be the most important, for example, while constructivists might expect belligerents' history of conflict to be crucial. Quantitative and formal studies of proneness to war have focused on the issues at stake and contiguity, and

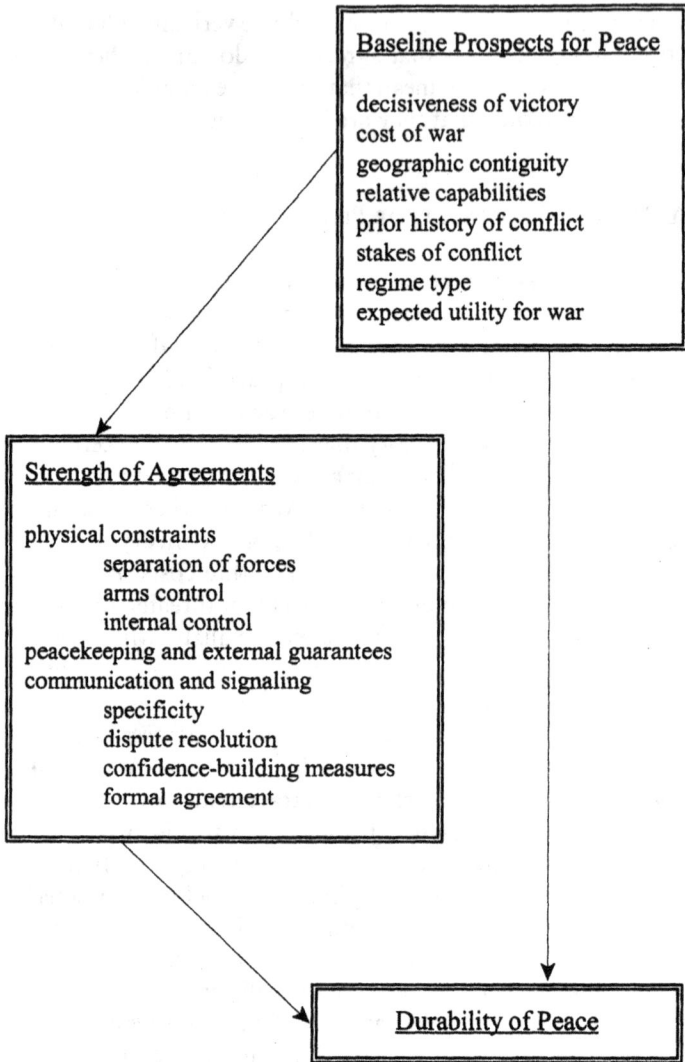

Figure 1.1 Summary of the Argument

on expected utility calculations, respectively. Inclusion of these variables is not intended as a comprehensive test of these theories. Rather I have tried to integrate some of these ideas into the cooperation theory of maintaining peace, and have tried to ensure that the test of my own theory not be biased by omission of situational variables indicated by alternative explanations.

The situational factors should help us understand when peace will be most difficult to keep, that is, what kinds of situations are most predisposed to renewed conflict. These variables help answer the central question of this book: What determines whether peace lasts or war resumes? But their inclusion in this study is also crucial for an evaluation of the role of agreements. They allow me to assess the baseline prospects for peace so that I can test the counterargument and rebuttal discussed above, and they allow me to control for these baseline prospects when I test the effects of agreements on the durability of peace.

SUMMARY OF THE ARGUMENT

Maintaining peace in the aftermath of war requires cooperation, but cooperation is particularly difficult to achieve between deadly enemies. They have strong incentives to take advantage of each other and good reason to fear each other. Cease-fires operate on the basis of reciprocity and mutual deterrence. The prospect of a response deters belligerents from simply marching in and settling their dispute unilaterally; such a move will be met with force. But for reciprocity and deterrence to work, the cost of war must outweigh the gains of an attack, and both sides must believe this to be true of the other; it must be possible to distinguish compliance from noncompliance; and accidents must be prevented from setting off a vicious circle of retaliation that spirals back to war. I argue that belligerents can institute measures that help overcome the obstacles to peace by raising the cost of reinitiating conflict, reducing uncertainty about actions and intentions, and preventing and managing accidental violations of the cease-fire. Mechanisms within cease-fire agreements therefore matter in the construction of durable peace.

The counterargument rests on the contention that strong agreements will be drafted only when peace is likely to last in any case, so that any association with durable peace is spurious. The rebuttal contends that strong agreements are concluded not when the baseline prospects for peace are good, but when they are most dim. Belligerents will invest in stronger measures to help them overcome the obstacles to peace when it would otherwise be most precarious. In order to assess the effects of agreements on whether war resumes or peace lasts, we must know something about the baseline prospects for peace at the time of the cease-fire.

This study therefore consists of an investigation of the three relationships summarized in figure 1.1. It asks three empirical questions: First, how do aspects of the situation between the belligerents at the time of the cease-fire affect the baseline prospects for peace? In other words, what are the effects of the situational variables on the durability of peace? This question is answered in chapter 3. Second, how do these baseline prospects affect the content of agreements? Are stronger agreements concluded when the prospects for peace are good or when peace would otherwise be precarious? The competing hypotheses of the counterargument and rebuttal are tested in chapter 4. Third, controlling for its baseline prospects, how does the content of agreements affect the durability of peace? Do stronger agreements yield more durable peace? Do specific mechanisms to alter incentives, reduce uncertainty, and prevent accidents actually help maintain peace? These questions are addressed in chapters 5 and 6. The following chapter discusses how I go about answering these three empirical questions.

CHAPTER TWO

INVESTIGATING THE DURABILITY OF PEACE

THE CENTRAL ARGUMENT of this book is that mechanisms incorporated into cease-fire agreements affect the durability of peace. How would we know if this argument is right or wrong? For a number of reasons the evidentiary issues are not entirely straightforward. As with most social science we usually cannot observe the direct causal connection between independent and dependent variables, but rather must infer that unobservable connection. Wars start (and conversely peace holds) for reasons numerous, complex, and often idiosyncratic. We cannot get inside decision makers' heads to observe their calculations of the costs and benefits of an attack or of restraint. To make matters worse, decisions about war and peace are made in secret, with documentary evidence likely kept classified. This is especially true in cases, like most of those studied here, in which political and territorial issues remain disputed (as in Kashmir, or the Golan Heights). This makes it unlikely that we will find evidence that definitively proves or disproves the argument. The absence of "smoking gun" evidence makes the research task more difficult, but it cuts both ways. Direct evidence will be hard to find either to refute or to support our hypotheses. This problem therefore does not bias the results one way or the other.

A second issue, however, does bias the findings. As in studies of deterrence, it is much more obvious when efforts to maintain peace fail than when they succeed. Not only do we notice it when war breaks out, we study it. Historians investigate in detail the factors at work when leaders go to war, but tend to ignore the factors at work when leaders "go to peace." We know much more about Anwar Sadat's decision making about war with Israel in 1973, for example, than about Gamal Abdul Nasser's in 1962. Much more has been written about the outbreak of the Falklands/Malvinas war than about the absence of war between Argentina and Britain in the years since. This means that in the available information there is a general bias toward finding evidence of the failure of efforts to maintain peace, rather than success. When peace-maintaining measures are in place, it is easier to argue that they have failed if war breaks out than to argue that they have succeeded if peace holds. For example, it is obvious that the presence of UN monitors did not keep peace between India and Pakistan in 1965, when the second Kashmir war broke out, but it is less obvious whether their presence helped maintain peace throughout the 1950s. This means that the available evidence may be biased against the argument made here. It should be easier to find information suggesting that the main hypothesis of this book is wrong than that it is right. If we do find evidence that it is right despite this bias, we can have all the more confidence in it, knowing that the "true" relationship is likely stronger than the one discovered here.

A third concern is the one raised by the counterargument that any apparent effect of agreement mechanisms on peace is likely spurious. This argument raises the issue of endogeneity and requires that we have some gauge of the baseline prospects for peace. The situational variables evaluated in chapter 3 provide a measure of the difficulty of maintaining peace. I then use this gauge to address the endogeneity issue in two ways. First, I test the relationship between these situational variables and agreements directly. Chapter 4 treats the overall strength of agreements and their individual mechanisms as dependent variables to see whether stronger agreements tend to be reached when peace is otherwise expected to be easy or more difficult. Second, I include the situational variables as controls when I test the effects of agreements on the durability of peace. This allows me to test the independent effect of agreements, given a particular set of situational characteristics. This issue of endogeneity is the reason for the three-question structure of the book: examining first how features of the situation between the belligerents shape the baseline prospects for peace; second, how these baseline prospects affect the content of agreements that are put in place; and third, given the baseline prospects for peace, whether stronger agreements lead to more durable peace.

This fix is not perfect because the endogeneity issue affects even the first of these questions. The tests in chapter 3 of how situational variables affect the prospects for peace deliberately omit consideration of any efforts to improve its chances through cease-fire agreements and the mechanisms within them. If these efforts work, as I argue they do, then this omission may bias the results presented in chapter 3. For example if a variable such as prior conflict makes peace less durable but also tends to inspire stronger agreements, and we ignore those agreements, we will underestimate the effect of such conflict because it, in a sense, corrects for itself. We must therefore be sensitive to this bias in conclusions reached in chapter 3.[1] Note, however, that this bias works against my overall argument. For reasons explained in chapter 4, this bias favors the counterargument that

---

[1] The tests in chapters 5 and 6 in which agreement variables are included in the model can be used to check this problem.

agreements are epiphenomenal and will make it harder to find evidence that they are a functional response to need. Again this bias means that we can have more confidence in evidence for the functional hypothesis.

How, then, would we know whether the hypotheses outlined in chapter 1 are supported, and how would we know if they are wrong? This study employs three complementary research methods: quantitative analysis, in depth-case studies, and what I call "large-N qualitative" comparison, or a qualitative survey. On its own, each of these has limitations, but they dovetail so that the strengths of one compensate for the weaknesses of the others. By using all three we can triangulate to get better answers to the questions at hand.

Of these three, two are "large-N" methods surveying the full universe of interstate cease-fires in the post–World War II period, and one is a "small-N" method researching a couple of cases in greater depth. Of the three, one is quantitative, relying on mathematical models and coded data, while the other two are qualitative. The two large-N studies allow for a comprehensive survey of a population of cases, giving the big picture, indicating general patterns and tendencies, and providing information on whether particular cases are typical or unusual. Many factors might be expected to influence how long peace lasts in the aftermath of war. Analysis of a large number of variables calls for a large number of cases. Furthermore, most of the relationships investigated here are likely to be probabilistic rather than determinate. Demilitarized zones, to take one example, will not guarantee lasting peace in every case, but they may well enhance durability on average. It is difficult to evaluate probabilistic relationships with a small number of cases.

The case studies, however, allow for depth that is not available in large-N studies, whether quantitative or qualitative. By examining the India-Pakistan and Israel-Syria cases in detail I can take into account context and nuances that get lost in large-N studies. Details such as Israel's contentious relationship with the United Nations, the role of the superpowers, or the asymmetrical geography of Kashmir that are important for understanding these conflicts cannot be gleaned without in-depth study.[2] A significant amount of evidence is available only through case study research. The justifications given by negotiators for their actions, or the day-to-day events along a cease-fire line, for example, shed light on the questions examined here, but finding this information requires digging, and extensive digging is feasible only for a small number of cases.

---

[2] The time period examined here means that the Cold War operates as a constant in the quantitative analysis (only the Gulf War and the Azeri-Armenian conflict occur outside the Cold War context). However, the implications of the strategic rivalry between the United States and the USSR can be explored in the cases.

There are similar advantages to combining both quantitative and qualitative methods. Statistical methods are capable of modeling complex relationships among variables, and crucially for this study, of controlling for a number of variables at once. Duration models such as those used here are also able to handle censored data, an issue discussed in greater detail below. But qualitative research is useful in investigating the causal relationships between cease-fire agreements and the duration of peace rather than just the association between them. Qualitative analysis, both the small- and large-N varieties, also gives insight into vagaries of individual cases, allows investigation of elements that are not easily quantified, and provides a check on how others are quantified. Reducing an issue as complex as why peace lasted or fell apart to a series of numbers for quantitative research entails the loss of much information, information that can be employed in qualitative analysis. To give one example, the durability of peace is measured in the statistical analysis as the length of time until another war by the same parties. After the Yom Kippur War of 1973, Israel and Syria fought again in Lebanon in 1982. The quantitative analysis thus treats the disengagement agreement reached in 1974 as failing eight years later. But even though Israel and Syria were at war in Lebanon, the cease-fire held along the Golan Heights, where the agreement mechanisms were implemented. A more nuanced sense of what it means to say peace lasted or fell apart is possible in a qualitative study. The case studies can use the fact that peace held in one place while war broke out in another to explore the role of mechanisms within cease-fire agreements.

By pursuing both quantitative and qualitative research together, this study is able to avoid some of the common pitfalls of either approach taken alone. The statistical analysis helps ensure that case selection and omitted variables do not bias the findings derived from the case studies. The qualitative research ensures that the econometric findings are not artifacts of crude data and allows investigation of the putative causal mechanisms connecting independent and dependent variables.

The drawback of using several methods together is posed by time constraints. It has not been possible to extend the scope of the quantitative study back to the beginning of the century or to include smaller conflicts or civil wars to enlarge the data set. The relatively small number of cases puts limits on the data analysis that is possible.[3] Time and funding constraints have also meant that fieldwork and extensive archival research have not been possible for the case studies. Time constraints notwith-

[3] The small number of cases poses statistical problems, as the assumptions of quantitative methods rely on the asymptotics of large numbers. Individual cases are also more likely to drive findings in small samples. However, the data set used here represents all of the interstate wars in the period, not a sample, thus minimizing inference problems.

standing, the complimentary nature of the multimethod research design is particularly appealing, given that this study is the first to address systematically the role of cease-fire agreements in the durability of peace. While each method has its limitations, the strengths of each compensate for the weaknesses of the others.

I. Quantitative Analysis

The Econometric Model

This book examines the duration of peace—why some cease-fires fall apart quickly while others last longer. Early studies of durability judged the success or failure of peace by whether the conflict resumed within some time period.[4] The use of an arbitrary time period is problematic, however. A five-year criterion, for example, treats peace that falls apart in five and a half or six years as just as successful as peace that lasts 20 years, or even permanently, while a cease-fire that fails in a month is no more a failure than one that holds for four years. Furthermore, what one chooses as the time limit to judge success can significantly affect results. In the cease-fire cases examined here, 30% of the wars that resume do so between five and ten years; should these be considered successes or failures? In another 25%, peace lasts for more than 10 years but eventually fails. These cases are clearly not as successful as those in which peace has lasted to date.

We could instead use the criterion of whether war has ever resumed to distinguish permanent peace from any cease-fire that fails. This method also lumps very short cease-fires together with peace that lasts much longer before it eventually fails, but at least there is an analytic rather than arbitrary distinction between the two categories. However, this method runs into another problem, the issue of "censored data." Peace that has lasted to date may not continue to hold. This is particularly a problem for recent cases, but even if peace has lasted quite a long time, we do not know for certain that it will continue to last. An armistice has held in Korea for 50 years, but renewed warfare is conceivable. Israel and Syria have not fought a full-fledged war in 20 years, but they might yet. "Censored" cases are those in which peace lasts until observation ends. When this study began, peace between India and Pakistan had lasted since 1971. But another war broke out in the spring of 1999. If censoring were not taken into account, a study of durability conducted in 1998 would

---

[4] Kozhemiakin 1994 uses a 30-year cutoff; Maoz 1984 divides stability into less than 5 years, 5–10 years, and more than 10 years. The war termination literature (for example, Stedman 1991) often defines "successful" agreements as those that last at least 5 years.

erroneously have treated this peace as permanent. The resumption of war between the United States and Iraq as this book went into production only underlines the importance of this issue.

Fortunately, a class of econometric models exists that avoids all of these problems. Duration models (also known as hazard rate or survival time models) were developed for engineers to study issues such as the failure rates of different types of equipment and for medical researchers to study the survival times of patients undergoing various treatments. Duration models estimate the effects of independent variables on a dependent variable measuring a length of time, and they can incorporate our uncertainty about how long a phenomenon (in this case peace) will continue into the future.[5]

There are several duration models to choose from depending on the assumptions one makes about the shape of the hazard function. The hazard function is the distribution of the probability of failure across time. For example, the exponential distribution assumes that the hazard rate is constant, that the probability of failure does not change as time goes by. This is a problematic assumption for the study of peace. Intuitively, we might expect peace to be most fragile right after a cease-fire and that the probability of renewed warfare decreases as peace lasts. On the other hand, one implication of Fearon's rationalist explanation would be that war is least likely to resume soon after a cease-fire because the preceding war will have revealed private information about capability and resolve.[6] I use the Weibull distribution because it requires no a priori assumption about whether peace is more or less likely to last given that it has lasted up to some point. I can therefore test the duration dependence of peace: does peace become more stable over time, or is the hazard rate flat, with war equally likely to resume in every period, or does the probability of war actually increase as peace survives longer?

The Weibull model assumes that the hazard rate is monotonic, but it is possible that peace is particularly unstable at first, then gets safer, and then slowly gets more precarious. Because we do not know the shape of the hazard distribution, I checked whether results differed when a Cox proportional hazards model is used.[7] There is no substantial difference in results between the two models, suggesting that the assumptions of the Weibull model are warranted. I report Weibull estimates because they are more precise in a small data set like the one used here.[8]

---

[5] For a technical explanation of duration models, see Greene 1993. For a good introduction to their use in political science, see Box-Steffensmeier and Jones 1997.

[6] Fearon 1995.

[7] The Cox model is what is known as "semiparametric" because it does not specify or "paramaterize" the shape of the distribution. It therefore rests on a looser set of assumptions.

[8] Box-Steffensmeier and Jones 1997, 1434.

The quantitative tests in chapters 3, 5, and 6 use this hazard analysis to estimate the effects of situational variables and various aspects of cease-fire agreements on the duration of peace. In these tests, situational variables and mechanisms within agreements are independent variables. In chapter 4, however, I treat these aspects of agreements as dependent. To test the effects of situational variables on the content of agreements, I use several econometric models, depending on the form of the agreement variable under consideration: ordinary least squares (OLS) for continuous variables; logistic and ordered logistic regression for dichotomous and ordinal variables, respectively.[9]

The Cease-Fires Data Set

Testing the hypotheses outlined in chapter 1 required a data set that included information on cease-fires and how long they lasted, on the situation between the belligerents at the time of cease-fire (their history of conflict, the decisiveness of military victory, etc.), and changes over time (in military capabilities, for example), as well as a great deal of information on the nature and content of any agreement that accompanied the cease-fire or was reached later on. Information on situational variables was available in existing data sets, but no one had systematically compiled information on cease-fire agreements. There are no comprehensive lists of peace agreements, let alone descriptive surveys of the content of cease-fire agreements. I therefore created the Cease-Fires data set by researching each case myself.[10]

The data cover 48 cease-fires in international wars ending after 1946 and before 1998. A cease-fire is defined as an end to or break in the fighting, whether or not it represents the final end of the war. It need not be accomplished through an explicit agreement. I began with the Correlates of War Version 3 (COW) list of interstate wars to identify cases.[11] Note that this is not a sample of wars, but rather covers all of the cases of interstate wars in this time period, using the COW definition.[12] In the Cease-Fires data set each case is a cease-fire between a pair of belligerents.

---

[9] For all of the quantitative analysis I use the statistical package STATA (version 6).

[10] The data and data notes are available at <www.columbia.edu/~vpf4>.

[11] COW data are available at <www.umich.edu/~cowproj/>.

[12] The COW definition is a war between members of the interstate system with at least one thousand battle deaths among all the participants. Small and Singer 1982. One war from the COW list is dropped because it never reached a cease-fire as an interstate war. The war between Vietnam and Cambodia "ended" with the installation of a pro-Vietnam government, but the fighting between this new government and the Khmer Rouge continued as a civil war. The line between civil and interstate wars is not always a thick one. I follow COW's classifications, for example excluding the wars in the former Yugoslavia as civil wars.

Multilateral wars in the COW list are therefore broken into separate dyads. COW lists every participant in each armed conflict, no matter how minor; for example, COW lists 16 participants in the Korean War, yielding 28 dyads.[13] In order to minimize overcounting these wars, I have kept only the principal belligerents in each war; so, for example, I keep four dyads from the Korean War (the United States and South Korea vs. China and North Korea).[14]

COW wars in which fighting stopped and started again are divided into separate cases, one for each cease-fire. In 1974, during the Turco-Cypriot War, the fighting stopped at the end of July when Turkey, Greece, and Britain reached an agreement known as the Geneva Declaration. The cease-fire held for two weeks, but was shattered when Turkish forces occupied the north of the island. The war ended two days later with Turkey's declaration of a unilateral cease-fire on August 16. I treat these as two distinct cases. History tends to forget the failed cease-fires, focusing only on the ones that succeeded in ending the war. Omitting cease-fires that failed so quickly that the next round of fighting was considered part of the same war would truncate the variation in durability, potentially biasing our results. Whether a war stopped and started again was discerned from COW dates on which participants "reentered" the war and my own research on each case.[15]

It is possible that I have missed cases of very short cease-fires. If so, the resulting selection bias should work against my own argument because the missing cases are almost certainly extremely weak agreements. Stronger agreements are much more likely to be publicized. The war between Armenia and Azerbaijan provides a good illustration. Between December 1991 (when the interstate war started) and May 1994 (when it ended) there were at least nine cease-fires reported in passing in the press. All but one of these either never went into effect at all, or broke down within a day or two, sometimes within hours. One reached in March 1992

[13] China and North Korea fought against the United States, South Korea, the United Kingdom, the Philippines, Turkey, Australia, Canada, the Netherlands, France, Belgium, Greece, Thailand, Ethiopia, and Colombia.

[14] Including all 28 dyads would only strengthen my findings as the Korean armistice is a very strong agreement that has lasted a very long time. The criterion defining a principal belligerent is that the number of troops committed by a country be more than one-tenth the number contributed by the largest provider of troops. Troop contribution figures are from Clodfelter 1992. In a few cases, a country that met the one-tenth criterion would not otherwise be considered a principal participant because it might seem unlikely to sign an agreement or to fight again without its ally (for example, Libya in the Ugandan-Tanzanian war, or Cuba in the Ethiopian-Somalian war). Excluding these cases makes little difference to the results, and the one-tenth rule provides an objective criterion.

[15] The stated COW criterion for marking a break in the fighting is a pause of 30 days or more. Small and Singer 1982, 66. However, the COW data includes the two-week break in the Turco-Cypriot War.

lasted about three weeks.[16] I have included the three-week cease-fire in the data set, as well as the end of the war in 1994. Including the others would add eight very weak (implementing few if any of the measures studied here) and very short-lived agreements. This would only strengthen the finding that weak agreements fall apart very quickly.

That each dyad in a multilateral war and each cease-fire in a repeated conflict is a separate observation means that the observations are not all independent of one another. Whether Israel and Jordan go to war is affected by whether Israel and Egypt go to war. To correct for the problem of autocorrelation (technically, that the error terms are correlated with one another, violating the assumptions of the statistical models and biasing standard error estimates) I calculate robust standard errors (using Huber's method) in the quantitative tests. Cases are clustered by conflict, so that all of the Arab-Israeli wars are a single cluster, those between India and Pakistan another, and so on. Robust standard errors are calculated on the assumption that each cluster is independent from the others, but that cases within clusters are not independent.[17] Because there have been many wars in the Middle East, and these have tended to be multilateral, the Arab-Israeli conflict dominates the data. In the statistical analysis and the large-N qualitative study I have checked whether particularities of the Arab-Israeli cases are driving results.[18]

In the Cease-Fires data set, each observation is a time span of a year or less after a cease-fire. This allows me to record changes over time, annual military capability data, for example, or changes in the number of peacekeepers, or the fact that a new agreement has been reached implementing new measures. These are known as *time-varying covariates* in the duration analysis lingo. Each of the 48 cease-fires is thus a subject for which there are multiple observations over time, for a total of 876 observations.[19] The duration models treat these subjects as a continuous history, focusing on whether peace survived each period.

[16] Thanks to Megan Gilroy and Arman Gregorian for research assistance on this case, and to Dr. Gerard J. Libaridian, former senior advisor to President Ter-Petrossian of Armenia and lead negotiator on Karabakh, for providing an insider's perspective.

[17] In general, it is better to include the cause of these linkages in our model rather than rely only on robust standard errors. There are only two ways cases can be linked in the data: multiple dyads in a war, or multiple wars in a dyad (or both). The former is controlled for with a dummy for multilateral wars (see below), and by checking whether results are robust when only one randomly selected dyad is included. The latter is more or less the dependent variable; another war means peace has failed, so it would make no sense to try to control for this linkage. Thanks to Erik Gartzke for advice on this issue.

[18] The case studies include one Middle East case and one non–Middle East case as a further check on whether these cases are atypical.

[19] The time spans run from the date of a cease-fire or new agreement to the end of the year, or the implementation of a new agreement, or to the outbreak of a new war, whichever comes first. Independent variables are thus constant within time spans but vary between them.

The cases are listed in appendix A. Also listed are the dates of 15 major follow-up agreements reached after an initial cease-fire. For example, after the cease-fire in 1973 that ended the Yom Kippur War, Israel and Egypt reached a disengagement agreement in 1975 and then, after the Camp David process, signed a peace treaty in 1979.[20]

I use a slightly different version of the data for some tests. In this time-constant form, each cease-fire is coded only once. This version is used for much of the analysis in chapter 4 (in which cease-fire agreements are the dependent variable) and to see how the war between India and Pakistan in 1999, after the other version is censored (see below), affects results.[21]

DURATION OF PEACE

The duration of peace is measured from the date of the cease-fire to the start of another COW war between the same two belligerents, if there was one.[22] This objective measure avoids the issue of whether the second round of fighting was over the same political disagreement as the first, that is, whether it was another round of the same conflict. However, in practice, all of the cases of war resumption examined here involved, at least in part, the issues of their predecessors.[23] There are 26 cases in which peace has lasted to date.[24] The duration of peace is censored in 1998 in the time-varying data (because country-year data is only available until then) and in 2000 in the time-constant version of the data.[25]

[20] These follow-up agreements mark substantial changes in agreement codings. Smaller changes in agreement mechanisms are coded in the time-varying data, but are not listed in the appendix because of space limitations.

[21] The war between North and South Vietnam is treated differently in the two versions. In the time-constant version this is treated as a case with no new war to date. In the time-varying data this case is censored at the time of the cease-fire because South Vietnam ceased to exist.

[22] I use the COW dates that participants "left war" and "entered war" to determine cease-fire dates and the start of another war. The COW data set runs through 1994, I checked the SIPRI yearbooks and sources on specific cases to determine whether dyads fought again between 1994 and 2000. SIPRI 1994–2000. In only one case has war resumed in this period: the fighting between India and Pakistan in Kargil in the summer of 1999 qualifies as a full-scale war under COW's criteria. Peace between Israel and Lebanon ends in 1982 even though COW does not list this as an interstate war. See Maoz 2001, 10, for comments on correcting this case. The Gulf War resumed in 2003, after the analysis for this book was completed.

[23] The most debatable case is perhaps the 1971 war between India and Pakistan over the secession of Bangladesh, but the unsettled nature of the Kashmir issue in the two previous wars was a major reason the conflict over Bangladesh resulted in war, and fighting occurred in Kashmir as well as what would become Bangladesh.

[24] Twenty-seven in the time-varying version, as it is censored before the Kargil war in 1999.

[25] Missing data effectively censors some tests earlier, as capability data is only available to 1994.

DATA ON AGREEMENTS

As noted above, data on the various aspects of agreements comes from my own research on each case.[26] I investigated each aspect of agreements in a systematic fashion, answering a series of questions for each case (for example: Was a demilitarized zone established? Did it run the full length of the cease-fire line? How wide was it?). To prevent my own knowledge of outcomes from biasing my coding, I coded the cases "blind." I omitted any references to proper names or other information that would allow me to identify the case. I then printed the notes on each measure separately and assigned values without knowing which case I was coding.[27]

I researched and coded the following characteristics of the cease-fire: the extent to which forces were withdrawn after a cease-fire (partially, to the status quo ante, or beyond), demilitarized zones, arms control measures, peacekeeping (whether a monitoring mission or a peacekeeping force, numbers deployed, and by whom), third-party involvement in peacemaking or as a guarantor of the peace, the detail and specificity of any agreement, whether it was formal or tacit, dispute resolution procedures, confidence-building measures, and measures to control possible rogue action. I also coded whether the agreement was an armistice or a peace agreement, and whether the political issues over which the war was fought were settled.[28] Note that I coded mechanisms as they were actually implemented, which sometimes differed from the terms of the agreement text. The agreement signed at the end of the Vietnam War, for example, called for a demilitarized zone, but it was never implemented. Measurement details are given in appendix B.

Not all of the cease-fires are accompanied by agreements, of course. The data set includes a number of cases in which fighting stopped by a

[26] Sources included references surveying international conflict in the postwar era, such as Brogan 1992; Butterworth 1976; Goldstein 1992; Miall 1992; and Tillema 1991; secondary works on each conflict; and primary documents including the texts of cease-fire agreements.

[27] Blind coding ensured that when, as is inevitable, judgment calls needed to be made about what value to give for a particular variable I was ignorant of outcomes and could therefore not even subconsciously "cook" the data to fit my theory. Unfortunately it was not financially feasible to hire someone to duplicate my research to check intercoder reliability, although I did have a research assistant spot-check randomly selected cases. During the original research, and on the rare occasion during the actual coding that something peculiar to a case made it obvious which observation I was coding, and a judgment call needed to be made, I tried to err against the argument that agreements affect the durability of peace.

[28] In a few of the multilateral wars all of the dyads signed identical agreements at the time of cease-fire. For example, all five dyads agreed to the same cease-fire in 1948 during the first Arab-Israeli war, and in the Korean War, all belligerents were subject to the armistice agreement. To ensure that including each case as a separate observation does not affect the results by overcounting these wars, I also ran statistical tests with just one (randomly chosen) dyad from each of these wars. For most of the tests inclusion or exclusion of these duplicate agreements makes no real difference to the results. Where it does, this is discussed in the findings.

unilateral decision, or simply fizzled to an end with no explicit cease-fire. In such cases, the mechanisms under discussion here are generally coded as zero, unless measures were implemented in the absence of an agreement (for example, Libya withdrew its troops after the Uganda-Tanzania War though it ended with no explicit agreement).

Overall agreement strength is measured in two ways. The first is simply a count of the mechanisms implemented, so that an agreement gets a point for a demilitarized zone, another for arms control measures, another for a formal agreement, half for a monitoring mission or one for an armed peacekeeping force, and so on. This measure is crude but has the benefit of being objective and replicable by others. It ranges from 0 to 10 with a mean of about 4.

The second measure is my own subjective coding of the extent of the measures implemented. This measure of strength is coded on a five-point scale. At the weakest end, coded as "none," are cease-fires with no mechanisms at all (Russo-Hungary, for example). "Very weak" describes those with just a few paltry measures: withdrawal of forces to the status quo ante, or a partial DMZ, for example, but little else (Ethiopia-Somalia and the Six-Day War are examples). Those with more or somewhat more extensive provisions are coded as "weak," perhaps involving a peacekeeping mission, some measure of dispute resolution, or attempts to control possible rogue groups (examples here include the Sinai War and the Sino-Indian War). Even more substantial mechanisms, a formal and specific agreement involving peacekeepers, say, and/or a wider DMZ or concrete measures to disarm rogue groups, are coded as "moderate" (e.g. Iran-Iraq and the Football War). The strongest agreements, those that are formal and very detailed, that implement large peacekeeping missions, arms control provisions, and CBMs, and so on, are coded as "strong" (Israel and Egypt after 1973, the Korean Armistice, and the Gulf War fall in this category). This coding is subjective, but probably gives a more accurate, and less mechanical, sense of the robustness of the provisions implemented in each case. The objective and subjective measures are highly correlated (.92). By using both in my analyses I can ensure that the subjective coding of strength is not biased, and that the objective index is fairly accurate. Note that neither of these measures includes political settlement (whether the agreement was an armistice or a peace treaty, or whether it settled the fundamental political issues of the conflict).

Of the 48 initial cease-fires and 15 major follow-up agreements, over half of the cases (61%) involved a formal agreement, whether a signed document or formal acceptance of a cease-fire proposal. Belligerents withdrew their forces from the cease-fire line in almost half of the cases, usually to the status quo ante, but in a few cases beyond that. The most extensive withdrawals took place in the Sinai in the follow-up agreements after the Yom Kippur War. In 19 cases a demilitarized zone was established along the cease-fire line, and in another 16 cases a partial or very narrow DMZ was created. Some sort of arms control provisions were implemented in half of the cases, although in some this involved only an arms embargo or stand-fast agreement. In 16 cases there were areas limited to defensive forces or other limits on armaments near the cease-fire line. Only in the Gulf War were more stringent arms control measures imposed, and these were highly asymmetric.

Peacekeeping was relatively common, with 10 cases of armed peacekeeping forces and another 29 with monitoring missions deployed. The number of peacekeepers ranged from about 30 (the Organization of American States [OAS] monitors deployed between Honduras and El Salvador) to 6,500 (in the Sinai in 1973). Third-party guarantees of the peace are relatively rare; only four cases, the Football War and its follow-up agreement, the Israel-Egyptian Peace Agreement in 1979, and the Paris Peace Agreement in Vietnam involved explicit guarantees by outsiders. Third parties played some role in mediating or restraining belligerents in 23 cases, but there was no external involvement in over half of the cease-fires.

The specificity of agreements, measured here by the length of the agreement,[29] varies significantly: in 13 cases with no document or plan specificity is coded as 0; the other cases range from four paragraphs to 230 with most falling between one and 20 paragraphs. Most cease-fire agreements contain no provisions to deal with rogue forces or the possibility of involuntary defection. Some (20 cases) state that responsibility for such defection lies with the signatories, but in only a few (Israel and Egypt in 1956, the Football War and its follow-up agreements, for example) were concrete measures taken to deal with this issue. Similarly, confidence-building measures to provide information were relatively rare: in eight cases there were provisions for exchange of information on mines, troop rotations, or maneuvers; four established hot line communication links; and four (the Gulf War cases and the agreements between Israel and Egypt after the Yom Kippur War) involved on-site inspection or aerial surveillance. Dispute resolution is more common, with 12 cases of ongoing third-party mediation and 16 in which the belligerents themselves set up a joint commission for resolving disputes pertaining to the cease-fire.

Six wars ended with no agreement, and the majority (40) ended with an armistice or cease-fire agreement. Only two ended with peace treaties that renounced the use of force or restored diplomatic relations, though 14 follow-up agreements met this definition of a peace treaty. However, surprisingly few wars ended with settlement of the political issues over which they were fought. In 13 cases the issues were settled by force or

---

[29] This measure is somewhat crude; simply adding words does not necessarily make an agreement more specific, but the length of the text does generally accord with a more subjective evaluation, and has the advantage of being replicable by others.

unilaterally, but this settlement was not officially accepted by the losing side (the Falklands War and the Sino-Indian War fall in this category). But in only four wars (involving seven dyads or follow-up agreements) did the belligerents formally accept a settlement of the root issues. The Israeli-Egyptian peace agreement is exceptional in that it was a truly negotiated settlement. In 1991, Iraq formally accepted a settlement of the Shatt-al Arab waterway dispute that had sparked the Iran-Iraq War; Iraq also formally, if grudgingly, accepted UN Security Council Resolution 687 relinquishing claims to Kuwaiti territory after the Gulf War; the Soviet Union and Hungary signed a Treaty of Friendship in 1967 officially settling their differences; and Jordan and Israel eventually signed a peace treaty in 1994. In most cases in this period, however, war has been a singularly ineffective way to resolve differences. Most disputes have continued to fester long after the fighting stopped.

DATA ON SITUATIONAL VARIABLES

I was able to draw on existing data sets to measure most of the situational factors. This entailed adapting some measures to the needs of this study, but has the advantage of using well-known variables to test the alternative explanation: that the duration of peace is a function only of these situational variables. Decisiveness of victory is measured with a dichotomous variable coded 1 if the war ended in a tie as opposed to a victory for one side. Another dummy variable marks the most lopsided military outcomes. The measure of the cost of war is based on total battle deaths. There are other material costs to war as well, of course, but loss of life is arguably the most important, and is also a good indicator of the other costs, as more expensive and destructive wars also tend to have higher death tolls. I also measure the duration of war, a variable highly correlated with the death toll. A dummy variable notes whether the dyad was part of a larger, multilateral war or the only one involved in the fight. Geographic contiguity is denoted with a dichotomous variable indicating whether the belligerents are neighbors. The measures of relative capabilities use the COW national material capabilities index.[30] Both preponderance of power at the time of the cease-fire, and changes in relative capabilities over time are noted.

The history of conflict between belligerents before the war measures the extent to which their shared history is marked by militarized interstate disputes (MIDs).[31] As an indicator of the stakes of the conflict, I use Brecher and Wilkenfeld's coding of "gravity of highest value threatened" in their International Crisis Behavior data set, particularly their coding of

---

[30] Version updated in 1993. This index is based on an average of each state's share of the interstate system's total population, urban population, iron and steel production, energy consumption, military manpower, and military expenditures.

[31] Jones, Bremer, and Singer 1996.

whether the war threatened either side's existence.[32] The MID data set's coding of "revision type" is used to indicate territorial conflicts. Information on democracy and change in regime type over time comes from the Polity III data set.[33] Bennett and Stam's EUGene data generation program was used to obtain measures of expected utility for war based on Bueno de Mesquita and Lalman's model.[34] Measurement details on the situational variables are provided in appendix B.

In about three-fifths of the cases in the Cease-Fires data set, war ended with a military victory for one side rather than a tie. The cost of war ranges from 271 deaths in the second part of the Turco-Cypriot War to 1,250,000 in the Iran-Iraq War. Two-thirds of the cases are part of larger, multilateral wars, and in over three-quarters the belligerents are contiguous. Relative capabilities range from very even cases, such as Iran and Iraq, to very lopsided cases such as the Soviet Union and Hungary, Turkey and Cyprus, or the United States and North Korea. The history of conflict ranges from cases such as China and South Korea or France and Egypt with virtually no disputes before the war to cases like Israel and Syria in 1967 with over three disputes per year since Israel's independence. The mean is about one dispute a year. The stakes are quite high in most of the cases in the data set; almost 40% involved the threat of grave damage, and 35% threatened one side's very existence. Three-quarters of the wars were fought over territory. About two-thirds of the cease-fires involved one democratic state. The cataloguing of these cases creates a data set that allows a detailed look at the complex relationship between situational variables, the content of agreements, and the durability of peace.

Because information on situational variables comes from existing data sets, most of which go back before 1946, I was able to test the effects of situational variables on the durability of peace over a much longer time period. I used Zeev Maoz's dyadic version of the MID data set, selecting cases of full-scale war, and EUGene to create a time-varying data set of 304 cease-fires (and 9,618 observations) between 1816 and 1992.[35] The structure of this data is the same as the Cease-Fires data. Each case represents the history of a dyad from the cease-fire to another war, if any, between the same belligerents. Wars that stop and start again are split into separate cases. The data are censored at the end of 1992. The independent

---

[32] Brecher and Wilkenfeld 1992. Note that not all dyads in each war have the same stakes threatened. For example, the fight between North and South Vietnam threatened existence, while the fight between the United States and North Vietnam threatened grave damage. See also Gelpi 1997.

[33] Jaggers and Gurr 1996.

[34] Bennett and Stam 2000a; Bueno de Mesquita and Lalman 1992. EUGene is available at <www.eugenesoftware.org>.

[35] Maoz's data is available at <http://spirit.tau.ac.il/poli/faculty/maoz/maoz.html>. Note that Maoz's data is based on COW version 2 (1992) rather than version 3 (1994).

variables are measured in the same way as in the Cease-Fires data.[36] The quantitative analyses of the baseline prospects for peace presented in chapter 3 use both the longer data set and the Cease-Fires data set so that differences between the two can be explored.

II. LARGE-N QUALITATIVE ANALYSIS

Increasingly, studies in international relations combine statistical analysis and case studies. But even together, these techniques miss some of the available evidence. This study therefore also draws on the information left out both by the reduction of complex realities into numerical data and by case studies that can only focus on a very small number of cases. The universe of cases in the time period studied here is relatively small, and while this is a drawback for statistical work, it makes possible a qualitative survey of all of the cases. In order to construct the data set used for the quantitative portion of this study, I researched each of the cease-fires, creating a series of "minicases." Rather than ignore this qualitative information once the cases were coded, this large-N qualitative method draws on it to find patterns missed by the two other methods. By arraying the cases systematically one can see, for example, that peacekeepers are sent not just to conflicts with less decisive military victories, but that the cases without any peacekeeping tend to be extremely lopsided outcomes, or cases in which one belligerent is a permanent member of the UN Security Council. In principle, these relationships are discernable through purely quantitative analysis, but they jump out at one in any systematic look at the cases as wholes rather than as numbers. This systematic "eyeballing" of the universe of cases serves as a check on the validity of case study and quantitative findings, and also suggests new relationships and hypotheses to be tested with the other two methods. It allows for more consideration of the context and the idiosyncrasies of particular cases, while still giving the big picture of general trends in the full range of cases.

This qualitative examination shows the range of circumstances faced by belligerents and the immense variety of cease-fire agreements. The cases include cease-fires imposed by overwhelming military force, such as the Soviet Union's intervention in Hungary, in which a new government was established and the matter was put to rest, and the similar outcome, despite very different circumstances, when Tanzania overthrew Idi Amin in Uganda, ending the 1979 war. Libya had intervened on Uganda's side in

---

[36] I have not eliminated minor participants in this data, so note that the world wars play a large role in any analyses. There are 42 dyads in World War I and 66 in World War II. The stakes variable is not available for the longer time period and is not included in this data.

this war and reportedly paid the Ugandan National Liberation Forces (the anti-Amin forces previously in exile) $20 million to pull out of the country without being attacked.[37] Neither of these cases involved mechanisms to maintain peace.

Some cease-fires were brokered by outsiders: a UN commission mediated in Kashmir in 1949, and U.S. Secretary of State William Rogers developed the plan to end the War of Attrition between Israel and Egypt in 1970. In other cases, the belligerents reached agreements on their own, as in Korea and the Falklands. The Korean armistice agreement is a very detailed document spelling out the military demarcation line and demilitarized zone, specifying the timetable for withdrawing troops, halting the introduction of new weapons into Korea, detailing provisions for handling the exchange of prisoners of war, establishing a Neutral Nations Supervisory Commission made up of representatives from Sweden, Switzerland, Poland, and Czechoslovakia, and a military armistice commission and joint observer teams staffed by the parties themselves to implement the agreement and hammer out problems as they arose.

The Falklands War ended with Argentina's unconditional surrender in 1982, with no formal agreement or other measures to keep peace. But in 1989 and 1990, Britain and Argentina formally ended hostilities and implemented a number of confidence-building measures, giving advance warning of military maneuvers near the islands, setting up procedures for maritime and air search-and-rescue operations, and establishing working groups on issues of joint concern such as fisheries. Ethiopia and Somalia also strengthened their cease-fire agreement a decade after hostilities ended. In 1978, they ended their war with an informal agreement in which Somalia withdrew from the Ogaden, and Ethiopian and Cuban forces promised not to cross the border. In 1988, they signed a formal agreement in Mogadishu establishing a 10–15 km wide demilitarized zone along the border and setting up a joint military committee to supervise disengagement.

In some of the multilateral cases, all of the belligerents signed the same or identical agreements, as in the first cease-fire and later the armistice agreements in the first war in Palestine, or the Korean War; in others the separate dyads reached separate cease-fires, as after the Yom Kippur War, or most dramatically in Vietnam—the United States and North Vietnam ended their fight in 1973 with the Paris Peace Agreement and America's withdrawal, but the fighting did not end between North and South Vietnam until 1975 when the North overran the South.

The cease-fires surveyed in this study cover a wide range, from no agreement at all to detailed agreements implementing an array of mea-

---

[37] Brecher, Wilkenfeld, and Moser 1988, 336.

sures, including demilitarized zones, peacekeeping, withdrawal of forces, dispute resolution procedures, and so on. What explains this variety in cease-fires and cease-fire agreements? And does this variation matter in the construction of durable peace? Combined with statistical analysis and case studies, a qualitative survey of all of the cases helps us answer these questions.

III. CASE STUDIES

Case Selection

The in-depth case studies focus on India and Pakistan, and Israel and Syria. These particular cases were chosen for several reasons, the most important being that they provide a hard test of the theory presented here. The conflicts in South Asia and the Middle East have been the most intractable in the postwar era, and within the Middle East conflict, Israel's relations with Syria have been more difficult than with any other state. Relations between both India and Pakistan and Israel and Syria are marked by deep hostility in which conflict began before independence and animosity has only intensified over time. Both conflicts touch on the very existence of the states involved. In short, peace is especially difficult to maintain in these two cases.

All of the cases in this study involve enemies. By definition participants in a cease-fire are adversaries, but Israel and Syria, and India and Pakistan are enemies worse than most. The dispute that first brought India and Pakistan to blows has never been resolved, and their relationship has deteriorated over the course of this conflict from one of siblings squabbling over their inheritance rights to one of hardened enmity. Israel and Syria have also been enemies from the beginning, their entire history as independent states marked by violent conflict and deep animosity. Their relationship is the most acrimonious in a region marked by extreme interstate antagonism. These cases therefore stack the deck against the argument made here. Skeptics might argue that while cease-fire agreements can have some marginal effect helping to keep peace when that job is relatively easy, in the really tough cases they will be inconsequential. Critics of institutionalist theory have charged that while it might apply when cooperation is easy, "the theory is of little relevance in situations where states' interests are fundamentally conflictual."[38] It is hard to think of states with more fundamentally conflictual interests than India and Pakistan or Israel and Syria.[39]

---

[38] Mearsheimer 1994–95, 15.

[39] The relationship between Egypt and Israel would provide a better case for studying the transformation of deadly enemies into something approaching friends. But it is precisely

For reasons explained in chapter 4, we should also expect the counter-argument—that belligerents will have more difficulty concluding strong agreements the worse are their relations—to be most likely to hold at the most adversarial end of the spectrum. Choosing the worst enemies thus favors this counterargument and works against the argument that belligerents will be more likely to draft strong agreements when these are most needed. If I find evidence that belligerents draft stronger agreements when the prospects for peace are worst and that these agreements are consequential in the toughest cases, then we can have much greater confidence that the argument will hold in other cases.

Another reason for selecting these two cases is itself a result of the intractable nature of these conflicts. Because in each case there have been several wars over time, and therefore several cease-fires, there are multiple observations and variation within the two cases. Indeed the primary comparisons in the study are within-case comparisons, not between the two cases. A criticism made by area studies scholars and others of statistical analysis in the social sciences is that it fails to account for the idiosyncrasies of specific cases, especially those that are hard to quantify such as culture or the emotional significance of a piece of disputed territory, or even particularities of geography. According to this argument, treating the India-Pakistan conflict as equivalent to, say, the Falklands War is highly suspect. In comparisons across observations within each case study, however, particularities such as these are held constant. This is not to say that such idiosyncrasies can be ignored; they are the stuff case studies are made of, but inferences about the effect of the 1974 disengagement agreement between Israel and Syria, for example, are possible because it can be compared to cease-fires in 1948, 1949, or 1967, between the same states, fighting over the same basic issues, locked in the same deeply rooted conflict with the same emotional resonance among the same two peoples.

As noted above, inclusion of one of the cases within the Arab-Israeli conflict is also important because the Middle East wars dominate the large-N studies. It is therefore important to know whether the causal mechanisms hypothesized in this study hold up there, and whether unique features of that conflict are driving the results of the study.

A third reason for choosing these cases is also related. In neither of the two cases examined in depth in this study have the political issues fundamental to the conflict ever been settled. Agreement on the issues over which the war was fought constitutes a decision to alter the nature of conflict by dealing with the issues at its roots. The finding that settlement of fundamental political issues fosters lasting peace is neither sur-

---

because Israel and Syria have never settled their political issues that this case provides insight into how even the most intransigent enemies can sometimes cooperate to maintain peace.

prising nor especially helpful. The case studies therefore focus on evaluating the effectiveness of measures to keep peace in the absence of a political settlement. The intractable hostility and repeated wars in the Middle East and South Asia have had tragic consequences for the people of both regions; this unfortunate characteristic makes them particularly useful examples in which to study how such conflicts can be managed to prevent the recurrence of war. The next two sections provide an overview of the history of these two conflicts as context for the material that follows in later chapters.

India and Pakistan

BACKGROUND: PARTITION AND THE ACCESSION OF KASHMIR

Tragic communal violence accompanied independence and the split between India and Pakistan in 1947. Relations were poisoned from the beginning by the bitter ideological divide between the "one-nation" theory that formed the basis for the secular state of India and the "two-nation" theory that motivated the Muslim state of Pakistan. In this flammable context, the Princely State of Jammu and Kashmir provided the spark for war. Most of the princely states that made up one-third of British India reached settlements to accede to either India or Pakistan before the transfer of power in August 1947. In three regions, however, it was not clear to which side the princely state would accede. In both Junagadh and Hyderabad, Muslims ruled over majority Hindu populations.[40] In Kashmir the reverse was true; a Hindu leader, the vastly unpopular and repressive maharaja, presided over a Muslim majority.[41] Of these three, Kashmir was the only territory bordering both India and Pakistan.[42]

Independence was set for August 14, 1947, for Pakistan, and the following day for India. As the transfer of power approached, the maharaja of Kashmir dithered in indecisiveness about accession, and an armed revolt broke out in the Poonch region of Kashmir.[43] The rebellion against the

---

[40] In Junagadh, the ruler's accession to Pakistan was rejected and Indian control was ratified in a plebiscite in February 1948. In Hyderabad, the Muslim Nizam declared independence, but this was put down by an Indian blockade and then military occupation.

[41] Muslims are a majority in the state of Jammu and Kashmir as a whole, but not in each of its regions. The Vale of Kashmir is overwhelmingly Muslim; Jammu province was about 60% Muslim in 1941 but by the 1960s had a Hindu majority (although the Poonch region, which now falls on Pakistan's side of the cease-fire line, is a Muslim area). Ladakh is overwhelmingly Buddhist; Baltistan is majority Muslim; and the mountain region of Gilgit is almost entirely Muslim. Lamb 1966, 19.

[42] Kashmir's mountainous border (K2 lies just on the Kashmiri side) with China to the east and north is disputed; India and China would fight over it in 1962.

[43] Kashmiri opinion was divided on the issue of accession. The secularist National Conference Party, led by the preeminent political figure in Kashmir, Sheikh Mohammed Abdul-

maharaja's rule formed the nucleus of the Azad Kashmir (Free Kashmir) liberation army.

By September 1947 this revolt took on communal overtones, as violence in the Punjab spread. Massacres by Hindu and Sikh bands killed or caused to flee over 200,000 Muslims in Jammu. In October, some two thousand Pathan (Pashtun) tribesmen from Pakistan invaded Kashmir in support of the Azad Kashmir rebellion. Their rapid advance and the brutality of their attack caused panic in the summer capitol, Srinagar. The maharaja, reportedly "prostrated by indecision," asked India for help.[44] India responded by sending forces, on the condition that Kashmir provisionally accede to India until law and order was restored and the invasion cleared out. At that point, "the State's accession should be settled by a reference to the people."[45]

Pakistan did not accept the maharaja's accession to India, arguing essentially that it was achieved under duress and did not reflect the will of the people.[46] Individual Pakistani soldiers began fighting along with the Azad Kashmir and Pathan forces against India. By May 1948, regular Pakistani units were involved, turning the rebellion into an international war between two states less than a year old.

THE FIRST KASHMIR WAR, 1948–49

Indian troops prevented Kashmir from being overrun but could not expel Pakistani and Azad forces completely. The war between India and Pakistan was restricted to Kashmiri territory; commanders of both the Pakistani and Indian armies were British and did not want a wider India-Pakistan war, nor did Jawaharlal Nehru and Liaquat Ali Khan, leaders of the newly independent nations.[47] The war escalated toward the end of 1948, when Pakistan moved troops up from Lahore to fight in Jammu province, exposing itself to possible attack in the Punjab. However, before the war spread beyond Kashmiri territory, and before a conclusive military outcome was reached on the battlefield, a cease-fire was arranged by

---

lah, did not believe in the need for a separate Muslim state in Pakistan, while the Muslim Conference supported joining Pakistan. The maharaja, however, had thrown both Sheikh Abdullah and leaders of the Muslim Conference in jail.

[44] Lamb 1966, 38, 45.

[45] Governor-General Mountbatten's letter to the maharaja accepting accession, October 27, 1947. In Lakhanpal 1965. Jawaharlal Nehru affirmed that "the fate of Kashmir is ultimately to be decided by the people." Quoted in Lamb 1966, 47.

[46] When India sent forces into Kashmir to repel the invasion, Mohammed Ali Jinnah's immediate reaction was to order his own troops to respond. However, at this point the armies of India and Pakistan were still under the same command and Army Supreme Commander Auchinleck was able to restrain Pakistan temporarily by threatening to withdraw all British officers from Pakistan.

[47] Lamb 1966. Pakistan's founder, Mohammed Ali Jinnah, died in September 1948.

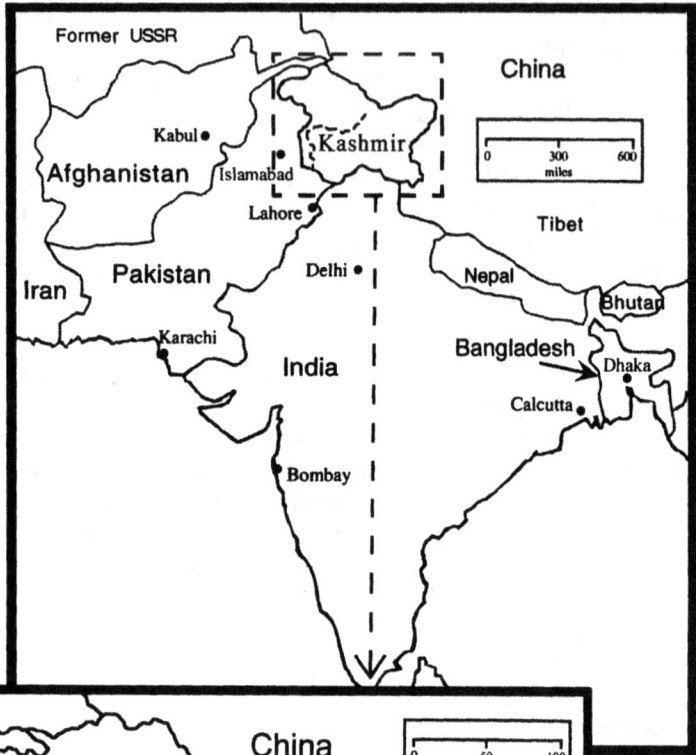

India and Pakistan

the United Nations Commission for India and Pakistan (UNCIP), a five-member body sent by the UN to help resolve the conflict.

The fighting stopped on January 1, 1949, on the basis of two UNCIP resolutions calling for a cease-fire, withdrawal of forces, and a plebiscite. The cease-fire agreement did not contain a plan for withdrawal, but merely agreement to principles for the future negotiation of a "truce agreement" on withdrawal of forces from Kashmir. Once these withdrawals had taken place, the future status of Kashmir would "be determined in accordance with the will of the people." However, the cease-fire was the only provision implemented; India and Pakistan never withdrew and the plebiscite was never held.

When the war ended, Kashmir had been de facto partitioned by the cease-fire line. Azad Kashmir forces set up a government in Muzaffar-abad on Pakistan's side of the line, while the prominent Kashmiri leader, Sheikh Mohammed Abdullah, led an administration on India's side from Srinagar.[48]

In July 1949, India and Pakistan signed a formal agreement in Karachi and began a series of negotiations over the "truce agreement" and withdrawals, and the political future of Kashmir. These negotiations lasted 10 years and involved countless proposals and a series of UN appointed mediators and special representatives; all to no avail. The Pathan tribesmen were withdrawn from Kashmir in the months following the cease-fire, and both India and Pakistan withdrew some units. But nothing more than this very limited pullback took place. India insisted that withdrawal of Pakistani troops and the disbandment of Azad Kashmir forces was a prerequisite for the holding of a free and fair plebiscite, while Pakistan feared that this would leave India and Sheikh Abdullah in control of the outcome.

Reading the reports of the negotiations in retrospect, it seems remarkable that India and Pakistan kept the talks going over all those years with no discernable progress.[49] However, while the negotiations were going on, both sides believed in the possibility of a resolution and neither side attempted to settle it by force; peaceful settlement was preferred to war. There were moments of hope for a resolution interspersed with tense periods when war seemed likely. Throughout this period India-Pakistan relations fluctuated between sincere attempts to settle outstanding issues, with talk of brotherhood between the two peoples, and, when these efforts failed to resolve the conflict, fraught periods full of vitriolic rhetoric.

[48] "The partition of Kashmir was as much a division of the territory between the two main Kashmiri parties, the Muslim Conference and [Sheikh Abdullah's] National Conference, as it was between Pakistan and India." Lamb 1966, 68.

[49] For accounts of the negotiations see, for example, Blinkenberg 1972, chap. 4; Korbel 1954; and UN documents S/1453, 1950; S/1791, 1950; and S/2375, 1951.

In October 1962, after several years of tension and clashes along an
ill-defined border, China attacked India, took control of the disputed
territory, and withdrew its forces unilaterally.[50] India's defeat was
swift and decisive. Pakistan refrained from taking advantage of India's
vulnerable military position by attacking in Kashmir. Rather, President
Mohammad Ayub Khan agreed to another set of negotiations apparently
in the hope that a chastened India would make concessions at the bargaining table that would enable a peaceful resolution. Talks in late December 1962 concerned possible ways of partitioning the territory of Jammu
and Kashmir. Despite serious diplomatic pressure from the United States
and Britain, Indian concessions were not forthcoming, and Pakistan
refused to consider accepting anything less than the bulk of the Vale of
Kashmir.[51]

The failure of these talks convinced Pakistan that a peaceful settlement
of the Kashmir problem was not possible. India was more or less satisfied
with the status quo, that is, with de facto partition along the 1949 cease-
fire line, and was gradually incorporating its territory in Kashmir into
legal and administrative union with India proper. Pakistan decided it
would have to force the issue. China's attack against India shifted Cold
War calculations, potentially undermining Pakistan's position as the key
bulwark against communism in South Asia. Moreover, in the aftermath
of defeat at the hands of China, India began a large armament program,
with considerable military assistance from the United States and Britain.
A classic security dilemma resulted: India's military buildup to counter
the Chinese could only be seen as a threat by Pakistan.

In early 1965 there were a number of skirmishes and shooting incidents
along the border between India and Pakistan. In April there was rather
serious fighting, including tank battles, in an area known as the Rann of
Kutch. While it is somewhat unclear how the episode started, the crisis
appears to have been a limited probe by Pakistan to test India's fighting
capacity and will.[52] A cease-fire was reached in May. At the end of June,
India and Pakistan signed an agreement restoring the status quo as of
January 1965, and calling for arbitration if the two sides could not reach

---

[50] The territory in question lies in the Aksai Chin region and the North East Frontier
Agency. China asserted control of approximately 14,000 square miles. Ganguly 1986. For
more details on this conflict see Hoffmann 1990. On its impact on India-Pakistan relations
see Brines 1968, chap. 9.

[51] See Lamb 1991, 239, for particulars of the offers and demands in these negotiations.

[52] Ganguly 1986; Brines 1968. The border was disputed here, but the area was strategically useless; *rann* means "desolate place," and the area is mostly flooded during the mon-
soons. Casualties, both dead and wounded, reached 93 for India and 350 for Pakistan,
according to an Indian source. Mankekar, cited in Brines 1968, 288.

a settlement on the border.[53] From the beginning of 1965 the cease-fire line in Kashmir was very tense, with hundreds of incidents and violations taking place each month.

THE SECOND KASHMIR WAR, 1965

Infiltrations into Indian-controlled Kashmir by *mujahedin* increased over the first half of 1965, and in August at least a thousand raiders crossed the cease-fire line from Azad Kashmir. Though Pakistan denied it, by all impartial accounts, Pakistan instigated and coordinated this guerilla attack in the hopes of triggering a revolt on whose behalf it could then intervene. The Pakistani plan failed to produce the hoped-for rebellion, however; Kashmiris were increasingly unhappy with Indian rule, but they were not yet interested in armed revolt. India responded to the infiltration by attacking across the cease-fire line to cut off the guerillas. By the beginning of September regular forces from both sides were fighting each other, and on September 6 India attacked across the international border, escalating the war beyond the confines of Kashmir itself. The war quickly reached a military stalemate.[54]

There was strong diplomatic pressure for a cease-fire, as the United States and the USSR reached a rare moment of Cold War consensus. The UN called for a cease-fire on September 4 (Resolution 209), but Pakistan attached as a condition that all troops be withdrawn from Kashmir and the territory be administered by a UN force until a plebiscite could be held, a condition that India would not consider. The UN Security Council then demanded a cease-fire (Resolution 211). In the face of continuing diplomatic pressure, India agreed, despite opposition from some within the military. Pakistan was beginning to run out of ammunition, and could see that the war would turn to favor India over the long haul.[55] A somewhat farcical ultimatum by China to India over a border issue (which included the demand of the return of eight hundred sheep and 60 yaks reportedly stolen from Chinese territory) provided some political cover for Ayub, allowing him to accept a cease-fire from an apparent position of strength. A UN promise to seek a future political settlement on Kashmir also allowed Pakistan to save face and accept the cease-fire. It came into effect on September 23, 1965.

---

[53] A tribunal did in fact convene in 1968, after the next war. It found generally in favor of India. The border was demarcated and formally accepted in 1969. Lamb 1991, 255–57; Brines 1968, 294–95.

[54] Lamb 1991, 259ff.

[55] U.S. military aid to Pakistan deliberately limited stockpiles of ammunition and spare parts so that Pakistan could use armaments to repel a possible communist attack, but not to wage a lengthy war with India. Brines 1968, 356.

The cease-fire was quite fragile, and it was clear that the danger of full-scale war re-erupting was very high. Soviet Premier Alexei Kosygin offered to mediate, and the heads of state, Lal Bahadur Shastri and Ayub Khan, met at Tashkent in January 1966. The Declaration of Tashkent, announced on January 10, did not settle the conflict; it only expressed commitment to restore peaceful relations and to forego the use of force. This was in fact a major concession by Pakistan, since no settlement of the Kashmir issue was really in sight. The declaration restored diplomatic relations and called for an end to hostile propaganda. The most important measure was an agreement to withdraw all forces to their August 1965 (i.e., antebellum) positions.

Shastri's death on the day after the Tashkent declaration was signed sanctified the agreement, and bilateral relations were improved temporarily by the "Spirit of Tashkent." But the chill would quickly return. Indo-Pakistani relations were relatively uneventful from 1966 through 1970. Pakistan seemed willing to leave the Kashmir issue on the back burner, and both countries were preoccupied with internal politics.[56] Within Kashmir there was growing, and increasingly violent opposition to Indian control. At the end of January 1971, an Indian plane was hijacked to Pakistan and then blown up. The Kashmiri hijackers may have been set up by India itself, but the episode was used by India as justification for refusing to allow flights between the two wings of Pakistan to pass through Indian airspace.[57] Rather than Kashmiri politics, it would be the growing divide between East and West Pakistan that would provide the occasion for the next Indo-Pakistani war.

THE THIRD WAR, BANGLADESH, 1971

In March 1969, in the face of serious opposition, both over the compromise at Tashkent and over the internal crisis between East and West Pakistan, President Ayub handed power over to General Agha Mohammad Yahya Khan. The economic disparity between the two halves of Pakistan, as well as ethnic and cultural differences, had led to increasing calls for regional autonomy in the beleaguered east. In December 1970 the military regime held elections to restore civilian rule and unify the country. Unfortunately, the election results rather deepened the split, as the proautonomy Awami League candidate won a landslide in the east, while a hard-liner, Zulfikar Ali Bhutto, won a majority in the west.[58] In the face of West Pakistani intransigence about recognizing the Awami League's electoral victory, East Pakistani demands hardened into calls for outright secession.

[56] Blinkenberg 1972; Lamb 1991.
[57] Lamb 1991, 287ff.
[58] Ganguly 1986, 111.

In March 1971 the military regime unleashed a massive military operation against secession of the eastern wing, now beginning to refer to itself as Bangla Desh. The crackdown was brutal and caused hundreds of thousands of people to flee across India's border into West Bengal. The number of refugees would reach 9.8 million.[59] India intervened in this crisis partly in response to the humanitarian crisis and domestic pressure to protect Bengalis in East Pakistan, partly to stem the tide of refugees who threatened to upset India's ethnic balance, and largely as a way to undermine its foe Pakistan. Training and support of the Mukti Bahini, the Bangladeshi secessionist force, was seen as retribution for Pakistan's support of Kashmiri separatists.[60]

There were border clashes between Indian and Pakistani forces in October and November 1971, and by then India was supporting the Mukti Bahini openly. Most analysts consider all-out war to have started with a preemptive Pakistani attack on Indian airfields on December 3, 1971, though both sides claimed the other struck first. India responded the next day, and once again the two were in full-scale war. The 1971 war was a disaster for Pakistan. The Indian victory was quick and decisive; Pakistan surrendered on December 16, and Bangladesh was born as an independent state.

India did not push for military gains in Kashmir because it feared the collapse of the Pakistani regime should Pakistan be forced to swallow both loss of its eastern wing and loss of Kashmir at the same time.[61] Bhutto, who had become president of Pakistan just after the war, and Indira Gandhi met between June 28 and July 3 to restore peace. The resulting Simla Agreement was a rather vague document resolving that conflict be settled peacefully and calling for resumption of communications, trade, and so on. In Kashmir, it set the cease-fire line of December 17 as the "line of actual control," making this line the de facto border.

After its humiliating defeat and dismemberment in the 1971 war, Pakistan was in no position to contest developments within Indian-held Kashmir, which was being incorporated more directly into the state of India.[62] Meanwhile, the continual Indo-Pakistani arms race took on a particularly dangerous dimension with India's nuclear explosion in May 1974.

---

[59] Ganguly 1986. Lamb 1991 claims this number is exaggerated, but Clodfelter 1992 puts the number at 10 million.

[60] Lamb 1991.

[61] Schofield 1996, 212–13. Bhutto's opponents in Pakistan charged him with secretly agreeing to the status quo as a settlement in Kashmir.

[62] In the face of increasing dissent in Kashmir, including riots and demonstrations, Gandhi patched up relations with Sheikh Abdullah and concluded the "Kashmir Accord" of 1975. The accord gave Kashmir nominal autonomy to legislate many domestic matters, but India retained veto power. Lamb 1991.

Relations between India and Pakistan remained fractious. Serious clashes took place in the early and middle 1980s on the Siachen Glacier in the mountains of Kashmir. And from 1980 on there were clashes along the cease-fire line itself in Kashmir.[63] The crisis over India's "Brass Tacks" military exercises exacerbated tensions in the mid-1980s. In 1988–89 Indo-Pakistani relations improved somewhat, and Benazir Bhutto and Rajiv Gandhi negotiated agreements not to bomb each other's nuclear installations and to respect the Simla accord reached by their parents. But in 1990 India and Pakistan were, according to some analysts, dangerously close to the nuclear brink.[64] A number of confidence-building agreements were reached in the 1990s, requiring advance notice of military exercises, and prohibiting chemical weapons, among other things.[65] But nuclear tests in May 1998 aggravated relations between two now openly nuclear enemies. Meanwhile, nationalist sentiment in Kashmir has complicated the conflict. What was originally primarily a territorial dispute between India and Pakistan has become also a civil conflict as Kashmiris struggle against Indian rule.[66]

THE FOURTH WAR, KARGIL, 1999

In the spring of 1999 the fragile peace between India and Pakistan faltered for a fourth time. While not as full-blown a war as the previous three engagements, the fighting marked a distinct escalation from the low-level skirmishes and incursions by irregular forces that had become common in Kashmir. It also meets the standard COW definition of war, as it entailed over one thousand battle deaths.[67]

In early May, India discovered that Pakistani troops and Kashmiri insurgents had infiltrated across the line of control and taken strategic positions in the snowy heights of the Batalik, Dras, and Kargil sectors. India fought back, using air power for the first time in Kashmir since 1971, and slowly and painstakingly recaptured most positions in June. Much of the fighting took place at altitudes of 16,000 feet. Pakistan had hoped to avoid blame for starting the conflict, but the international community, including the United States, insisted that Pakistan withdraw. In mid-July Pakistan complied, though it refused at the time to acknowledge that reg-

[63] Lamb 1991.
[64] Schoffield 1996, 235; Bajpai 1996, 23.
[65] See Krepon and Sevak 1995.
[66] The secessionist civil war in Kashmir started in earnest in 1989 after fraudulent elections. See Ganguly 2001. The terrorism that India had exaggerated in the early 1970s to justify its actions in Kashmir thus became a reality. Lamb 1991.
[67] Battle death estimates range from over one thousand to over two thousand. In the 1999 SIPRI yearbook (generally a conservative source on death tolls), Taylor Seybolt lists combatant deaths at "about 1,100" not including civilian deaths.

ular Pakistani forces had been involved. By the end of the month the conflict was over. Pakistan seems to have instigated the fight as a limited probe, not expecting a vigorous Indian response, apparently believing its nuclear weapons would deter any significant escalation by India. According to Ganguly, Pakistan also hoped the crisis would revive the flagging Kashmiri insurgency.[68]

In May and June 2002, the actions of Kashmiri insurgents threatened to spark another, possibly nuclear, war on the subcontinent. Terrorist attacks by Kashmiri secessionists, including one on the Indian Parliament in December 2001, took both states back to the brink.[69] Over half a century after the maharaja's indecision about accession, the political status of Kashmir is still hotly contested, clashes along the cease-fire line continue to be frequent, and yet another war seems all too possible.

Israel-Syria

BACKGROUND: BRITAIN'S MANDATE AND ISRAEL'S DECLARATION OF INDEPENDENCE

The fundamental cause of the Arab-Israeli conflict is that two peoples claim one land as home. Britain's contradictory promises to Arabs and Jews during World War I sowed the seeds of what would become the international community's most intractable conflict later in the century.[70] In the face of intensifying Arab nationalist feelings and an influx of Jewish immigrants striving to create a national home, Britain declared that its mandate would end on May 15, 1948, and turned to the new United Nations to help resolve the dilemma of competing claims on Palestine.[71]

In a contentious vote, the UN General Assembly resolved to partition Palestine into an Arab and a Jewish state.[72] The Arabs, both those in Palestine, and the Arab states, including Syria, objected vehemently. The partition resolution and the phased withdrawal of British troops sparked armed clashes between Arabs and Jews.[73] Britain was not willing to en-

---

[68] For these arguments and a summary of the war see Ganguly 2001, chap. 6.

[69] See for example, "All Fronts: Nuclear Poker; at the Brink in Kashmir," *New York Times*, May 26, 2002, Week in Review, sec. 4, 1; Nicholas Kristof, "August 1914 in Pakistan," *New York Times* editorial, June 20, 2002, A12.

[70] The British promised the Arabs independence in exchange for the Arab revolt against the Turks in 1916, and in 1917 in the Balfour Declaration promised "the establishment in Palestine of a National Home for the Jewish people." Meanwhile Britain also concluded the secret Sykes-Picot Treaty divvying up Arab lands with France.

[71] For an overview and comprehensive bibliography on the Arab-Israeli conflict, see Peretz 1996.

[72] UN General Assembly Resolution 181 (II), November 29, 1947.

[73] Khouri 1985, 59, 68; Bar-Yaacov 1967, 13–26; Peretz 1996.

force a plan against the wishes of either group, and the United States backed away from partition once the seriousness of objections was realized. Despite the lack of a solution acceptable to all parties, Britain went ahead with its plan to withdraw.

THE FIRST ARAB-ISRAELI WAR, 1948–49

On May 14, 1948, just as the British were leaving Palestine, Israel declared its independence. The following day Syria, along with Egypt, Lebanon, Jordan (then known as Transjordan) and Iraq sent forces to help Palestinian Arabs resist the new state. The UN had been trying to negotiate a truce between Arabs and Jews before the conflict became an interstate war, and it now turned to obtaining a cease-fire among the states. The UN mediator, Count Folke Bernadotte, arranged a temporary four-week truce beginning June 11, 1948. Israelis favored the break in the fighting as they were not faring well militarily, while the Arabs accepted it under diplomatic pressure.[74] This cease-fire was successful in the sense that it lasted the full four weeks as originally intended, but it was not extended, despite Bernadotte's efforts. Fighting recommenced on July 9.

While both sides ignored the prohibition against acquiring new arms and fighting personnel during the temporary truce, Israel benefited most from the break, consolidating its forces and purchasing arms from Czechoslovakia. Israel thus emerged on the offensive and made substantial territorial gains before the Security Council determined that the war constituted a threat to international peace and ordered a cease-fire.[75] Bernadotte set July 18, 1948, as the date for this halt in the fighting. The July 18 cease-fire was essentially imposed by the international community: it was accepted by Israel and the Arabs because of the threat of sanctions under Chapter VII of the UN Charter.

The Security Council and Bernadotte tried unsuccessfully to work out an acceptable political solution. But the cease-fire collapsed when Israel, claiming an Egyptian violation of the cease-fire, launched an offensive into the Negev on October 15, and into western Galilee by the end of the month.[76] Regular Syrian forces were only involved in a limited way at this stage of the fighting and were "badly mauled" by Israeli forces. Throughout the war, Syria relied largely on irregular forces rather than its own army.[77] Except for continuing battles between Egyptian and Israeli forces

---

[74] Because this cease-fire was intended to last only four weeks, it is not included in the Cease-Fires data set. For its terms, see UN document S/829, 1948, reprinted in Bailey 1990, 88–89. See also Bailey 1990, 25–27; and Bar-Yaacov 1967, 27.

[75] UN Security Council Resolution 54, July 15, 1948. In this stage of the fighting, thousands of panicked Arabs fled, creating an enormous refugee problem that festers to this day.

[76] Bailey 1990, 46; Khouri 1985, 87, 91.

[77] Khouri 1985, 91; Ma'oz 1995, 19.

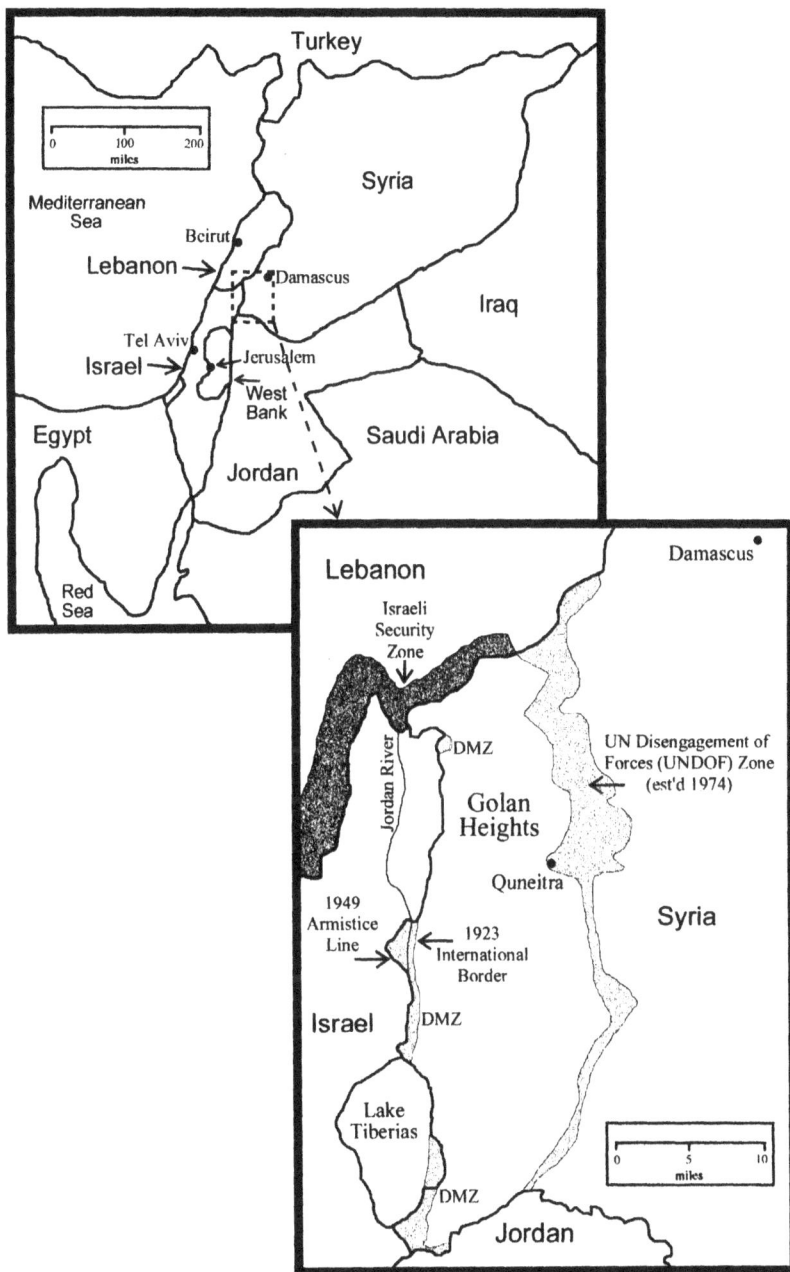

Israel and Syria

in the Negev, most of the fighting died down by November.[78] Egypt and
Israel began armistice negotiations early in January 1949, and the other
Arab states followed suit. Syria was the most reluctant to negotiate with
Israel, but a cease-fire came into effect on April 13, and Israel and Syria
signed an armistice agreement on July 20, 1949.

The armistice was meant to be a temporary arrangement while negotiations took place to find a political solution to the problem of Palestine,
but as with so many other cases, no solution was ever found. The armistice regime consisted of the UN Truce Supervision Organization
(UNTSO) observers monitoring the cease-fire line and demilitarized
zones, and an Israel-Syria Military Armistice Commission (ISMAC) to
resolve disputes. Most incidents and armed clashes along the Israel-Syria
Armistice Demarcation Line concerned civilian activity in the demilitarized areas: over fishing rights in Lake Tiberias (Sea of Galilee), between
Arab and Jewish farmers in the demilitarized zones, and over Israel's civil
engineering projects within the demilitarized areas.[79] By the mid-1950s
the armistice regime had largely eroded, with Israel refusing to participate
in meetings of ISMAC.

Despite a military pact with Egypt in 1955, Syria refrained from attacking Israel during the 1956 Sinai War, largely because Syria feared
invasion by Britain and France. In February 1958, Syria and Egypt united
into one state, creating the United Arab Republic (UAR). The threat of
war between the UAR and Israel seemed high, especially during a crisis
in early 1961 over an Israeli raid on the Syrian village of Tawafiq in the
demilitarized area. However, the experiment in Arab unity had failed by
September, and Syria split away from Egypt, much to Israel's relief.

By the time of their second war, the conflict between Israel and Syria
was firmly embroiled in the Cold War. While the United States and the
Soviet Union often restrained their respective proxies to avoid being
dragged into a nuclear confrontation in the Middle East, their support
also contributed to an arms race and to intransigent positions in the region. Their vetoes at the UN stymied efforts by the international community to help resolve the conflict.

THE SIX-DAY WAR, 1967

The 1967 war is a classic case of the security dilemma leading to unwanted war. Serious clashes took place along the Israeli-Syrian cease-fire
line in early 1967 over Israel's plans to divert the Jordan River. Israeli
noises about the need to overthrow the radical Ba'th regime in Syria and
misinformation from the Soviet Union that Israel was amassing troops on

[78] Herzog 1984, 89–91.
[79] For detailed accounts of these disputes see Bar-Yaacov 1967; and Kinsolving 1967.

Syria's border led Arab leaders to believe an Israeli attack against Syria was imminent. Egyptian President Nasser, under harsh criticism within the Arab world for not standing up sufficiently to Zionism and for hiding behind a UN force, put troops on alert and requested the withdrawal of the UN Emergency Force (UNEF) stationed in the Sinai after the war in 1956. Nasser also announced that he was closing the Gulf of Aqaba to Israeli shipping.[80]

In the face of these moves and ongoing hostile Arab rhetoric, Israel launched an all-out attack on June 5, 1967. Israel's surprise attack immediately destroyed the bulk of Egypt's air force, and after occupying the entire Sinai and the West Bank, Israel took the Golan Heights from Syria on July 9. The Soviet Union considered intervention against Israel's forces advancing through Syria, and the United States pressured Israel to accept UN calls for a cease-fire before it came to that.[81] Israel halted its advance on July 10. There was no formal cease-fire agreement, but UNTSO observers demarcated the new cease-fire line, and this brief dramatic war was over.

In November 1967 the UN Security Council passed Resolution 242, affirming the principles of Israeli withdrawal from "territories occupied in the recent conflict," termination of the state of belligerency, and recognition of "every State in the area and their right to live in peace within secure and recognized boundaries free from threats or acts of force." This "land for peace" formula has been the basis of most attempts to negotiate peace since, but it has never been implemented. Syria did not formally accept Resolution 242 even in principle until after the 1973 war, while Israel accepted it initially but later backed away from willingness to give up the Golan.[82]

In the aftermath of the 1967 war the conflict between Israel and Syria intensified. Israel's position on returning the Golan hardened, and Syria endeavored to challenge the status quo by supporting Palestinian guerilla attacks against Israel. Israel retaliated with land raids and air attacks against Syria.

THE YOM KIPPUR WAR, 1973

After suffering humiliating defeat in 1967, both Syria and Egypt looked to restore their lands and their pride. Syrian president Hafez al-Asad and

---

[80] Ovendale 1984, chap. 10; Bailey 1990, 187–221. Israel had never countenanced UNEF deployments on its side of the line. UN Secretary-General U Thant now suggested that UNEF could move onto Israeli soil to continue to provide a buffer between Egyptian and Israeli troops, but Israel refused to consider this.

[81] UN Security Council Resolutions 233–36, 1967. See Khouri 1985, 265; and Bailey 1990, 229–40.

[82] Ma'oz 1995, 103–4.

Egypt's Anwar Sadat began planning for war, rebuilding their militaries with Soviet military aid. Meanwhile, the United States armed Israel but also pursued ties with Egypt.

On October 6, 1973, Syria and Egypt launched a surprise attack against Israel. Their armies met with initial success on the battlefield, but within a few days, Israel was able to turn the tide, driving back Arab advances and pushing beyond the 1967 lines. While maneuvering to protect their proxies' interests, the United States and the Soviet Union agreed to what would become Security Council Resolution 338 (October 22, 1973) calling for an immediate cease-fire, implementation of Resolution 242, and negotiations "aimed at establishing just and durable peace in the Middle East." Egypt and Israel accepted the cease-fire resolution promptly, Syria only reluctantly.[83] Fighting continued between Egypt and Israel for a few more days as Israel attempted to gain a bit more ground, but the cease-fire was effective by October 24.[84]

In the years following the war, Egypt and Israel worked out disengagement agreements and eventually, much to Asad's chagrin, the Camp David Accords and the Egypt-Israel Peace Agreement in March 1979.[85] Disengagement negotiations between Israel and Syria, mediated by Henry Kissinger, were much more difficult and were accompanied by frequent clashes along the cease-fire line.[86] But an agreement was signed on May 31, 1974, under which Israel withdrew back to the 1967 lines, and from the town of Quneitra, occupied in 1967. The UN sent a peacekeeping force, the UN Disengagement Observer Force (UNDOF) to oversee the withdrawal of forces and to take up positions between the opposing forces.

FIGHTING IN LEBANON, 1982

While Israel and Syria have managed to avoid war over the Golan since 1973, they fought again in Lebanon in 1982. Civil war erupted in Lebanon in 1975 between right-wing Christian Maronites and Phalangists on

---

[83] The Soviets pushed for a quick cease-fire to protect the Arabs, while the United States delayed proposals so as to help the Israeli offensive. Ma'oz 1995, 130–31; Khouri 1985, 370–71; Bailey 1990, 326.

[84] The superpowers came close to military confrontation as the Soviet Union moved to protect Egypt and the United States responded by going on alert. Khouri 1985, 370; Bailey 1990, 330–32.

[85] Sadat had achieved what he wanted from the war; he launched a limited war to challenge the status quo and to persuade the United States to pressure Israel to give up the Sinai. Asad, however, had hoped to take back the Golan by force and to pressure Israel into giving up the West Bank, and was sorely disappointed. Despite Israel's decisive victory over Syria, it was the Israeli leadership (Golda Meir and Moshe Dayan) who resigned after the war, while Asad's prestige was strengthened by his willingness to take on Israel. Ma'oz 1995, 133–34.

[86] Ma'oz 1995, 132; Kissinger 1982, chaps. 21, 23.

the one hand and Muslim Lebanese and the Palestine Liberation Organization (PLO) on the other. After a failed attempt at reconciliation, Syria intervened militarily in 1976 to prevent the Muslim and Palestinian forces from defeating the Maronite-Phalange side.[87] Syria had American support for this intervention, and Israel acquiesced because it protected Israel's own interests. With American mediation, Israel and Syria reached a tacit agreement to avoid conflict. Known as the Red Lines Agreement, it consisted of Israel's acceptance of Syrian troops in parts of Lebanon, so long as they did not cross a line running from south of Sidon to Aishiya, did not bring surface-to-air missiles into Lebanon, and refrained from using air power.[88]

After the end of the first round of fighting in Lebanon, Syrian troops remained as the bulk of an Arab peacekeeping force, and Syria renewed its ties with the PLO and the Lebanese leftists. The rightist Christians now looked to Israel for support.[89] In 1978, when Israel invaded Lebanon in response to Palestinian raids, Israel and Syria were at first careful to avoid direct confrontation. But clashes in 1979 strained the Red Lines Agreement, and the tacit agreement collapsed by April 1981, when Israel attacked Syrian helicopters.[90] In 1981, Israel annexed the Golan Heights, extending Israeli jurisdiction and administration, and signaling its refusal to consider handing the territory back to Syria.

Israel launched a full-scale invasion of Lebanon in June 1982. The Israeli cabinet approved only a limited war against Palestinian guerillas threatening settlements in the north, but Defense Minister Ariel Sharon had plans to push Syria out of Lebanon and install a Lebanese government that would agree to peace with Israel. Israel's attack on Syrian forces threatened to bring Soviet involvement, and the United States pressured Israel to cease fire on June 11. This cease-fire held for the most part in eastern and central Lebanon, but fighting continued around Beirut. In August, U.S. mediator Philip Habib arranged for the evacuation of PLO and Syrian troops from Beirut under the supervision of a multinational force (MNF I) consisting of the United States, France, and Italy. Israel withdrew from the quagmire in Lebanon in 1985, its image tarnished both internationally and domestically by the war.[91] Israel maintained a security zone in southern Lebanon, not withdrawing completely until May 2000.

[87] Syria feared that such a military defeat would lead to Israeli intervention, the possible partition of Lebanon, and the loss of Syrian control. Ma'oz 1995, 149; Khouri 1985, 386–87; Evron 1987; Avi-Ran 1991.
[88] Schiff 1984, 100; Evron 1987, 45ff.; Weinberger 1986, chap. 10.
[89] Ma'oz 1995, 167–68. On the Arab peacekeeping forces, see Pogany 1987.
[90] Schiff 1984, 102; Ma'oz 1995, 169.
[91] Schiff 1984, 104; Evron 1987, chap. 4; Avi-Ran 1991, chap. 9; Thakur 1987, chap. 4.

A new peace initiative moved forward after the end of the Cold War, and in the aftermath of the 1991 Gulf War. The October 1991 peace conference in Madrid represented the first public and direct negotiations between Israel, Syria, Lebanon, Jordan, and the Palestinians. A series of bilateral talks and multilateral committees have followed since, but Is-raeli-Syrian talks have moved only slowly when they moved at all. While Israel has indicated willingness to withdraw from at least parts of the Golan Heights, and Syria has agreed to the principle of peace, differences over the extent of withdrawal and timing of land for peace remain. In the context of the second Palestinian Intifada, hopes for a settlement between Israel and Syria seem very remote.

In over half a century, and four wars each, neither India and Pakistan nor Israel and Syria have been able to resolve their political differences. Despite continual tension, they have managed for long periods to avoid war. But efforts to maintain peace have also met with dramatic failure.

Questions and Evidence

The case studies address in depth the same three questions answered in breadth by the large-N analyses: (1) how were the baseline prospects for peace shaped by aspects of the situation between the belligerents at the time of the cease fire? (2) how did these baseline prospects influence the content and strength of agreements reached? and (3) did mechanisms within cease-fire agreements affect the durability of peace?

In-depth examination of the role played by situational variables on the prospects for peace serves two purposes. It provides a check on the quanti-tative findings, particularly important as the measures used in the statisti-cal analysis are somewhat rough. Tracking the history of conflict between enemies as it developed over time gives a much better reading than count-ing disputes, for example. It is also important for the rest of the case analysis to know how the situational variables operated in a particular instance. For example, while I find only moderate evidence that geo-graphic proximity affects the duration of peace across all cases, particular-ities of the geography of Kashmir and the Golan Heights are clearly im-portant for understanding the prospects for peace in both places.

Exploration of how the baseline prospects for peace between India and Pakistan and between Israel and Syria affected the agreements these coun-tries put in place also gives a much richer understanding of the competing hypotheses on endogeneity. In the case studies it is possible to get a better sense of the prospects for peace at a given time than it is using the statisti-cal indicators of situational variables. The causal link between these pros-pects and the agreements drafted can also be examined directly. The his-torical record on the negotiations is often explicit about why various measures were or were not put in place. We can therefore ask whether political differences and animosity made it difficult for India and Pakistan or Israel and Syria to agree on mechanisms such as withdrawal of forces or demilitarized agreements, or whether they turned to these measures when the risk of war was higher. Were they only able to reach vague agreements, or were they more specific about the terms of the cease-fire when tensions were high? Were peacekeepers opposed because they might alter the military balance or because of sensitivities over sovereignty? When tensions rose after the cease-fire agreement was in place, were there efforts to enhance mechanisms to keep peace, or were the measures already in place likely to fall by the wayside?

In answering the third and most important question, about the effect of agreements on peace, direct evidence is sometimes available linking causal mechanisms to decisions about whether to go to war. For example, in 1973 Israel decided not to launch a preemptive attack as it had in 1967 because it did not want to lose international support by firing first. But, as noted above, the political and military sensitivities that continue to surround the conflicts studied here make direct evidence particularly hard to come by. As with most inferences in social science, less direct evidence must be relied on to assess effects. The case studies explore whether the process by which Israel and Syria, and India and Pakistan maintained peace and went to war is consistent with the theory presented here. Does a comparison across cease-fire observations within each case support the idea that stronger agreements foster more durable peace? In both cases, evidence for the effects of agreements can also be seen by examining the smaller details. For example, were tensions and skirmishes along the cease-fire line reduced when troops pulled back to create a demilitarized zone? Did it matter whether the demilitarized area ran the full length of the cease-fire line? In some cases evidence for the effects of agreements can be seen in the breach, in the efforts belligerents took to circumvent the measures they had set up. By looking at what happened when new measures were put in place or existing ones fell into disuse we can also discern their role in keeping peace.

The case studies provide depth to complement the breadth of the large-N analysis. Where the statistical and survey work indicates general trends and associations in all international cease-fires since World War II, the India-Pakistan and Israel-Syria cases show how the various mechanisms operate within a particular context. Because the contexts chosen are the most difficult cases, we can have greater confidence in the applicability of the findings to other, easier cases. Together, these three methods provide rich evidence about the ways in which enemies can and do maintain peace.

CHAPTER THREE

THE BASELINE PROSPECTS FOR PEACE

NOT ALL CEASE-FIRES are created equal. Peace is easier to maintain after some wars than others. Cease-fire agreements aside, we would probably expect peace to be easier to keep after the Falklands War, for example, than after the first Kashmir war between India and Pakistan. This chapter investigates the factors that affect the baseline prospects for peace.

Evaluating variables other than the cease-fire agreement is important for two reasons. First and foremost, it gives us a more complete answer to the primary question asked in this book: what determines whether peace lasts or war resumes? Second, because the content of agreements may be related to the baseline prospects of peace, a valid assessment of the role of the former is impossible without an understanding of the latter.

I use the term *situational variables* to refer to aspects of the situation between the belligerents other than their agreements or mechanisms intended to enhance the durability of peace, aspects over which those who would maintain peace have little or no control. These include both characteristics of the situation at the time of the cease-fire (which will be especially important for evaluating when stronger or weaker agreements are reached) and factors that change over time. We might think of the former as preexisting conditions that shape the baseline prospects for peace, and the latter as exogenous shifts that alter its chances. Preexisting condition variables fall roughly into three categories. Some of them are characteristics of the war that has just been fought: its death toll, whether it was a multiparty war or a bilateral conflict, and the military decisiveness of victory. Some are aspects of the relationship between the parties: the stakes of the conflict between them, the issue over which they are in dispute, and their history of conflict before the war. Others are material conditions such as relative capabilities and geographic contiguity. These variables represent the cooperation problem faced by belligerents before an attempt is made, through an agreement, to make peace more durable. Exogenous changes that occur after a cease-fire is in place but that might affect its durability include shifts in relative power, in the expected utility for peace, and regime change.

I. Hypotheses

If we were assigned the task, like that of an actuary, of assessing the chances for lasting peace of a particular cease-fire, what would we want to know? Setting aside for the moment the deliberate efforts to maintain peace embodied in a cease-fire agreement, in what kinds of situations might we expect peace to be most fragile, and when most likely to last?

The discussion of obstacles to peace in chapter 1 suggests some answers to this question. More generally, many of the factors that make war more likely in the first place might also make it more likely to resume. To some extent, then, gauging the baseline probability of war entails analyzing the causes of war. This has been the primary question addressed by the field of security studies, and there is a vast literature on which to draw.[1] The hypotheses that follow are derived from the literature on war-proneness, from existing studies of the durability of peace, and from cooperation theory. What kinds of wars are most likely to resume? What about states' relationship makes them more likely to fight anew? What material factors make peace more fragile? And what changes after a cease-fire is in place make peace more likely to break down?

Characteristics of the War and Stability of the Peace

DECISIVENESS OF VICTORY

Much of the existing work on the durability of peace has focused on the decisiveness of victory as an explanatory variable. Most analyses of the durability of peace after militarized international disputes and civil wars have found empirical evidence that disputes or wars that end with a clear winner are less likely to resume than those that end in a stalemate or tie.[2] Theories that treat war as part of a rational bargaining process emphasize that if actors could know perfectly what the outcome of war would be before fighting, they could save themselves the trouble of battle by settling their disputes accordingly. Rational leaders fight inefficient wars because they do not know ahead of time who will win.[3] Decisive victories presumably reveal reliable information about who would win another war, which

---

[1] For good overviews of this literature, see Levy 1989; Vasquez 1993 and 2000.

[2] Maoz 1984; Licklider 1995; Kozhemiakin 1994; Stinnett and Diehl 2001.

[3] Fearon 1995; Goemans 2000. According to Blainey 1973, 122–23, wars "begin when fighting nations *disagree* on their relative strength," and they "end when the fighting nations *agree* on their relative strength." States might come to agree that they are evenly matched in a stalemate, but decisive victories are likely to reveal more information than less decisive outcomes.

should make peace more durable, while fighting that stops before this likely outcome is known with certainty should be more likely to resume.

That decisive victory should be associated with stability is not beyond debate. Advocates of "peace by empire" argue that complete victory is the best means of achieving stability, while others argue that "prudence in victory" requires the winner not to impose terms on the loser that are overly harsh.[4] However, this debate is less over the military outcome itself than over how the victor, if there is one, should behave toward the vanquished.[5]

In her discussion of the effects of stalemate or victory on stability, Suzanne Werner suggests that Zartman's concept of "hurting stalemate" as a factor contributing to conflict resolution might lead us to expect stalemates to yield more stable peace. Zartman uses the hurting stalemate concept to explain decisions to negotiate an end to war rather than fighting on in the hopes of victory.[6] If wars that bogged down in hurting stalemate are likely to lead to stable peace, that would seem to have more to do with the "hurting" part than the "stalemate," a hypothesis discussed below. Moreover, if Werner's own argument about power shifts upsetting peace (also discussed below) is correct, we should expect wars that end in stalemate to be more susceptible to breakdown than those in which one side was beaten soundly. This yields this chapter's first hypothesis:

HYPOTHESIS: *Peace is more stable after decisive victories than after less conclusive military contests.*

Note that I am distinguishing the military outcome from the agreement, if any, reached at the end of a war. These are often conflated, with agreement and decisive victory treated as opposites.[7] While these may be correlated, they are conceptually distinct.[8] Wars ending in decisive victories sometimes yield negotiated agreements (as after the Yom Kippur War)

---

[4] Raymond Aron 1966 is credited with the first argument, while Nissan Oren 1982 has argued the second. On this debate, see also Kegley and Raymond 1999; Maoz 1984; and Towle 1997.

[5] Kozhemiakin 1994 separates the concepts of decisiveness and punitiveness, finding that both decisive victories and settlements that are not overly punitive lead to more durable peace.

[6] Werner 1999; Zartman 1989, 1995.

[7] See, for example, Maoz 1984; Hensel 1994; and Licklider 1995. Licklider defines and measures "negotiated settlement" as "an end to the violence reached while both sides had significant military capabilities remaining and therefore presumably could have decided not to stop fighting if the terms were unacceptable." He is thus testing the effects of decisiveness, not negotiations.

[8] Interstate wars that end without a victor are, in fact, no more likely to yield a formal agreement to cease fire than are those that end with a victory for one side, nor are they significantly more likely to yield a peace agreement rather than a cease-fire or truce.

and military draws occasionally end with no negotiations (the first Sino-Vietnamese war ended in stalemate with China's unilateral withdrawal in 1979, and in the second, clashes simply fizzled out in 1987).[9]

COST OF WAR

There are conflicting hypotheses on the cost of war and the durability of peace. On the one hand, avoiding the high cost of war, particularly in lives, is the main incentive to cooperate. The cooperation theory outlined in chapter 1 suggests that states will be less inclined to fight again when doing so is expected to be very costly. While it is difficult (both for states and analysts) to measure future costs, the cost of the fighting just ended may be a good gauge of the expected costs of war if it resumes. This suggests that

HYPOTHESIS: *More deadly conflicts are less likely to resume.*

Moreover, war weariness among the societies that bear the brunt of fighting may also make reinitiating a costly fight more difficult for domestic reasons.[10] But the opposite hypothesis is also possible. More costly wars may be the result of more entrenched conflicts that are more difficult to resolve. Costly wars may also increase the domestic pressures not to concede on issues for which so many have died.[11]

HYPOTHESIS: *More deadly conflicts are more likely to resume.*

MULTILATERAL WARS

Similarly, the effect of the number of states at war might go in either direction. Studies of cooperation have suggested that increasing the number of players diminishes its prospects. Detecting cheating and coordinating retaliation become more difficult.[12] The unit of analysis in this study is the dyad; each pair of states that have fought is treated as a separate case.

HYPOTHESIS: *Conflicts between dyads that are part of a multilateral war are more prone to resumption than are bilateral conflicts.*

[9] By distinguishing between the military outcome, treated here as a situational variable, and the form of the cease-fire (whether no agreement, a negotiated cease-fire, or a peace agreement) or the formality of that agreement, we can test their separate effects. I find that both decisiveness and political settlement (explored in chapter 6) lead to greater stability.

[10] However, Levy and Morgan 1986 found no empirical support for a related war-weariness hypothesis, that fighting war makes great powers less likely to fight again soon.

[11] On these competing hypotheses, see Werner 1997. See also Hensel 1994.

[12] Oye 1986a, 18–20. The realist argument about numbers and stability is about poles in the international system and has not generally been applied to relations between specific states.

However, the argument that cooperation is more difficult with more players may only apply to the difference between a few and many, not to the difference between two and three or four.[13] A competing hypothesis would be that multilateral conflicts are more likely to include states that were drawn by alliances into wars not of their own making. While these states may be pulled in again, they are probably less likely to fight again than are other dyads.[14]

HYPOTHESIS: *Dyads in multilateral conflicts are less prone to renewed conflict.*

The Belligerents' Relationship and the Prospects for Peace

HISTORY OF CONFLICT

Intuitively, we might expect that peace will be much harder to maintain between belligerents who share a long history of conflict than between actors who enjoyed relatively pacific relations before the war. The literature on "enduring rivalries" suggests that a context of historical conflict should affect the postwar relations of actors.[15] A history of conflict may be an indicator, reflecting the intractable nature of the issues over which states are fighting. If they have been unable to resolve the conflict over a long period, this may indicate that it is a tough issue to solve. Or it may be that repeated conflict is an actual cause of instability, tending to breed future conflict. Wars create new issues of dispute, over occupied territory, prisoners of war, reparations, and so on. They may make leaders less likely to trust each other to maintain peace. Repeated wars and disputes may also lead to a more visceral sense of historical animosity between the two societies, creating domestic pressures for war.[16] Fighting against each other changes the very nature of the relationship from that of opponents to that of deadly enemies. In either case we should expect that between states whose relations have been marked by repeated conflict, peace will be more difficult to keep.

HYPOTHESIS: *Peace is less durable among belligerents with a history of conflict.*

---

[13] Collective action problems arise when the number of players makes it difficult to monitor compliance and to mobilize retaliation. Olson 1965.

[14] See also Werner 1997; and Gartner and Siverson 1996. Stinnett and Diehl 2001 find support for a related hypothesis: that states joining a dispute after it has begun are less likely to become involved in an enduring rivalry than are the initial parties to the dispute.

[15] See, for example, Goertz and Diehl 1993.

[16] The proposition that entrenched hatreds contribute to repeated conflict has more often been made for civil than for international wars. For a critique, see Walter 1994.

ISSUES AT STAKE IN THE CONFLICT

A growing literature has emphasized the importance of territorial conflicts as opposed to conflicts over other issues.[17] This literature has argued that territorial disputes are particularly salient and are therefore especially prone to escalation and war and especially difficult to resolve. Hensel found that disputes over territory are more likely to recur and to recur quickly than are other types of conflicts, while Stinnett and Diehl found that disputes over territory are more likely to develop into enduring rivalries.[18]

HYPOTHESIS: *Wars fought over territory are more likely to resume than wars fought over other issues.*

A related hypothesis puts the emphasis on the stakes of the conflict. The value of what would be gained if one attacked, or lost if one were attacked, might affect the prospects for maintaining peace. When a state's very existence is on the line, fear of cheating makes cooperation much riskier than when the war is over less vital issues.[19] If one side can be eliminated in war, reciprocity and deterrence will not work.

HYPOTHESIS: *The higher the stakes of the conflict, the more quickly war will resume.*

Material Factors and the Prospects for Peace

GEOGRAPHIC CONTIGUITY

Neighbors are more likely to fight than nonneighbors. In his study of "war-proneness," Bremer found that of all the variables he tested, geographic contiguity was the strongest predictor of whether a dyad went to war.[20] If contiguous states are more likely to fight in the first place, they might also be more likely to fight again after a cease-fire. The study of "politically relevant dyads," including contiguous states and major powers, is predicated on the logic that contiguous states are both more likely to have potential issues of conflict and can reach each other to fight more

---

[17] For reviews of this literature and summaries of its findings, see Huth 2000; and Hensel 2000.

[18] Hensel 1996; Stinnett and Diehl 2001. See also Werner 1997.

[19] For a formal treatment of a related argument about the likelihood of war when one side might be "absorbed" by another in battle, see Smith and Stam 2001.

[20] Bremer 1992. See also Hensel 2000 for a review of related empirical findings on geographical proximity, and Stinnett and Diehl 2001 on contiguity and the development of enduring rivalries.

easily.[21] It is easier for actors that are contiguous to attack each other, whereas distance provides a natural buffer that raises the cost of attack. A shared border is also more prone to incidents and misunderstandings that could spark renewed war.

HYPOTHESIS: *Peace between states with a common border is less stable than peace between states that are farther apart.*

This hypothesis is closely related to the notion, discussed above, that territorial issues are more prone to renewed conflict. Neighbors are more likely to have territorial disputes than are states far away from each other. But the two hypotheses are based on different causal mechanisms—one contends that it is the salience of territorial issues themselves that make them more difficult to resolve peacefully, the other that proximity makes conflict over any issue more likely because it allows militaries to reach each other or makes accidents more likely.[22] By separating these two claims we can better test what it is about geography that affects the prospects for peace.

RELATIVE CAPABILITIES

Relative power is the variable that many international relations scholars, particularly those in the realist tradition, look to first for explanation and prediction. In the causes-of-war literature, there are competing theories as to whether a preponderance of power or a balance of power makes for a more stable environment.[23] This debate has been applied both to the systemic level and to relations among pairs of states. A preponderance of power may make disagreements about who has the capacity to win another round of fighting less likely.[24] Bremer found that statistically, a preponderance of power makes a given dyad less likely to go to war.[25] However, a balance of power may deter either side from initiating a new war. Relative capabilities at the time of the cease-fire may therefore affect the durability of peace in either direction:

HYPOTHESIS: *Peace is more stable when one side has a preponderance of power.*

---

[21] Maoz and Russett 1993. One reason that civil wars re-erupt may be that the parties cannot even separate to opposite sides of a border after a cease-fire. Following this logic, we might expect civil conflicts that end with the secession of one side and the creation of two separate states to be less likely to resume (all else equal) than civil wars that leave the state intact.

[22] On this distinction see Diehl 1991; Hensel 2000; and Vasquez 1995.

[23] See, for example, Claude 1962; and Organski 1968.

[24] Capabilities give no information about resolve, however. Stronger powers are often defeated by weaker foes with greater commitment to fight. Rosen 1972.

[25] Bremer 1992.

Alternatively,

HYPOTHESIS: *Peace is more stable when relative capabilities are balanced.*

Changes over Time

The foregoing hypotheses refer to characteristics of the situation between the belligerents at the time of the cease-fire. But changes that take place in the years that follow are also likely to affect the prospects for peace. Suzanne Werner argues that the stability of peace is best analyzed as a decision to resume war. To reach peace, states must decide to stop fighting; if they decide to start again, this must reflect a change in circumstances.[26]

CHANGES IN RELATIVE POWER

Werner's study of the durability of peace found shifts in relative capabilities to be especially destabilizing. She argues that a settlement at the end of a war reflects the belligerents' expectations about how each would fare if they kept fighting. However, if power shifts after a cease-fire is in place, states' expectations about what kind of bargain they can obtain will shift, giving the newly powerful state an incentive to contest the settlement, perhaps by force.[27] This argument parallels power transition theories that focus on wars caused by a stronger power's losing its dominant position as a revisionist state rises.[28] Following these arguments:

HYPOTHESIS: *Peace is more likely to break down when belligerents' relative capabilities change markedly.*

However, it is possible that the causal arrows run the other way; that the outbreak of war (or its immediate anticipation) affects capabilities, rather than the other way round.

EXPECTED UTILITY FOR WAR

In a similar vein, Bueno de Mesquita and Lalman's expected utility theory of war starts from the premise that decisions to go to war are made in the face of cost-benefit calculations. At any point in time, rational leaders choose whether to make demands, to acquiesce, to fight, or to capitulate by calculating which strategy will give them the highest ex-

[26] Werner 1997.
[27] Werner 1999. We might ask, however, why states cannot reach a new bargain without resort to war if they both know about the shift in power. For a related argument, see Gartzke 1999.
[28] Gilpin 1981; Maoz 1984; Organski 1968.

pected utility. In *War and Reason*, Bueno de Mesquita and Lalman develop an "international interaction game" that can end in negotiation, capitulation, or war.[29] They use the similarity of alliance portfolios to estimate state preferences, and combine this information with capability and alliance data to estimate a state's utility for each outcome vis-à-vis other states. They then use this estimated expected utility to predict whether states will go to war with one another in a given year. This same process can be followed for states that have already fought one another to predict when they are most likely to fight again.

HYPOTHESIS: *Peace is likely to fall apart when war is predicted in Bueno de Mesquita and Lalman's international interaction game.*

DEMOCRACY AND THE DURABILITY OF PEACE

Perhaps the strongest empirical regularity in the study of war is that democracies do not fight each other.[30] It follows that there are no cases of cease-fires reached between two democracies. Regime type at the time of the cease-fire is therefore not a particularly helpful piece of information for assessing the prospects for peace. But because regime type can change over time, it sometimes occurs that both former belligerents become democratic. The democratic peace literature suggests that once this happens, war will not resume.

HYPOTHESIS: *If both belligerents become democracies, war will not resume.*

On the other hand, Mansfield and Snyder have shown that the process of becoming democratic can be particularly dangerous for peace, as can shifts toward greater autocracy.[31] This suggests that

HYPOTHESIS: *Peace is more likely to break down if a belligerent is democratizing or becoming more autocratic.*

Characteristics of the war, including decisiveness of victory, its cost, and whether it was a multilateral conflict; aspects of the belligerents' relationship, especially their prior history of conflict and the stakes of their

---

[29] They also distinguish between capitulation by A as opposed to by B, and between wars initiated by A as opposed to by B. Bueno de Mesquita and Lalman 1992. On the international interaction game and a more recent test of its predictions, see Bennett and Stam 2000b.

[30] On the democratic peace see, for example, Russett 1993; and Brown, Lynn-Jones, and Miller 1997.

[31] Mansfield and Snyder 1995.

dispute; material factors such as relative power and geography; and changes over time, in relative capabilities, calculations of expected utility for war, and regime type—each of these variables is hypothesized to affect the baseline prospects for peace. Do they? I now turn to an empirical investigation of these hypotheses to begin to answer the question of why peace sometimes lasts and sometimes falls apart.

II. Empirical Findings

I test the hypotheses presented above both qualitatively and quantitatively. The quantitative tests use both my own data set of cease-fires between 1946 and 1998 and, to give a longer perspective, the Maoz/EUGene data set consisting of wars between 1816 and 1992. Tables 3.1 and 3.2 show statistical results of time-varying covariates duration analysis using a Weibull model (see chapter 2 for discussion of the model and data sets and appendix B for coding details).[32] Table 3.1 shows the effects of variables in place at the time of the cease-fire. Table 3.2 shows the effect of changes over time. Both tables report estimated hazard ratios and robust standard errors. Statistical significance is indicated with asterisks.

The interpretation of hazard ratios differs from that of coefficients that take negative and positive values. Hazard ratios are interpreted relative to a baseline of 1.0. Variables with hazard ratios greater than 1.0 increase the risk of war; those with hazard ratios less than 1.0 decrease the risk of war. For example, a dummy variable with a hazard ratio of 2.0 would indicate a doubling of the hazard of renewed fighting, while a hazard ratio of 0.66 would mean that a variable reduced the hazard by a third. Variables with hazard ratios indistinguishable from 1 have no effect on the risk of war.[33]

Characteristics of the War

DECISIVENESS OF VICTORY

At first glance, the quantitative evidence in favor of the hypothesis that decisive military outcomes lead to stable peace is surprisingly mixed. The

[32] Tests were also run to check robustness to different model specifications (including or excluding independent variables, dropping duplicate agreement cases, etc.). Where these affect the results, this is discussed in the findings below. The analysis in table 3.1 is equivalent to a time-constant model.

[33] That the shape parameter P (toward the bottom of the table) is less than 1.0 indicates that the hazard rate decreases over time. The exception (column 2 in table 3.2) is the result of missing data bias. This finding is discussed further in chapter 5.

TABLE 3.1
Baseline Prospects for Peace at the Time of Cease-Fire

	Weibull Hazard Ratios (robust standard errors)			
	Cease-Fires, 1946–1998		Maoz/EUGene, 1816–1992	
Tie	25.022***	34.879***	0.658	0.683
	(6.069)	(11.024)	(0.249)	(0.257)
Cost of war				
Deaths	0.521***		0.928*	
	(0.092)		(0.038)	
Duration		0.885***		0.974***
		(0.028)		(0.008)
Multilateral war	0.978	0.489	1.137	1.018
	(0.488)	(0.224)	(0.323)	(0.278)
History of conflict	3.134***	2.892***	1.181	1.267*
	(1.076)	(0.924)	(0.157)	(0.164)
Territorial conflict	1.003	1.080	1.290	1.226
	(0.958)	(0.930)	(0.311)	(0.285)
Existence at stake	5.398***	10.470***		
	(2.766)	(4.784)		
Contiguous	1.950**	1.867	1.471	1.426
	(0.641)	(0.776)	(0.426)	(0.409)
Preponderance of power	1.523	1.804	1.126	1.303
	(1.295)	(1.481)	(0.401)	(0.478)
P	0.725*	0.763	0.510***	0.526***
	(0.118)	(0.131)	(0.045)	(0.046)
N	876	876	9,255	9,609
No. of subjects	48	48	292	303
Log likelihood	−49.163	−47.389	−295.132	−291.695

Note: Cases are clustered by conflict in Cease-Fires data, by dyad ID number in Maoz/EUGene data.
* Statistically significant at the .10 level.
** Statistically significant at the .05 level.
*** Statistically significant at the .01 level.

first row of table 3.1 shows the effects of a variable coded 1 for wars that end in a tie, 0 for those that end in victory for one side. Statistically, wars that end in a draw have tended to resume more quickly in the last 50 years. The hazard of renewed warfare in such cases is estimated to be almost 25–35 times that for decisive victories. But this finding does not appear to hold up over a longer time period. In fact, if one looks back to

1816, wars that end in draws may even yield more stable peace rather than less (the hazard ratios are less than 1.0)—exactly the opposite of what we would expect.[34] Note, however, that almost all of the wars without clear victors occur after World War II. War ends in a draw in less than 5% of the dyads (10 cases) between 1816 and 1945. After 1945 over 52% (46 cases) end in a draw.[35]

Because indecisive outcomes are so rare in the earlier periods, it is hard to come to strong conclusions, but examining the relationship between decisive victory and the duration of peace by time period suggests that wars with clear winners and losers tend to yield more stable peace, with the notable exception of the period from 1900 to 1920.[36] In this period only one war (involving two dyads) ended in a draw: the Central American war of 1906 between Guatemala and both Honduras and El Salvador. This war did not resume. The World War I cases dominate the data in this period, representing 42 out of 68 dyads. The experience of this war and the Versailles treaty inspired the "prudence in victory" argument, and it seems quite likely that the apparently deleterious effects of decisive victory in this period have more to do with the punitive nature of the political settlements imposed than with the military outcome itself. So while the relationship between decisiveness and stability is somewhat murky before 1945, in part because of the crude nature of our measures,[37] the relationship after World War II is quite clear. A closer look at the cases confirms that decisive military outcomes are generally more stable in the postwar era, though there are important exceptions to the rule.

The South Asia cases fit the general rule. Both the first and second wars between India and Pakistan ended before a decisive military outcome was reached. This left the possibility of another round of fighting to settle the score more definitively in the future. As one observer put it, the indecisive military outcome in 1949 left "a red-hot cinder smoldering in the kindling of India-Pakistan relations."[38] After the 1965 cease-fire, there was domestic pressure (both from the public at large and from the military) on both governments to renew the war in order to achieve a more decisive outcome.[39] These wars stand in stark contrast to the Bangladesh War of 1971,

---

[34] Other measures of decisiveness based on differences in battle deaths do not fare well in either data set.

[35] This percentage is a bit higher than in the Cease-Fires data because all of the dyads in the Korean War are included in the Maoz/EUGene data.

[36] The hazard ratio for ties is about 3 in both the nineteenth century and the period from 1920 to 1992, though it is not quite significant in the former because there are so few cases (results not shown).

[37] To my knowledge, the only attempt to separate measures of military outcomes and punitiveness exists in an unpublished paper, Kozhemiakin 1994.

[38] Clodfelter 1992, 1088.

[39] Lamb 1991, 268.

which ended in the dramatic defeat and dismemberment of Pakistan. While even this decisive defeat did not officially settle the issue of Kashmir (the war was not primarily over the disputed territory after all), Pakistan was forced to accommodate Kashmir's de facto partition after 1971, as well as its loss of Bangladesh. Moves in 1975 by India to incorporate its portion of Kashmir into its governance structure that might well have sparked renewed war could only be protested weakly by a defeated Pakistan.[40] Only with a measure of military parity provided by nuclear weapons has Pakistan been able to press its claims on Kashmir, as it did in May 1999. The India-Pakistan case provides strong evidence in favor of the decisiveness hypothesis. Stalemates have led to peace that fell apart quickly, while decisive victory has led to more durable peace.

The cease-fires reached in 1948 during the first Arab-Israeli war support this finding as well. They were unstable because "each of the contestants was convinced that, had it not been for the truce imposed by the Security Council, it would have achieved complete victory on the battlefield."[41] Israel had begun to turn the military tide against Arab forces when the UN demanded a cease-fire in July 1948. In the negotiations that followed, Israel thus held out for a favorable territorial settlement. But Arab leaders, and perhaps more important the Arab public, were not convinced of Israel's superior force and refused to give in.[42] Israel decided to settle the matter by force and broke the cease-fire. The renewed fighting ended with a much clearer defeat of Arab forces, which settled the matter, at least for a time.

The Six-Day War provides a counterexample, however. Of the Arab-Israeli wars, by far the most decisive outcome was Israel's quick and categorical victory in 1967. Golda Meir reportedly hoped that this victory was decisive enough that Israel would never have to wage war again.[43] Her hopes were quickly dashed in the War of Attrition with Egypt in 1969–70, and in yet another regional war in 1973. Israel again won both of these wars, though much less decisively than in 1967.

Khouri argues that decisiveness in fact undermined stability in the Arab-Israeli conflict, because the extent of the Arabs' original defeat in 1949 damaged Arab pride in a way that made compromise and conciliation extremely difficult. Resounding defeat in 1967 made Syria and Egypt even more belligerent, while victory only increased Israeli intransigence. The relatively more even outcome of the 1973 war, on the other hand, made it easier for Arab states to contemplate peace.[44] The 1967 outcome

[40] Lamb 1991, 308.
[41] Bar-Yaacov 1967, 30.
[42] On these negotiations, see Khouri 1985, 81–86.
[43] Bailey 1990, 240.
[44] Khouri 1985, 373.

was the most punitive from the Arab perspective, and one could easily argue that it was occupation of territory, not the decisiveness of the war, that engendered so much instability.

A survey of all of the cases since World War II suggests, the Six-Day War notwithstanding, that decisive victories are unlikely to be followed by renewed warfare. At one end of the decisiveness spectrum there is a set of extremely lopsided military outcomes, not just military victories but routs: the elimination of South Vietnam by the North, the overthrow of the Nagy government by the Soviet Union in Hungary in 1956, the over-throw of Uganda's Idi Amin by Tanzania in 1979. None of these wars has restarted. Other resounding defeats include Pakistan's unconditional surrender and the loss of Bangladesh in 1971, the unconditional surren-ders of Argentina to the United Kingdom in the Falklands, and of Iraq in the Gulf War in 1991, and India's loss to China in 1962. Most of these victories were literally decisive, in the sense that they decided the conflict for good (but see below on punitive victory).

Not all wars that end in stalemate have repeated; Vietnam and the United States did not fight again after 1973. Nor has there been a second Korean War, despite the fact that the first ended in a draw. Both of these examples suggest that it was the "hurting" in lives lost, rather than the stalemate, that led to a reluctance to fight again. The "hurt" of Vietnam made the United States extremely reluctant to fight again, even elsewhere. El Salvador and Honduras did not fight again after their military draw in 1969, though they came close in the 1970s. Peace between Iran and Iraq has held despite the inconclusive nature of their war, but this is attribut-able to Iraq's other security problems. On the other hand, the lack of a clear victor in the first Sino-Vietnamese war led to very unstable peace, with ongoing clashes and skirmishes, and then another full-scale war. The first cease-fire in the Turco-Cypriot War in July 1974, when neither side had the clear upper hand, fell apart within two weeks, while the cease-fire after Turkey's much more decisive victory in August has been shaky but has held.

With some exceptions, the evidence suggests that decisive military out-comes are much less likely to be followed by renewed warfare than are more even military outcomes. The policy implications of this finding pre-sent a dilemma for peacemakers. Putting pressure on belligerents to cease fighting before a decisive outcome will save untold lives in the present, but may jeopardize stability in the longer term.

The qualitative evidence on the question of punitive versus prudent victory is mixed, with perhaps a stronger empirical case for the prudence argument. The most punitive settlement in the cases examined here is probably UN Security Resolutions 686 and 687 (1991) calling for Iraq to dismantle its weapons of mass destruction, compromising Iraqi sovereignty through the enforcement of no-flight zones within Iraq itself, and maintaining crippling economic sanctions. This punitive policy may have kept Iraq from starting another war in the Gulf, but it has also led to ongoing hostilities between Iraq and the United States, with recurrent air strikes in the decade after the war. Peace failed as this book went to press. A punitive peace may require the continued use of force on the part of the victor.[45] The punitive nature of Israel's victory in 1967 in Arab eyes at least, particularly its occupation of the West Bank, the Golan Heights, and the Sinai, led to the 1973 war. Note, however, that imposed regime changes (as in Uganda and Hungary) by the victor have tended to lead to stable peace. Punishing the leadership appears to have different effects than punishing the country as a whole.

In sum, indecisive wars are not doomed to repeat, and decisive ones are not invulnerable, especially if the victor punishes the loser. However, more even outcomes are generally more likely to be followed by renewed warfare, all else equal.

COST OF CONFLICT

The human cost of the previous war has a clear effect on the duration of peace. The longer and more deadly the war, the more stable the peace. The higher the death toll of war, the lower the risk of renewed warfare, all else equal (table 3.1, second row). This finding holds true whether one uses a measure of the total toll of the war, or only those deaths within a particular dyad. In the longer data set the effect of the cost of war is smaller but still significant.[46] The duration of war is highly correlated with the death toll, and longer wars are also associated with more stable peace.[47]

While there are some relatively low-cost wars that do not repeat (for example, the Falklands War, and the war between China and India in 1962) and there are some costly wars that do (the first Sino-Vietnamese war, for example), in general, wars toward the more costly end of the spectrum are less likely to resume than those at the less costly end. Those with truly horrific death tolls, such as Korea and Vietnam, which killed

[45] This is one conclusion of Maoz 1984. See also Towle 1997.

[46] Interestingly, as wars have gotten more deadly over the last two centuries, this relationship has shifted. In the nineteenth century, peace was generally less stable after more deadly wars, but in the twentieth century the reverse was true. In the subset of data from 1900 to 1992, the hazard ratio for the cost of war is significantly less than 1.0.

[47] Dubey 2002 found the intensity of fighting to have a quadratic effect on the duration of peace after civil wars (i.e., the hazard increases, flattens, and then declines as intensity increases). I find intensity (measured as deaths/duration) to have no effect on the stability of interstate peace, quadratic or otherwise.

about one million people each, and the Iran-Iraq War, in which 1.25 million perished, have fortunately been one-time-only catastrophes.

That the ghastly toll of World War I did not prevent Europe from fighting again shortly after reminds us that this is in no way a deterministic relationship. Many have argued that the desire to avoid the high price of war after World War I contributed to appeasement and the outbreak of World War II. However, the statistical relationship between higher death tolls and more stable peace holds for all of the twentieth century (notwithstanding the presence of the World War I dyads), not only after 1946, suggesting a strong general tendency.

The circumstantial evidence from the case studies of India and Pakistan, and Israel and Syria supports the conclusion that high-cost wars yield more stable peace. The need to put aside their conflict and its accompanying arms expenditures so as to get on with the business of developing their countries comes through clearly in the rhetoric of Indian and Pakistani leaders;[48] much less so in the Middle East. But in neither case is rhetoric necessarily a reliable indicator of decision making.[49]

There is not much direct causal evidence from the case studies that the cost of war in terms of casualties has been a major consideration or deterrent to war. But as with the study of deterrence, it is easier to see when costs did not prevent war than when they might have restrained leaders. In 1965, Pakistan was clearly not deterred by the cost of war when it decided to contest the status quo in Kashmir. The first Kashmir war had been relatively inexpensive, and the rising cost of war does seem to have been considered by India in 1971. In this case, however, the status quo was itself quite costly, as India was faced with millions of Bengali refugees flooding across the border. One analyst has argued that as the Pakistani crisis deepened, "India decided at last that it was cheaper to go to war than to absorb the refugees into its already bloated population."[50] More recently, some have argued that the development of nuclear weapons on the subcontinent means that the anticipated costs of a possible nuclear confrontation provide a major deterrent to hostilities between India and

---

[48] See for example, Ayub Khan's new year's message to Pakistan, in the very tense situation right after the 1965 cease-fire, emphasizing how neither side could afford the disastrous consequences of renewed conflict. Blinkenberg 1972, 277.

[49] While one might expect those bearing the costs of fighting directly to be most attentive to its costs, in both South Asia and the Middle East, popular sentiment has been in favor of standing firm on an issue over which blood has been spilt. Domestic politics has generally provided more of an incentive for war than a constraint. The legitimacy of the Syrian government rests in part on its strong stand against Israel, and Israel has tended to step up aggressive action against Syria in election years. Leaders in India and Pakistan have come under equally strong political pressure to maintain a strong stance in Kashmir.

[50] Ganguly 1986, 135.

Pakistan.[51] This has not stopped their brinkmanship, nor did it prevent war in May 1999, though it may have helped to keep the war from escalating further than it did. The nuclear deterrent may make total war less likely, but in so doing so may make it safer for India and Pakistan to fight at lower levels along their disputed border.[52]

In the Middle East, there is some evidence that the concern for heavy casualties entered into calculations about initiating warfare, both in 1967 and in 1982.[53] This fits the general pattern we have observed, as in each case the previous war was quite costly. The comparatively low cost of the 1967 war may also have convinced leaders that limited war could be waged without major losses in 1973.[54] While not large in absolute numbers, the toll of war in Lebanon in the 1980s relative to the security gains eventually led many Israelis to question their country's military policy. Lebanon became in some ways Israel's "Vietnam," and concern over casualties restrained Israel later in the decade.[55]

Akin to the mixed effect of a nuclear deterrent in South Asia, the restraining involvement of the superpowers in the Middle East has dampened somewhat the concern for extremely costly fights. Superpower patronage reassured both sides that costs could be contained, as the United States and the Soviet Union were unlikely to allow dire losses to their respective clients before either imposing a cease-fire or extending military support.[56]

Overall the evidence refutes the hypothesis that more costly wars reflect intractable conflicts that will be harder to resolve. Rather, longer and more costly wars give greater incentives to cooperate and maintain peace. States are chastened by high-cost wars into maintaining peace.

MULTILATERAL WARS

Whether a war was fought between just two states or among several does not have a strong effect on the durability of peace. In the years since World War II, the multilateral wars can be divided into two categories, those between Israel and its neighbors, and the rest. The former have been particularly prone to renewed warfare, while the latter have been very stable. Almost all of the Arab-Israeli wars were multilateral, with several Arab states fighting Israel in 1948, 1967, and 1973, or Israel fighting

[51] Bajpai 1996, 23.

[52] This is a good example of the "stability/instability paradox" that while nuclear weapons make all out war less likely, they make limited conflict more likely. Snyder 1965.

[53] See for example Evron 1987, 38, 87; and Ma'oz 1995, 99.

[54] Because it was so short, the 1967 war's death toll was much lower than either the 1948 or 1973 wars. For a detailed account of casualties, see Clodfelter 1992, 1032–75.

[55] Khouri 1985, 249, 306–7; Ma'oz 1995, 195.

[56] See, for example, Ma'oz 1995, 129.

along with Britain and France against Egypt in 1956, and of course almost all of these cease-fires eventually broke down. However, of the other cases of multilateral conflict, Korea, Vietnam, Uganda-Tanzania (in which Libya fought with Uganda), Ethiopia-Somalia (in which Cuba joined on the side of Ethiopia), and the Gulf War, only the last has resumed to date.

In general then, more belligerents do not seem to make resumption more likely. The problems of detecting cheating and coordinating retaliation among many players that make multilateral cooperation difficult in other settings do not seem to affect the maintenance of peace in the aftermath of war. Note, however, that in the post-1945 period we do not have a good test of the "ally drawn into war not of its own making" hypothesis outlined above. For not only are allies of initial belligerents less likely to fight again, rarely do any of the parties to the multilateral wars fight again. It is not the case that the war resumes but reluctant allies this time stay out of the fray.[57] Rather, it may be that one of the uncertainties that can lead rational states to irrational war, namely, who will join the fight if a conflict escalates to war,[58] has been cleared up in the first war, thus making resumption less likely.

The conflict over Palestine and the right of Israel to exist was not a matter of a bilateral conflict that other states joined as allies. Rather the conflict was, especially at its inception, between the nation of Israel and an Arab nation (lowercase *n*) represented by multiple states. With regards to Israel, the interests of Syria, Egypt, and for a time Jordan were close to identical. Syria and Egypt were even joined as one state between February 1958 and September 1961. That Syria stayed out of the Sinai War when Egypt was under attack was the exception rather than the rule. Nor did the Sinai War involve reluctant allies; Israel, France, and Great Britain were co-conspirators in that conflict. However, the fact that Britain and France did not fight with Israel again in 1967 makes clear that states that fight together once need not always.

The relevant uncertainties in the Middle East were generally not who would fight, but rather concerned the resolve and capabilities of those virtually certain to fight if war broke out. And here problems of misperception do seem to have been exacerbated by the multilateral nature of the conflict. While it is impossible to know how history would have played out had the Arab states been a single entity, or had only one of them battled against Israel, the number of players does seem to have contributed to miscalculations that led to war. Assessing accurately their own military strength relative to Israel was often a challenge for the Arab states as they jockeyed amongst themselves for position as leaders in the struggle against Israel.

---

[57] With the notable exception of the Gulf War in 2003.
[58] Iklé 1991.

The 1967 war provides an example of Egypt and Syria drawing each other into provocative action, but not as "reluctant" allies. Israeli noises about overthrowing the Ba'th regime in Syria, along with misinformation from the Soviet Union that Israel was amassing troops on Syria's border, led Arab leaders to believe that an Israeli attack against Syria was imminent. Egypt acted in response to that perceived threat to Syria, put troops on alert, requested that the UN peacekeeping force leave, and closed the Gulf of Aqaba to Israeli shipping.[59] Israel's response to Egypt's provocations started a war that automatically involved both Egypt and Syria. Security dilemma dynamics seem to have been exacerbated in this case by the multilateral nature of the conflict. The dynamics of the Arab-Israeli conflict do not generalize well to other multilateral conflicts, however. Overall, there is no clear and consistent relationship between the number of states that fight and the baseline prospects for peace.

The Belligerents' Relationship

HISTORY OF CONFLICT

Knowing something about the belligerents' history before the war provides quite a good gauge of the chances that peace will last. In the various hazard analyses testing the baseline prospects for peace, prior conflict consistently indicates a higher risk of renewed warfare. The more the combatants' history before the war was marked by serious disputes, ceteris paribus, the more quickly war between them resumed.[60]

Peace has been remarkably stable among states with a lower than average record of conflict. In the set of deadly enemies surveyed here, the average rate of conflict is just under one dispute per year. In only two cases with fewer prewar disputes than this has fighting resumed: between China and Vietnam (who had two disputes in 25 years before 1979), and between Turkey and Cyprus (three disputes in 14 years). The latter exception proves the rule, as it was driven largely by the historical enmity between Greece and Turkey. In comparison, in four-fifths of the cases of higher than average conflict, peace eventually broke down. This category includes the Arab-Israeli wars in which the belligerents' history was marked by severe conflict even before independence, and the wars between India and Pakistan, whose conflict began with the violence surrounding partition at independence from Britain (more on these below). It also includes the two cease-

---

[59] Bailey 1990, 187–221; Ovendale 1984, chap. 10.

[60] This effect is large and statistically significant in tests run on post-1945 cases, but is somewhat less pronounced and occasionally fails tests of statistical significance in the data going back to 1816. The average level of prewar conflict rises over time, particularly after World War I, but this is partly an artifact of the measure, as disputes prior to 1816 are not counted.

fires between Armenia and Azerbaijan, the first in 1992 that faltered after only a few weeks, and the second that has held tenuously since 1994. Violent struggles at independence are particularly inauspicious for peace.[61]

Neither the quantitative results nor an overview of the cases can tell us whether a history of conflict is merely an indicator of intractable issues under contention, or whether it is itself a cause of instability, but the case studies shed light on this question. In both the Middle East and South Asia, the underlying conflict has been and continues to be particularly difficult to solve, but in both there is also clear evidence that the violence itself intensified and bred new conflict.

The colonial history of South Asia and the trauma of partition give India and Pakistan a rather unusual shared history. From the very moment of independence the two countries were in conflict, and their founding ideologies were directly contradictory, pitting secular India against Islamic Pakistan. The extraordinary violence surrounding partition and the mass movements of Hindus and Muslims to their respective sides of the partition line only made things worse.[62] Nonetheless, at partition, Pakistanis and Indians viewed each other more as family than as enemies. They had struggled together against British rule, and had more in common culturally and historically than that which divided them.

To some extent the conflict between Pakistan and India has endured because Kashmir poses a difficult problem. Indian and Pakistani leaders negotiated for a full decade after the first war, apparently in good faith and with sincerity, and were unable to devise an acceptable solution. Various proposals for partition have been considered, but the ideological implications of how to divide the heart of Kashmir, the Vale, have so far proven irreconcilable.[63]

However, Kashmir need not have become such an intractable issue. In 1947, as independence and partition of British India approached, and the maharaja dithered on the decision of which state to join, Lord Mountbatten informed him that the Indian States' Department would not object to Kashmir's joining Pakistan.[64] Once armed revolt broke out and tribesmen from Pakistan invaded to support the rebellion, the maharaja's panicked

---

[61] This finding is supported by Stinnett and Diehl 2001. Note, however, that it does not hold for anticolonial wars of liberation. None of the COW "extrasystemic" wars between a colony and the metropole have been repeated. These wars are not included in the data examined here.

[62] Estimates of the numbers of people killed in this violence vary considerably, but many analysts put the death toll in the range of 500,000 to 800,000. Sivard 1993, 21, for example, estimates 800,000 civilian deaths from 1946 to 1948. See Valentino 2002.

[63] For details of the early negotiations on partition, see, for example, Lamb 1991, esp. 239.

[64] Blinkenberg 1972, 72.

decision to ask India for military help sparked the first war between India and Pakistan. With a more decisive or popular Kashmiri leader, the accession question might well have been settled peacefully. Brines states that Pakistan "might have obtained Kashmir easily and bloodlessly" if it had not supported the tribal invasion in 1947. He notes that Indians were indifferent about Kashmir before 1948, but the war "intensified the strong fears within India that Pakistan would use force to expand [and] transformed Kashmir from a theoretical battlefield into an active battle area [and] inevitably strengthened the anti-Muslim elements in north India."[65] Kashmir was necessarily more important to both sides, and their need to save face greater, once they had invested blood and treasure in the fight.[66]

In the early years following the first Kashmir war, relations between India and Pakistan alternated between sincere amity and deep animosity.[67] But by the early 1960s, public opinion in both countries was consistently much more hostile, and the leaders of both sides faced increasing domestic opposition to any move that might be construed as giving up ground on Kashmir.[68] The 1965 war cemented the enmity. As one historian describes it,

> What had emerged from the events of 1965 was clear evidence that India and Pakistan really were *enemies*, people who killed each other with all the horrible weapons of 20th century warfare, not merely rivals for a disputed inheritance from the British Raj.[69]

By 1970 the dispute was no longer confined to the issue of Kashmir. It had become a zero-sum conflict between two deadly adversaries. India took advantage of internal turmoil in Pakistan to split its enemy in half in the Bangladesh War, not to gain ground in Kashmir. Animosity between the two successor states to British India was not inevitable, but once it began, it fed on itself. The first war made a second more likely, and the second cemented the Indo-Pakistani relationship as one of enemies. India's decisive victory in the third war settled matters for a time, but only fomented further mistrust. The most recent round of warfare, in May 1999, was a product of this mistrust. The fighting in Kargil scuttled na-

---

[65] Brines 1968, 80.

[66] "[For Pakistan] to withdraw from the territory won by arms, while India still held the Vale, could have produced a severe loss of internal prestige. . . . India, on the other hand, having successfully defended Kashmir, could not allow it to be assaulted again or captured, and still maintain face." Brines 1968, 92.

[67] Blinkenberg 1972, 168.

[68] See, for example, Lamb 1991, 230, 261.

[69] Lamb 1991, 277.

scent efforts between Indian and Pakistani leaders to improve relations, providing yet another example of hostility breeding hostility.

Between Israel and Syria we see a similar pattern. While relations between Arabs in Palestine and Jews were hostile from the beginning, relations between Syrian and Zionist leaders were not always so acrimonious. In the early years of the Zionist movement, some moderate and pragmatic nationalist leaders in Syria were willing to engage in dialogue and possibly to support the Zionist cause in exchange for Jewish help, along with the British, in forestalling French control.[70] Other Syrian nationalists, however, identified more strongly with Palestinian anti-Zionist ideology. As Jewish immigration to Palestine increased, Syrian sentiment turned increasingly against the perceived Zionist threat to the Arab cause. Early hopes for pacific relations between Syria and the Jews were thwarted when Zionists proclaimed their goal of a Jewish state and when Syria gained independence under radical leadership.[71]

Of the Arab states, Syria quickly became the most antagonistic toward the prospect of a Jewish state; Syria was the first to enact a boycott against the Jewish community and the first to mobilize troops along the border with Palestine after the announcement of a partition plan in 1947.[72] From before its independence, then, Israel saw Syria as an implacable enemy, bent on its destruction, while Syria viewed the state of Israel as an illegitimate usurper of Arab lands. The war in 1948 hardened these perceptions, both among the leadership of Israel and Syria, and among the general public.

In the first years after the war, Syrians and Israelis were at least able to work together within a Military Armistice Commission to address some of their disputes, but Syria interpreted unilateral actions by Israel in the demilitarized zones set up after the war as evidence of expansionist and aggressive intentions.[73] Syria's bellicose rhetoric did nothing to assuage Israeli fears. Over the years animosity between the two countries was exacerbated by a series of disputes and clashes, and particularly by guerilla (fedayeen) raids from within Syria and harsh retaliatory raids by

---

[70] For details of this dialogue, see Ma'oz 1995, 1–5.

[71] The newly independent Syrian republic was led by the radical Shukri al-Quwwatli, who used anti-Zionist, pro-Palestinian policies to bolster domestic support for his fragile regime and pan-Arab ideology to guard against the ambitions of other Arab leaders. But even he had expressed willingness to work out a settlement as long as the Zionist claims on Palestine were limited. He distinguished between a Jewish home *in* Palestine, and a Jewish home *of* Palestine. Ma'oz 1995, 4–17.

[72] Ma'oz 1995, 17.

[73] The first of many crises during the armistice came in 1951 over Israel's project to drain the Huleh marsh within the demilitarized area. Arab civilians fired on Israeli bulldozers, which led to fighting along the armistice line. See Kinsolving 1967, 24–32.

Israel. The resulting atmosphere of mistrust contributed directly to the security dilemma and the spiral that led to the 1967 war. Israel's attack against Egypt in 1956, its preemptive assault on Syria and Egypt at the start of the 1967 war, and then the Syrian and Egyptian surprise attack in 1973 merely confirmed Syrian and Israeli perceptions of each other as treacherous and hateful enemies. As in South Asia, the conflict became a basis for nationalist identity and legitimacy.[74]

And as in South Asia, the history of repeated violent conflict between Syria and Israel reflects in part the intractable nature of their dispute. The bone of contention until very recently was Israel's right to exist as a state, hardly an issue amenable to compromise. But the course of the Israeli-Syrian relationship also demonstrates how conflict breeds conflict. The war in 1948, and the series of clashes in its aftermath, contributed to the mistrust that caused the 1967 war, while that war planted the seed for the next. Once ensconced as implacable foes, the prospect of either of them gaining undue influence in Lebanon brought them to war yet again.

It is possible for states to alter even an entrenched relationship of belligerency; otherwise cycles of war and rivalry would never end. Israel and Egypt changed their relationship in a historic peace process that settled their conflict politically in 1979. Israel and Jordan have not fought outright since 1973, despite 25 years of conflict before that, and eventually reached a peace treaty in 1994. If the Palestinian issue is ever settled, Israel and Syria may yet reach peace, *insh'allah*. However, the ingrained nature of the competition within Israeli and Syrian society will be a difficult obstacle to overcome. Likewise, India and Pakistan may yet break out of their chronic cycle of war, but each round of fighting makes this task more difficult.

States are not inexorably doomed by their history to repeat conflict incessantly, but both the quantitative and qualitative evidence indicates that conflict does breed conflict, making it much more difficult to achieve lasting peace.

STAKES AND ISSUES

The results in table 3.1 show that territorial conflicts may be somewhat more prone to resume than are fights over other issues, but this is not a strong (nor statistically significant) indicator of the baseline prospects for peace. In the postwar period this finding is driven by the repeated disputes over only two pieces of land: Israel/Palestine and Kashmir. Other territorial conflicts such as those along the borders between China and India, between El Salvador and Honduras, between Ethiopia and Somalia, between Iran and Iraq, and over the Falklands/Malvinas, have not led to renewed war-

---

[74] See Barnett 1998.

fare, even though many of these borders and territories remain in dispute. Taking a longer view of history and looking at wars going back to 1816 suggests a similar pattern; there may be a weak relationship between territory and more fragile peace, but it is not statistically significant.

This finding contrasts with that of Hensel, who found territorial disputes to be more prone to resumption.[75] The difference may stem from the fact that he examines the resumption of all militarized disputes, while I am focusing only on peace after full-scale war. Territorial issues may be more salient than other issues over which states make claims and rattle their swords, but not significantly more salient than nonterritorial issues over which states have already decided it is worth fighting. Given that states have already fought, knowing whether they fought over territory or something else is not terribly helpful in predicting whether they will fight again.

A separate indicator of the stakes at issue, measuring how much states stood to lose or gain in the war, is a better predictor. As a cooperation perspective would predict, the more there is at stake in a conflict, the harder it is to maintain peace. The few wars examined here that threatened only a state's political influence (e.g., Israeli and Syrian influence in Lebanon in 1982) or its political system (as in the Ugandan-Tanzanian war) have yielded stable peace.[76]

Wars that threatened "grave damage" to one or both sides include some cease-fires that failed (the War of Attrition between Egypt and Israel, for example, and the Sino-Vietnamese war), but many that did not (Iran-Iraq, Yom Kippur, and the Sino-Indian War, for example). Those that threatened a state's territorial integrity but did not threaten grave damage have been relatively stable (e.g., the Falklands War, and the war between Ethiopia and Somalia over the Ogaden). But where the very existence of one of the belligerents was at stake (as in the first Arab-Israeli war over Palestine, and the Six-Day War), peace is much less likely to be durable. Once again, this finding is driven largely by the wars between Israel and its neighbors. But it is the existential nature of this conflict at least as much as the fact that the conflict involves competing claims to territory that accounts for the deep animosity between Israel and its neighbors. The quantitative analyses indicate that when one state could be obliterated in the war, peace is significantly less likely to last, all else equal.[77]

More subtle effects of the stakes of a conflict and its territoriality emerge from the case studies. In both the South Asian and Middle Eastern

[75] Hensel 1996. See also Stinnett and Diehl 2001.

[76] Because of the small number of cases in each, these categories are combined.

[77] Including dummies for the other values of the stakes variable indicates that higher stakes lead to less stable peace, but that the most important effect is that of threat to existence (results not shown). Unfortunately, we do not have a measure of the stakes of conflict that goes back to 1816.

conflicts, domestic political stakes and the extent to which a conflict touches on existential nerves is at least as important as is the "objective" value of disputed territory in material or strategic resources.

At its most basic level, the initial dispute between India and Pakistan was over a piece of real estate. Kashmir was of strategic value for the defense of the northern frontier of the subcontinent—hence the importance placed by India on control of the sparsely populated mountainous northern regions of the state. Pakistan's most important material stake in Kashmir concerned control of water.[78] However, this security fear was alleviated substantially by the Indus Waters Treaty of September 1960, which was respected even during subsequent wars.

The initial dispute was territorial and did not represent an objective threat to either state's existence. In symbolic terms, however, Kashmir touched on existential nerves, particularly for Pakistan.[79] Partition and the birth of two separate states on the subcontinent was the result of the bitter debate between the "one-nation" and "two-nation" theories of independence—essentially over whether Muslims and Hindus could live together in a single political entity. From the beginning then, the fight over Kashmir was a struggle not just over the physical territory of the State of Jammu and Kashmir, but over which theory of statehood was correct. India thus invested the struggle over Kashmir with significance for its claim as the true successor to British rule. An India that contained Kashmir proved the feasibility of the one-nation theory on which the secular state of India was founded. For the same reason, control of Kashmir and its majority Muslim population was even more important for Pakistan's two-nation ideology. If Muslims could live easily within India, then the raison d'être of Pakistan was in question.

Moreover, the cultural, economic, and religious links between the Kashmiris and Pakistanis made Indian rule there a travesty for Pakistan. The *k* in Pakistan's very name stands for Kashmir.[80] The domestic stakes of the conflict only grew over time as the dispute became entrenched.[81] Pakistani leaders could ill afford to be "weak" on Kashmir. Domestic opinion has consistently supported aggressive action and has contributed to the re-

---

[78] West Pakistan depends for its agriculture on the waters of the Indus and its tributaries, many of which flow through Indian-controlled territory before reaching Pakistan. India exploited this by cutting off water to the Lahore region in 1948. Lamb 1991, 235.

[79] Korbel 1954, 25ff.

[80] Bailey 1982, 59.

[81] We can see in the conflict over Kashmir an example of Snyder's 1991 concept of "blowback." Both India and Pakistan used rhetoric and propaganda against each other for nation-building purposes. The enmity between the two societies then came to constrain leaders. See Blinkenberg 1972; and Brines 1968. On the link between this sort of nationalist blowback and territorial conflict, see Huth 2000.

sumption of war. It has been difficult for India and Pakistan to resolve the issues dividing them, in part because the highest stakes of the fundamental conflict between them are largely symbolic and rhetorical. The physical territory of Kashmir can be, and in fact has been, divvied up. Symbolic pies are not so easily divided.

The imbalance in stakes between India and Pakistan has exacerbated the problem. From the beginning, Kashmir was more important to Pakistan than to India. If Pakistan had not supported the Pathan invasion in 1947, India would likely have let Kashmir go. India was also quite content to live with the de facto partition of Kashmir after 1949, while Pakistan had to agitate, in fact to start the 1965 war, to try to force a permanent settlement of the issue. The same sort of agitation to try to press a settlement in Kashmir appears to have motivated Pakistan's 1999 incursion to take heights in the Kargil region.

The domestic stakes of Kashmir continue to stand in the way of peace between India and Pakistan. Prime Minister Nawaz Sharif's decision to withdraw Pakistani troops from Kargil to end the 1999 fighting, taken under pressure from the United States, was extremely unpopular and contributed to his downfall in a coup in October.

At least at the beginning, the conflict in the Middle East was literally existential. Israel's very survival as a state was on the line in the war in 1948 and was at least perceived to be at stake in later years. Fear of annihilation certainly posed an obstacle to cooperation, making Israel particularly wary of depending on agreements or the international community for its security.[82] The stakes for Syria were not so dire in the early stages of the conflict, but once the adversarial relationship with Israel became entrenched, Syria had reason to fear efforts by Israel to overthrow its regime, if not to destroy it as a state.[83] Opposition to Israel has been central to Arab nation-building, making it essential for Arab states' legitimacy.

Over time the stakes for Israel and Syria were lowered somewhat by superpower involvement. Beginning in the early 1960s and increasing over time, Soviet protection of Syria and U.S. protection of Israel mitigated the risks of total annihilation or overthrow. By 1962, President Kennedy talked of a special relationship and a security guarantee for Israel, and in 1973 both superpowers rushed arms to their respective clients in order to forestall defeat.[84] But while superpower protection calmed fears

---

[82] David Ben-Gurion put his distrust of relying on others for protection this way: "Our future does not depend on what the Gentiles say but what the Jews do." Quoted in Ma'oz 1995, 46.

[83] One of the sparks that set off the 1967 conflict, for example, was the Syrian and Egyptian perception that Israel intended to attack Syria in order to overthrow the government. Khouri 1985, 244.

[84] Ma'oz 1995, 86; Peretz 1996, 73.

somewhat, it also removed a restraint on provoking or launching limited war. Knowing that the superpowers would quickly impose a cease-fire seems to have contributed to both the 1967 and 1973 wars.

After the Six-Day War, the dispute over the Golan Heights gave both Israel and Syria an important stake in that strategically important territory. From the international border in the Jordan River valley,[85] the land rises sharply to the escarpments of the Golan Heights, giving whoever holds this territory a large strategic advantage in either direction. Passage through the Golan is difficult, and the territory below is vulnerable to shelling from above. Between 1949 and 1967, the northern areas of Israel were thus exposed to attacks from the Golan. Since 1967, when Israel took the Golan, Syria has been keenly aware that its archenemy commands the heights 40 miles from Damascus. The Golan is also important for control of water in the region.[86] In addition to the material importance of the high ground, the Golan quickly took on political significance. For Syria, regaining territory lost to Israel was crucial to repair damaged prestige, and this had political ramifications, both domestically within Syria and within the Arab world. Meanwhile, by deciding to increase Jewish settlements in the Golan, Israel deliberately increased the political importance of the territory within Israel. The strategic and political importance of the Golan contributed to the breakdown of peace in 1967, giving Israel a motive for an offensive against Syria, and again in 1973 when Syria tried to take it back by force. It has also made it much more difficult for Israel and Syria to settle their differences. Thus territory that was originally useful as a buffer to protect northern Israel and to deny Syria the high ground became both a more valuable bargaining chip and a greater obstacle to a peace treaty. The status of the Golan Heights remains the most contested issue between the two states.

Syrian and Israeli involvement in the war in Lebanon was also motivated in part by geostrategic calculations. Political influence by either Syria or Israel in Lebanon threatened the other. The Biqa' Valley in Lebanon is a natural invasion route for the Israeli army to take toward Damascus, while Syria could attack or sponsor guerilla operations against Israel from southern Lebanon.[87] When civil war broke out in Lebanon, both Israel and Syria were therefore concerned not only with instability in that country, but also with the need to prevent its being used by the other to launch an offensive. However, while the fight in Lebanon in 1982 could

---

[85] With some exceptions created by demilitarized zones, the 1949 armistice line ran along this international border, originally the boundary between the mandatory territories of Palestine and Syria. See map p. 69.

[86] For a detailed analysis of the strategic significance of the topography, see Shalev 1994, chap. 11. On the water issues, see Ma'oz 1995, 113; and Shalev 1994, chap. 18.

[87] Ma'oz 1995, 162.

have escalated into a larger war between Israel and Syria, the stakes in that conflict were much lower than in previous fights, as neither country's homeland was directly threatened.

The stakes of the conflict between Israel and Syria have diminished over time, from the threat to one side's very existence, to more indirect threats to territory or to influence. This may offer some hope for the prospect of an eventual political solution between Israel and Syria, but the strategic importance of the territorial dispute, along with a history in which the belligerents threatened each other's existence, means that the conflict remains very highly charged.

Both the Syrian-Israeli and Indian-Pakistani conflicts are territorial, but in both it is because of the way in which territory is tied to existence, either for strategic or symbolic reasons, that peace has been elusive. As a general indicator of the prospects for peace, then, threat to existence is more important than territory itself.

Material Factors

GEOGRAPHIC CONTIGUITY

While territoriality may not be crucial, geography does play a role in determining whether war resumes or peace lasts. Proximity matters, at least to some extent. The risk of peace breaking down is higher for neighboring states than for others, though this finding is often not statistically significant.[88]

Since contiguity is a good predictor of war proneness to begin with, it is not surprising that over three-quarters of the pairs of states that have fought in the last half century are neighbors and that most of the others include a major power in a multilateral war that also involved neighbors.[89] But even within this data set, neighbors seem to be more likely to fight again. Half of the cases of contiguous dyads surveyed here experience renewed warfare, while the only cases of geographically separated states fighting again stem from Iraq's very limited participation in the first Arab-Israeli war. Noncontiguous cases such as the United States in Korea and in Vietnam, or Britain and France in the Sinai, have not been repeated, nor has the only case of a war with no contiguous belligerents, the Falklands/Malvinas war.

Most arguments about proximity and war-proneness emphasize the ability of states to reach each other militarily. Great powers and neighbors are more likely to fight because other states simply cannot project military

[88] This finding is much stronger from World War I on than before 1914. It is also stronger when the strength of agreements is controlled for, as in chapter 5.

[89] Exceptions since 1945 include Iraq and Israel, Cuba and Somalia, and Libya and Tanzania—all fighting in multilateral wars in which the other dyads were contiguous.

force. That proximity affects the recurrence of warfare suggests a slightly different argument. All of the dyads in these data are by definition able to reach each other. (This selection effect helps explain the relatively weak showing of this factor in the quantitative analysis.) That neighbors have a harder time maintaining peace suggests that proximity leaves cease-fires vulnerable to accidents and incidents that can spiral back to war. The skirmishes along the border following the first Sino-Vietnamese war provide a good example. These border clashes escalated to another full-scale war in 1986 and 1987.[90]

The instability of peace in both South Asia and the Middle East stems in part from the ill effects of shared borders and from the particulars of geography. The geopolitics of South Asia presented specific challenges for maintaining peace. The border between India and East Pakistan and connections between the population of West Bengal in India and Bengalis in Pakistan eased covert Indian support of secession in 1971. And the long and remote nature of much of the cease-fire line in Kashmir, and particularly the fact that it divided the Kashmiri population, made it conducive to infiltration by irregular forces. Such infiltration began both wars over Kashmir and continues to beleaguer the subcontinent. In the spring and summer of 2002, this issue took India and Pakistan to the brink of nuclear war.[91]

Kashmir's location and geography vis-à-vis India and Pakistan also hampered one avenue toward political resolution of the dispute. One of the reasons that a plebiscite was never held to determine Kashmir's status was that Pakistan insisted on demilitarization of the territory to ensure a free and fair vote. But India was unwilling to withdraw because its access to Kashmir was so much more difficult than Pakistan's; India's only route into Kashmir was a long and mountainous road, generally closed in winter. If Pakistan welshed on a demilitarization agreement and sent forces back in, it could overrun the territory before India could gets its troops back over the mountain passes.[92] Of course, the geography of Pakistan itself, a country consisting of two noncontiguous wings, played an important role in the secession of Bangladesh, which provided the context of the 1971 war between India and Pakistan.[93]

[90] The persistent nature of clashes along the border makes marking the start date of the second war somewhat controversial. COW lists the second war as starting in January 1987, but the related MID project gives a start date in October 1986. Incursions and retaliations along the border escalated into serious fighting in April 1983 and again in early 1984, with clashes continuing and escalating in 1986 and early 1987. Bercovitch and Jackson 1997, 212, 216.

[91] See, for example, "Still Raw from Attack, India Is Girding Itself for War," *New York Times*, May 18, 2002, A6; "The Kashmir Brink," *New York Times*, June 20, 2002, A12.

[92] Korbel 1954, 159.

[93] India delayed its intervention until after the monsoon season and until snow blocked China from crossing the Himalayas in response. Ganguly 1986, 120.

As with India and Pakistan, the particular geopolitical situation between Israel and Syria has affected their conflict. Israel found itself completely surrounded by hostile states, and this has led to an attitude toward security that borders on paranoia. And as in South Asia, the ease with which irregular forces, with varying levels of government backing, have been able to cross borders to carry out attacks has been an ongoing source of tension. Attacks by *fedayeen* on Israel from Arab states and Israeli retaliation across its borders have been a persistent attribute of the Arab-Israeli conflict.

In short, neighbors make for difficult partners in peace. Contiguous states are more likely to fight in the first place, and there is some evidence that they are also more prone to renewed conflict. Just as it is easier for states to keep peace than for combatants in civil wars who have to live on top of one another, it is somewhat easier for states separated by great distances to keep peace than for those separated by no more than a border.

RELATIVE CAPABILITIES

Surprisingly, whether there is a balance of power or a preponderance of power between the belligerents at the time of a cease-fire has no meaningful effect on the durability of peace. In some of the quantitative tests, more balanced power relations appear more stable, but this finding is not robust, nor is it statistically significant. It seems likely that any apparent association is the result of statistical chance rather than a true relationship.[94] Relatively balanced power, such as that between Iran and Iraq in 1988 or between Israel and Syria in 1967 is no more or less stable than very lopsided relationships, such as those between Turkey and Cyprus in 1974, between China and Vietnam in the 1970s and 1980s, or between the Soviet Union and Hungary in 1956. Despite the importance of relative power in international relations literature, the relative capabilities of combatants at the time of the cease-fire tells us little about the chances for stable peace. The effects of the balance of power at the time of a cease-fire is a separate question from whether shifts in capabilities after the cease-fire disrupt peace, a subject examined below.

Changes over Time

Our findings so far suggest that if we were assigned the task of assessing the likelihood of lasting peace at the time of a cease-fire, we would want to know whether the war ended in a decisive victory, how long and deadly it was, the combatants' prior history, whether it threatened the existence of either state, and whether it was fought between neighbors.

[94] This finding is consistent with Stinnett and Diehl 2001, who found no significant relationship between the balance of power and the development of enduring rivalries. Relative capabilities may affect when a cease-fire is reached and its terms, but not how long it lasts.

The prospects for peace are not static, however. As power shifts, as the expected utility of war shifts, and as regimes change, we might expect the likelihood of war to change as well. Table 3.2 shows a sample of the quantitative analyses done to test hypotheses about exogenous changes to the baseline prospects for peace. The first five variables listed in the table are highlighted here.

CHANGES IN RELATIVE CAPABILITIES

Large shifts in relative power are strongly associated with the failure of peace. In both the post-1945 period and in the longer data set, the measure of change in relative capabilities from the previous year has a large and significant effect on the hazard rate. But it is not clear from these tests whether shifts in capabilities lead to the breakdown of peace, or whether the start of a new war leads to shifts in capabilities. A lagged measure of change in the previous year may be more appropriate. This lagged variable does not have a statistically significant effect in the 1816–1992 data, and is associated with *more* stable peace in the Cease-Fires data set. (This is likely due to selection bias; the lagged variable is missing in cases in which a cease-fire fails within the year.)[95] Shifting capabilities in one year do not lead to war in the next. This could be interpreted in two ways. On the one hand, if shifts in capability lead to war, we might not expect that effect to be delayed to the next year, so this finding could be consistent with the hypothesis that shifts in power are destabilizing. On the other hand, it is also consistent with the argument that the causal arrow runs the other way, that our indicators of capability shift when wars break out. Did war break out between India and Pakistan in 1971 because Pakistan's capabilities dropped in that year, or did the measure of capabilities drop because Pakistan lost much of its territory, population, and resource base? The Correlates of War capability index data for this case suggest the latter. Pakistan's recorded population in 1971 is less than half that in 1970.[96] Moreover, components of the index such as population, energy consumption, iron and steel production, and urban population are not immediately convertible into military might. These inputs should lead to lagged rather than immediate shifts in war fighting capability. Without a more fine-grained measure of capabilities (measured on a monthly basis rather than annually, or a better measure of war fighting ability), quantitative tests are not well suited to determine which interpretation is correct. But the fact that the

---

[95] Note that in the year following a cease-fire, the lagged variable is by definition zero, so that it is impossible for it to explain peace that falters within a year.

[96] It is not clear from the COW annual data when during the year the measurements are taken. As the 1971 war occurred in December, the Pakistan data suggests measurements are for the end of the year.

TABLE 3.2
Baseline Prospects: Change over Time

	Weibull Hazard Ratios (robust standard errors)					
	Cease-Fires, 1946–1998			Maoz/EUGene, 1816–1992		
Change in relative capabilities	3.778*** (1.206)			3.684*** (1.116)	1.899*** (0.341)	
Lagged change		0.059*** (0.017)				0.998 (0.001)
Expected utility for war			0.984 (0.105)		1.490 (0.438)	1.480 (0.461)
Monadic democracy	3.195 (3.736)	0.916 (1.526)		4.514 (4.906)	0.895 (0.262)	0.875 (0.262)
Polity change	0.974 (0.021)	0.956 (0.028)		0.969 (0.023)	1.001 (0.062)	1.027 (0.060)
Tie	5.127 (7.955)	2.374 (3.309)	26.509*** (8.065)	5.802* (6.127)	0.532 (0.248)	0.488 (0.242)
Cost (deaths)	0.804 (0.234)	0.882 (0.312)	0.484*** (0.095)	0.774 (0.202)	0.895** (0.043)	0.920* (0.046)
Multilateral war	0.584 (0.490)	0.246*** (0.073)	1.557 (1.679)		0.783 (0.243)	0.666 (0.217)
History of conflict	2.613** (1.074)	5.919** (4.534)	2.977*** (1.178)	1.919** (0.523)	1.292 (0.205)	1.330* (0.228)
Territorial conflict	1.217 (1.429)	2.293 (1.642)	0.849 (1.403)		0.951 (0.272)	0.884 (0.267)
Existence at stake	2.791*** (1.068)	1.902* (0.715)	4.527 (4.676)	2.539*** (0.898)		
Contiguous	2.583 (3.405)	0.612 (0.324)	2.373** (0.959)	4.670*** (1.938)	1.374 (0.496)	1.332 (0.497)
Preponderance of power	3.103 (2.458)	3.600 (3.846)	1.100 (1.063)		0.951 (0.393)	0.711 (0.307)
P	0.795 (0.384)	1.427*** (0.195)	0.818 (0.104)	0.776 (0.365)	0.560*** (0.065)	0.539*** (0.103)
N	713	703[a]	556	713	8,626	8,409
No. of subjects	42	39	41	42	264	249
Log likelihood	−31.398	−24.860	−40.433	−31.789	−212.730	−185.213

Note: Cases are clustered by conflict in Cease-Fires data, by dyad ID number in Maoz/EUGene data.
[a] Affected by missing data bias.
* Statistically significant at the .10 level.
** Statistically significant at the .05 level.
*** Statistically significant at the .01 level.

lagged variable has no effect casts doubt on Werner's argument that shifts in capabilities lead to decisions to restart the war.[97]

A look at some of the cases suggests that shifts can sometimes be destabilizing, but there is not a clear or consistent relationship between power shifts and the breakdown of peace. Evidence from the case studies about the effects of changes in capabilities over time is mixed, and is complicated by the Cold War and arms control dynamics. Shifts in relative capabilities between Israel and Syria do seem to have helped provoke war in some cases. From early on, Israel has enjoyed greater military strength than Syria. Israel's desire to maintain its military dominance was one of the factors contributing to the 1967 war and to the war in Lebanon in 1982. In 1973, Syria and Egypt attacked when they had built their forces up and felt strong enough to challenge Israel. Israel stepped up provocations after the military pact between Syria and Egypt in 1955 in an attempt to expose its weaknesses.[98] Military weakness prevented Syria from initiating war in some instances, but it has also tended to push Syria to acquire arms, instigating arms races with Israel that contributed to war.[99]

The relative military capabilities of India and Pakistan have shifted over time, but these shifts have not consistently affected stability. The 1965 war erupted during a peak in India's relative power, while the 1971 war was fought when India's preponderance was less pronounced. But it was Pakistan that initiated the former and India that provoked the latter. While declining power and anticipation of further losses may have helped provoke these wars, there were large shifts that did not lead to war but were in fact associated with negotiations and agreements.[100]

Involvement of the South Asian conflict in the Cold War complicated the military picture considerably. Military aid from and alignment with the United States, the Soviet Union, and China as those powers attempted to balance against each other have been both credited with keeping peace and blamed for triggering arms races and precipitating war on the subcontinent. Lamb argues that U.S. aid to Pakistan in the 1950s undermined negotiations for a permanent settlement to the Kashmir issue, and that Pakistan's pact with China upset talks in 1963. Brines maintains that the

[97] Werner 1999. Note that these capability measures are bilateral and do not take into account the resources of allies. However, the expected utility measures, which do account for allied capabilities, fare no better. See below.

[98] Ma'oz 1995, 45. On the other hand, by signing the Egyptian-Syrian defense pact of 1966, Egypt attempted to restrain Syria; Nasser believed the Arab states were not prepared for war. Khouri 1985, 233.

[99] On arms race dynamics see, for example, Khouri 1985, 305.

[100] For example, India and Pakistan negotiated the Indus Waters Treaty in 1960 when India's relative power was falling after a peak, and fluctuations in the 1980s and early 1990s did not spark war.

pact between the United States and Pakistan postponed war for a decade by assuaging Pakistan's security fears, but also intensified India's efforts to incorporate Kashmir, thereby leading to war in 1965.[101] He also charges the Soviet Union with upsetting the military balance and increasing Pakistani security fears, causing it to initiate war. However, Western and Soviet aid also provided leverage in getting India and Pakistan to sign a cease-fire in 1965 and to negotiate an agreement in Tashkent.

Cold War dynamics complicated security relationships in South Asia, but the most detrimental effects were from the arms races that have plagued the subcontinent. India and Pakistan found themselves in a classic security dilemma. Pakistan's rearmament, with U.S. help, in the 1950s threatened India, and India's buildup after the Chinese attack could not but threaten Pakistan. A spiral of insecurity was clearly at work in the prelude to the 1965 war and again before the war in 1971. The military stalemate in 1965 should have convinced both sides that their security fears were somewhat exaggerated; instead it convinced each side of the other's belligerent intentions. The arms race therefore fed off and contributed to the hardening of India and Pakistan's adversarial relationship. Since 1971, this arms race has continued, and has become particularly dangerous with the development of nuclear capability. Nuclear weapons may help restrain both sides from total war, but have not kept them from serious skirmishes, nor from the Kargil war in 1999.

Likewise, entanglement of the Middle East conflict in the Cold War has had conflicting effects. The superpower rivalry exacerbated the conflict both by blocking constructive efforts in the United Nations and, more important, by contributing greatly to the arms race between Arab states and Israel.[102] On the other hand, the superpowers often acted to restrain their clients from precipitous action.[103] While shifts in military capabilities and Cold War considerations certainly affected the conflicts between India and Pakistan and between Israel and Syria, it is difficult to discern a consistent relationship between these factors and the probability of war. The jury remains out on the relationship between shifts in power and the resumption of war. There is clearly an association, but whether there is a causal relationship is much harder to determine.

EXPECTED UTILITY FOR WAR

Relative capability is presumably not the only factor in states' evaluations of whether to press for better terms from their enemies. Bueno de

---

[101] Brines 1968; Lamb 1991, 227, 241.

[102] See Khouri 1985, 280. For a detailed account of the Security Council debates, see Bailey 1990.

[103] The Soviet Union restrained Syria in late 1966, for example, and the United States tried to insist that in return for military aid, Israel not initiate hostilities. Ma'oz 1995, 87.

Mesquita and Lalman have formulated a complicated set of calculations based on capability and alliance data to estimate states' utility for peace, for making demands, and for war. Their "international interactions game" has been touted as a good predictor of war. In the quantitative tests performed for this study, however, I found little predictive value in the expected utility measures. Peace is no more likely to fail when the expected utility measures predict war than at other times (see table 3.2), nor are predictions of demands by one side destabilizing (results not shown). In some tests the war and demand predictions are actually associated with a lower risk of war, and in no case were these predictors statistically significant.[104] Measures of states' expected utility for war give us no purchase in predicting when war will resume.

DEMOCRACY

The democratic peace literature is based on the empirical finding that democracies do not fight each other. It follows that there are no cease-fires between two democracies (with one possible exception discussed below). Only in years after a regime change in at least one combatant is it possible for both to be democratic. Joint democracy is therefore quite rare in the data. It occurs for Russia and Hungary after 1991, for Britain and Argentina after the latter becomes a democracy in 1983, for El Salvador and Honduras after 1990, for Israel and Syria between 1954 and 1957, and for India and Pakistan briefly in 1956 and 1957. That none of these cases experience a failure of peace is consistent with the democratic peace theory.

However, two cases raise questions about the finding that peace is more stable in democratic dyads. Both Cyprus and Turkey are coded as democracies in 1974 in the Polity data on which my measure is based. A military coup took place in Cyprus on July 15 (a fact not recorded in the Polity data),[105] so the initial outbreak of war does not refute the democratic peace hypothesis.[106] However after the fighting began, the leader appointed by the coup-makers, Nicos Sampson, resigned, and Glafkos Clerides, the president of the House of Representatives became acting president of the republic. When the first cease-fire went into effect at the end of July, Cyprus was thus led by an elected representative, acting as president until the previous president, Makarios, returned after fleeing the

---

[104] This was true whether I used Bueno de Mesquita and Lalman's tau-b measure of alliance similarity in the calculations, or the measure (S) suggested by Signorino and Ritter 1999. Because of problems with multicolinearity, it is difficult to test the expected utility measures along with other changes over time in the smaller data set, hence the separate analyses reported in table 3.2.

[105] This is true both in the Polity III annual data, and in the Polity IV version that incorporates dates of regime changes.

[106] See Russett 1993, 20 on this case.

coup. This hardly represents robust democracy, but neither was Cyprus clearly nondemocratic at this point. This cease-fire is the shortest in the data set and therefore has a large influence on statistical findings. If Cyprus is considered a democracy in July and August 1974, then joint democracy is not associated with stable peace (in fact just the opposite, statistically). If it not considered a democracy, or if this case is dropped, then we find peace to be very stable between democracies.[107]

The second case is much more straightforward. The war between India and Pakistan in Kargil 1999 occurred when both were democratic. This case is not included in the time-varying data because it took place after the data are censored, but the outbreak of that war casts some doubt on the power of joint democracy to keep peace among bitter enemies.

Consistent with other empirical findings of the democratic peace literature, monadic democracy has no pacifying effect. In the post–World War II period, democracy on the part of just one state in a dyad is in fact associated with less stable peace, though not significantly so (see table 3.2). This finding is driven largely by the fact that both Israel and India are democracies and drops away when one looks at a longer time period. Democracy on the part of one belligerent has no consistent effect on the prospects for peace.

Jointly democratic dyads may enjoy more stable peace (the Kargil war between India and Pakistan notwithstanding), but what of the process of getting there? Mansfield and Snyder found that democratization itself can be highly destabilizing, as can the process of states becoming more autocratic. I find, however, that absolute changes in levels of democracy (polity change) have no discernable effect on the stability of peace.[108] Nor is the process of crossing the threshold to democracy associated with war.[109] This is somewhat surprising, as we might expect states with bitter enemies to be most prone to conflict while undergoing regime change.

As a predictor of the baseline prospects of peace, then, regime type is not very helpful. The process of democratization (or its opposite) has no effect, and there is no pacifying effect of democracy on the part of one state in the dyad. If both become democratic, peace is very stable, but this is rather rare in the data (and depends on the questionable coding in the

[107] So much so that the hazard ratio drops to zero—peace is predicted to last forever between democracies. Controlling for joint democracy by dropping democratic dyads does not affect the other results in the study.

[108] This measure records changes in either direction, both democratization and moves toward greater autocracy.

[109] In fact, in the time-varying data there are no cases of peace breaking down when a state crosses the democracy threshold, though the Kargil war would qualify as a case of democratic transition (in Pakistan) preceding war.

Cyprus case). The most recent war between India and Pakistan suggests that deadly enemies may fight even if both enjoy democratic rule.

In sum, the hypotheses on changes after a cease-fire is in place fare surprisingly poorly in the empirical tests. Regime change has no effect, and even the closest thing we have to an empirical law in international relations, that democracies do not fight each other, is called into question by the 1999 war between India and Pakistan. Expected utility measures give us no leverage in estimating the chances for peace. Shifts in relative capability appear to have a strong effect, but it is difficult to know whether this is because shifts in capability lead to war, or the other way round.

CONCLUSION

Table 3.3 summarizes the findings on situational variables that might be expected to affect the baseline prospects for peace. Peace is easier to maintain after wars that are long and costly, end with a clear winner, do not threaten the existence of either state, or are fought by states whose shared history is not overly riddled with conflict. If the war was fought between nonneighboring states or over issues other than territory, the subsequent peace is more durable, although the evidence on these points is weaker. Conversely, neighbors with a longstanding conflict, especially if they fought a high-stakes but relatively inexpensive war that ended in a stalemate, will have a much more difficult time preventing another round of fighting. The relative strength of the two sides at the time of the cease-fire is irrelevant, as is the number of belligerents. Changes in relative power over time may upset peace, but it is also possible that this relationship is spurious. Other changes after the cease-fire do not have a strong effect, with the possible exception of both sides becoming democracies.

Once belligerents cease fire, what determines whether peace lasts or war resumes? The situational variables examined here begin to answer this question. In general, characteristics of the war itself and of belligerents' relationship are more important than material factors and changes over time. The cost of war and the way it ends matter, as do contestants' past and whether the war touches on existential nerves. One material factor may be important: neighbors seem to have a harder time keeping peace than states separated by more than just a border.

These findings are generally consistent with the notion that maintaining peace requires cooperation. As this perspective would lead us to expect, the incentives to cooperate are greater when the cost of renewed fighting is very high. Cooperation is quite difficult when the stakes are high, when being "suckered" threatens a party's existence so that it might not be around to retaliate. Cooperation is also more difficult among actors

TABLE 3.3
Summary of Findings on Baseline Prospects for Peace

Variable	Effect on Peace	Evidence/Comments
Military tie	Less durable	Fairly strong evidence, with some exceptions
Costly/Longer war	More durable	Strong evidence
Multilateral war	No clear effect	
History of conflict	Less durable	Fairly strong evidence
Territorial conflict	Less durable	Weak evidence
High stakes	Less durable	Strong evidence
Contiguity	Less durable	Moderate evidence
Preponderance of power at time of cease-fire	No clear effect	
Changes in relative power	Less durable	Causal relationship unclear
Expected utility for war	No effect	
Joint democracy	More durable	Mixed evidence
Monadic democracy	No effect	
Democratization/ Polity change	No effect	

whose past makes them hesitant to trust each other. And proximity between enemies makes cooperation somewhat harder because militaries with little separating them are prone to low-level clashes and accidents that can escalate to war.

Not all cease-fires are created equal; peace is harder to maintain in some cases than in others. But knowing the decisiveness of victory, the cost and stakes of war, the belligerents' history of conflict, and proximity help us assess the baseline prospects for peace at the time of a cease-fire. With this assessment we can answer the other questions posed in this book: whether belligerents implement strong agreements when peace is easiest or most difficult, and how these agreements affect the durability of peace. It is to the first of these questions that I now turn.

CHAPTER FOUR

AGREEMENTS: EPIPHENOMENAL OR FUNCTIONAL?

CEASE-FIRE AGREEMENTS are not randomly applied to cease-fires like treatments in a laboratory experiment. They are put in place by deliberate agents, written by the belligerents who will be affected by them, perhaps with the help of international organizations or other interested states. They are the result of a bargaining process between deadly enemies. This makes it impossible to study their effects in isolation. We need to know why we get stronger agreements in some cases than in others. A full-fledged bargaining theory of the content of agreements is beyond the scope of this book.[1] But to know whether agreements matter, we need to know how they are shaped by other factors that also affect the ease or difficulty of maintaining peace at the time of the cease-fire.

Chapter 1 laid out two competing hypotheses about the relationship between the baseline prospects for peace and the strength of agreements. To recap briefly, the counterargument to my own argument that cease-fire agreements have an independent effect is that agreements are epiphenomenal. I label this argument *realist* because it is akin to realist arguments about international institutions. Strong agreements are reached only when peace would be easy to keep in any case.

HYPOTHESIS: *Strong agreements are concluded when the baseline prospects for peace are relatively good.*

The rebuttal suggests just the opposite. Agreements are a functional response to the obstacles to peace. Belligerents and the international community will invest more in mechanisms to keep peace when peace is most precarious. Strong agreements are most likely to be reached when peace would otherwise be most difficult to keep.

[1] For related work on the design of international institutions, see Abbott and Snidal 2000; Koremenos, Lipson, and Snidal 2001. Both sides are likely to prefer strong constraints on the other side while maintaining their own freedom of action. However, blatantly one-sided mechanisms are surprisingly rare in the cease-fire agreements studied here (with the notable exception of the measures imposed on Iraq after the first Gulf War). More than might be expected from a strict bargaining perspective, states accept curbs on their own side to achieve restraint on the other in the context of a cease-fire agreement.

HYPOTHESIS: *Strong agreements are concluded when the baseline prospects for peace are relatively dim.*

We may, of course, observe no relationship between the baseline prospects for peace and the strength of agreements, for one of two reasons. Agreements may, in fact, be exogenous, driven not by the baseline prospects for peace at the time of the cease-fire, but by other factors. The content of agreements may be "random" with respect to the baseline prospects for peace, driven by the political constraints, tastes, or ideas of particular leaders or mediators,[2] or other factors of the bargaining process not related to the baseline prospects for peace. Alternatively, the opposing logics may both be at work and may simply cancel each other out, so that when cooperation is more difficult the added incentives to implement strong agreements are counterbalanced by the greater difficulty in doing so. Conversely, in easier situations, while strong agreements are achievable, there is less need for them. Both of these possibilities suggest a null hypothesis:

HYPOTHESIS: *The content of agreements is unrelated to the baseline prospects for peace.*

The realist and functionalist hypotheses run in opposite directions, but rather than cancel each other out, a more interesting dynamic may be at work. The interaction between the ability to achieve cooperation and the need for it may mean that the relationship between the underlying probability of war and strength of agreements is not linear. Anne-Marie Slaughter has suggested that vague agreements are the result of either very friendly relationships in which parties trust each other enough to work out differences as they arise, or very contentious relationships in which no more can be agreed upon.[3] This implies a curvilinear pattern between relations and the strength of agreements (see figure 4.1). Good friends need not write specific agreements or implement mechanisms to make cooperation easier; they may not need agreements at all. As one moves toward the acrimonious end of the spectrum and the underlying probability of war gets somewhat higher, there is growing need for measures to maintain cooperation. At some point, the difficulty in agreeing to substantive measures outweighs this functionalist logic, and agreements among enemies will tend to be weaker in content. At the far end, parties may not

---

[2] The use of monitors between El Salvador and Honduras after the Football War is one example. Their use and especially their withdrawal was very much shaped by OAS Secretary-General Galo Plaza's prior job experience with UN peacekeeping forces in Lebanon and Cyprus. Wainhouse 1973, 590.

[3] Slaughter 1995.

Agreements

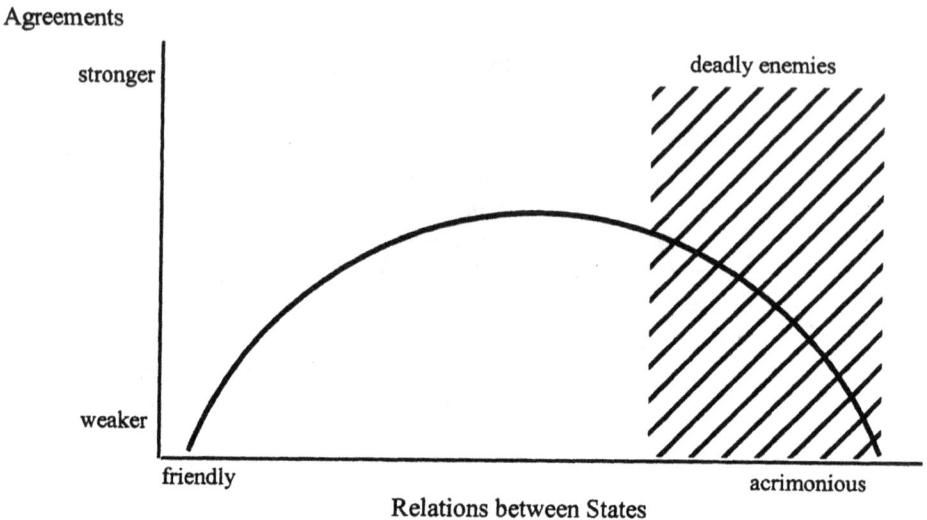

Figure 4.1 State Relations and Agreement Strength

be able to reach agreement at all, or may only be able to draft very weak agreements that paper over differences. Alternatively, states may decide that it is not worth investing in costly mechanisms to avoid war when they are almost sure to fail.[4]

This curve covers the full spectrum of state relations, from close friends to bitter enemies. However, by studying relations among recent combatants, I am selecting only the acrimonious end of this spectrum (the hatched portion of figure 4.1) where war is relatively likely. By definition belligerents have proven themselves to be enemies with seriously conflicting interests. Here, on the downward part of the curve, we might expect the obstacles to cooperation to determine the strength of agreements. Even if agreements are a functional response to cooperation problems among more friendly actors, among enemies we might expect the strength of agreements to be inversely related to the underlying probability of war. The selection of cases therefore provides an easy test for the counterargument that agreements are epiphenomenal and a hard test for the functionalist argument (and therefore for my own argument that agreements affect the durability of peace).

The previous chapter examined variables that influence the baseline prospects for peace. Many of these are characteristics of the situation between the belligerents at the time of the cease-fire, that is, when a cease-fire agreement is drafted and implemented. This chapter examines empiri-

---

[4] Thanks to an anonymous reviewer for this suggestion.

cally the relationship between these situational variables and the content of cease-fire agreements. Are strong agreements epiphenomenal, drafted in the easy cases only when they are irrelevant? Or are they functional responses, created in the hardest cases precisely because they are expected to be effective? The evidence presented below shows that agreements are to some degree exogenous. But to the extent that there is a relationship, stronger agreements are put in place when peace would otherwise be most precarious; they are not epiphenomenal.

The realist counterargument and functionalist rebuttal are posed in very general terms. The next section outlines in more detail how situational variables might be related to the content of agreements. The section that follows presents several large-N tests of the relationship between the baseline prospects for peace and the strength of cease-fire agreements. I then look at the India-Pakistan and Israel-Syria cases in more detail to see whether these enemies reached stronger agreements when peace would likely last in any case, or when the prospects for peace were relatively dim.

I. Situational Variables and the Strength of Agreements: Hypotheses

In the last chapter we looked at eight situational variables at the time of the cease-fire: the decisiveness of victory in the war just ended; its cost; whether it was a multilateral or bilateral conflict; the participants' history of conflict before the war; the stakes of the conflict; whether it was over territory; contiguity; and relative capabilities at the time of the cease-fire. These indicators give us a sense (albeit imperfect) of the baseline prospects for peace.

In chapter 3 we saw that the most important of these variables in terms of predicting the duration of peace are the cost of war, the belligerents' history of conflict, stakes (particularly if the war threatened one side's very existence), the decisiveness of military victory, and contiguity. The other variables were not strong predictors of the durability of peace. Nonetheless, in the statistical analyses that follow I include all of the situational variables. I do this for two reasons: first, even though some of these variables failed tests of statistical significance, the point here is to get as accurate a prediction as possible of the baseline prospects for peace, and these variables generally add *some* information to our predictions. Second, and more important, if there is a relationship between these variables and the content of agreements, and if agreements in turn shape outcomes, the effect of some situational variables on the durability of peace may have been hidden. For example, if the functional logic outlined above is correct, then variables that make peace more likely to fall apart will also lead to stronger agreements that offset this negative effect. Some of these variables may thus "control" for their own effects. As it is the first part of this relationship—the extent to which agreements are endogenous—that I am investigating here, it is important to include any aspects of the belligerents' situation that might affect the content of agreements.

For some situational variables, the implications of the counterargument and rebuttal are relatively straightforward. The counterargument that strong agreements are written when they are largely irrelevant would suggest that neighboring states will have a harder time reaching agreements with teeth than noncontiguous states, and those with a history of violent conflict should also tend to implement weak agreements. When the stakes are particularly high, it will be harder for parties to reach substantive agreements; it will be harder for them to compromise, and they will fear potential defection all the more. If territorial conflicts are distinct because territory is highly salient, then we should expect weaker agreements after wars over land. A preponderance of power should also be associated with more forceful agreements.

For each of these variables, the functionalist rebuttal suggests the opposite hypothesis. If stronger agreements are put in place when peace is most precarious, we should see more mechanisms to keep peace between contiguous states; we might expect measures to create buffers and separate forces to be particularly important for contiguous states. The functionalist logic would lead us to expect those with a long history of conflict to be more rather than less likely to implement agreements with teeth. In high-stakes conflicts belligerents might only cease fire in the first place if incentives to attack are altered, and when the stakes are high, they will require greater assurances about each others' intentions. We should see stronger agreements after territorial wars. Many institutionalists would likely concur in the hegemonic logic that suggests stronger agreements when there is a large imbalance of power,[5] but might also think that there would be a countervailing trend in which balanced power would lead to greater investment in agreements to help provide cooperation.

For several variables, however, the realist and functionalist hypotheses are less straightforward. Both arguments expect stronger agreements after multilateral wars, but for different reasons. The functionalist logic would be that, if cooperation is more difficult or accidents and misunderstandings more likely with more players, there is a greater need for strong agreements in multilateral conflicts. The realist logic would be that states

---

[5] For a discussion of the hegemonic theory of regimes, see Keohane 1984; and Gilpin 1981.

pulled into wars not of their own making (who are therefore less likely to fight again) will have an easier time drafting strong agreements than states whose fight is their own.

Following the functionalist logic, the higher the cost of war, the greater the incentive for parties to invest in ways to avoid that cost. Avoiding the high cost of war is the reason to try to cooperate in the first place. If a more costly war indicates a more acrimonious relationship between the belligerents, the realist argument would imply a negative association between cost and the strength of agreements. But we have already seen empirically that higher death tolls are associated with more stable peace. One could therefore argue that these hypotheses should be reversed. If realists contend that anything that makes peace more stable also makes it easier to reach strong agreements, they will expect a positive association, with the rebuttal contending the opposite. However, the theoretical connection between higher-cost wars and longer peace runs counter to realist logic; rather, it is indebted to institutionalist notions of realizing the gains from cooperation—that high-cost wars produce the incentives to maintain peace and therefore to draft stronger agreements. So the logically consistent expectation for the realist argument is that high-cost wars yield weaker agreements, and for functionalism that costly wars lead to strong agreements.

Functionalism would predict stronger agreements after wars that end in a draw than after decisive military outcomes, while the logic of the counterargument would predict the opposite. However, some realists might expect weak agreements at the most decisive end of the spectrum, with victors simply imposing a diktat. A decisive victor has the bargaining power to impose its preferred agreement. The victor is also likely to be the most satisfied with the status quo, and therefore most inclined to freeze it with a strong agreement restraining options for another war. But after very lopsided outcomes, the victor may feel it can impose peace unilaterally without a strong agreement. The Soviets needed no strong agreement to prevent a second Hungarian uprising. The realist expectation might therefore be a curvilinear relationship, with weak agreements associated with wars that end in a tie, stronger agreements after moderately decisive victories, but weak agreements after the most decisively imposed outcomes.[6] Table 4.1 summarizes the hypotheses, showing the relationship between situational variables and agreement strength expected by each argument.

---

[6] Note, however, that this downward bend at the most decisive end of the spectrum runs counter to the general argument that the strongest agreements will be reached in the easiest cases, since such thorough victories should be associated with very durable peace.

TABLE 4.1
Summary of Hypotheses on Endogeneity

Situational Variable	Hypothesized Relationship to Agreement Strength	
	Realist	Functionalist
Military outcome (relative to victory) Imposed	—	—
Tie	—	+
Cost of war	—	+
History of conflict	—	+
Stakes	—	+
Territorial conflict	—	+
Contiguity	—	+
Multilateral war	+	+
Balance of power	—	+

II. LARGE-N EVIDENCE

Effects of Situational Variables on Overall Strength of Agreements

A qualitative survey of the cases provides a first cut at evaluating these competing hypotheses. It suggests that stronger agreements are reached when peace is most precarious, not when it is easiest to keep. Table 4.2 shows the cases arranged by agreement strength. That the most decisive wars end with weak or nonexistent agreements is immediately apparent. After the Soviet Union suppressed Hungary, or Uganda overthrew Tanzania's government, or the United Kingdom clobbered Argentina, no one bothered to put in place mechanisms to keep peace. Only the weakest of agreements were implemented after the Israel's decisive victory in the Six-Day War or Turkey's partition of Cyprus. Both the realist and functionalist arguments predict weak agreements at this very decisive end of the spectrum. However, as functionalism, but not realism, would predict, stronger agreements are more likely in wars that end in a draw (Korea, the Football War, and the second Kashmir war) than in those with a more decisive outcome (Ethiopia-Somalia and the Israeli-Egyptian War of Attrition, for example). The only clear exceptions to this trend are the 1991 Gulf War, with a very strong agreement after an extremely decisive victory by the United States–led coalition (which neither argument would pre-

TABLE 4.2
Cease-Fires, by Agreement Strength

War	Agreement
Russo-Hungarian	None
Vietnam (North–South Vietnam)	
Ugandan-Tanzanian	
Sino-Vietnamese 2	
Yom Kippur (Israel-Jordan)	
Falklands	
Sino-Vietnamese 1	
Ugandan-Tanzanian (Libya)	
Six-Day (Israel-Jordan)	Very weak
Azeri-Armenian 1	
Turco-Cypriot 2	
Six-Day (Israel-Egypt)	
Ethiopian-Somalian (2 cases)	
Six-Day (Israel-Syria)	
Israeli-Egyptian War of Attrition	
Azeri-Armenian 2	
Lebanon (Israel-Syria)	Weak
Sinai (Egypt–U.K., France)	
Palestine 1 (all 5 cases)	
Sino-Indian	
Turco-Cypriot 1	
Bangladesh	
Sinai (Egypt-Israel)	
Iran-Iraq	Moderate
Kashmir 1	
Palestine 2 (Israel-Iraq)	
Palestine 2 (Israel–Egypt, Syria, Lebanon)	
Palestine 2 (Israel-Jordan)	
Football	
Kashmir 2	
Yom Kippur (Israel-Egypt)	Strong
Gulf War (all 3 cases)	
Yom Kippur (Israel-Syria)	
Korean (all 4 cases)	
Vietnamese (U.S.-North Vietnam)	

122 • Chapter Four

dict), and the Sino-Vietnamese wars, which ended indecisively but without strong efforts to maintain peace.

Greater effort is also made to shore up peace after the most deadly wars. The Korean War, the Vietnam War, and to a lesser extent the Iran-Iraq War, all ended with formal and detailed agreements and concrete provisions to improve the chances for peace, including demilitarized zones, arms control arrangements, and peacekeeping, among other things.[7] Meanwhile, relatively low-cost wars such as the Falklands and the second portion of the Turco-Cypriot War ended with much weaker agreements.

A bivariate relationship between the combatants' history of conflict and agreement strength is harder to see from an overview of cases. However, it does appear that in repeated wars between the same states, agreements tend to be stronger after the second or third war than the first (with the notable exception of very decisive victories). As states experience more conflict over time, they strengthen their attempts to avoid it. Perhaps this reflects a learning curve in reaction to earlier failed attempts to maintain peace.[8] Conflicts in which a state's very existence is at stake (whether Kuwait, North and South Korea, or Israel) also seem to yield stronger agreements than less serious conflicts, though again, this relationship is less clear-cut from just a survey of cases.

While the Arab-Israeli wars dominate the data set, agreements reached in the Middle East run the gamut from very weak to very strong, suggesting that they are not in a class by themselves in this regard. But note that wars in which the United States was involved: the Korean War, Vietnam, and the Gulf War, have ended with unusually strong agreements, an issue I will return to below.

Reviewing the post–World War II cases, one would be hard pressed to sustain the argument that the strongest agreements were reached when peace would otherwise have been most likely to last. To do so, one would have to argue that at the time of the cease-fire, we would have expected lasting peace between Iran and Iraq, between Israel and its neighbors in 1949 as well as 1973, between India and Pakistan after the Kashmir wars, on the Korean peninsula, or between El Salvador and Honduras after the

[7] The first Gulf War also fits this trend, although its high costs were borne entirely by one side.

[8] Within a case, agreements also tend to get stronger over time, with follow-up agreements generally more robust than their predecessors. Since the hazard of another war generally goes down over time, this trend runs counter to the functionalist logic (thanks to Amitabh Dubey for raising this issue). However, in many cases, agreements are strengthened in response to a perceived increase in the danger of war. For example, the follow-up agreement reached in 1976 in the Football War was a response to serious clashes and skirmishes that leaders feared would escalate to war. Martz 1978.

Football War, but that we would have expected fragile peace between the Soviet Union and Hungary after 1956, or after the Falklands War. This qualitative survey clearly supports the functionalist hypothesis over the counterargument.

Quantitative analysis of the relationship between the determinants of the baseline prospects for peace and the overall strength of agreements leads to the same conclusion. Two measures of strength, the more subjective coding of agreement strength and the more objective index of agreement mechanisms, are treated as the dependent variable.[9] Table 4.3 shows the statistical relationships between situational variables and these two measures, labeled *Agreement Strength* and *Agreement Index*, in ordered logit and ordinary least squares (OLS) regressions, respectively. For each measure three model specifications are shown: the first uses only the variables discussed in the previous chapter;[10] the second includes a dummy marking wars in which the U.S. was a belligerent (as we shall see, the U.S. cases are exceptional); the third adds a control for the most decisive or imposed outcomes to test the non-linear expectation of realism. The hypothesis that stronger agreements are put in place when conditions make peace particularly easy to maintain does not fare well in these tests. Rather, those relationships that are statistically significant support the functionalist argument that belligerents invest more in stronger agreements when peace is most precarious.

Both arguments predict weak agreements for the most decisive victories, unilaterally imposed settlements such as that by the Soviets on Hungary, by Britain in the Falklands, or Tanzania in Uganda. And indeed we see a negative coefficient for imposed outcomes. However, stronger agreements are implemented after wars that end in a tie rather than a decisive victory, and while this finding is much stronger when the control for U.S. involvement is included, the positive relationship is robust to numerous model specifications.[11] That imposed outcomes tend to have the weakest agreements, decisive victories short of this (the omitted category in the regressions) fall in the middle, and wars that end in a draw have the strongest agreements is exactly as the functionalist argument would predict. We do not find the curvilinear relationship predicted by realism.[12]

---

[9] See chapter 2 and appendix B for measurement details.

[10] The relative power measure "balance of power" is the inverse of the preponderance-of-power measure used in chapter 3.

[11] For example, adding or dropping independent variables, or duplicate agreement cases, or controlling for Middle East cases.

[12] Tests using quadratic terms to explore other possible curvilinear relationships did not yield strong results. There is very weak evidence for a slightly hill-shaped relationship between agreement strength and both the history of conflict and the balance of capabilities. The cost of war exhibits a slight U shape. None of these relationships is terribly robust, however.

Chapter Four

124 • Chapter Four

TABLE 4.3
Situational Variables and the Strength of Agreements

	Coefficients (robust standard errors)					
	Agreement Strength (ordered logit)			Agreement Index (OLS)		
Imposed			−1.718* (0.958)			−0.690 (0.665)
Tie	1.329 (0.986)	2.190*** (0.506)	1.138 (0.922)	1.529* (0.852)	2.122*** (0.618)	1.623* (0.785)
Cost of war	0.460*** (0.161)	−0.207 (0.652)	−0.176 (0.649)	0.336** (0.134)	−0.331* (0.188)	−0.341 (0.199)
History of conflict	1.032 (0.905)	1.937*** (0.674)	1.644** (0.719)	0.995 (0.611)	1.622*** (0.356)	1.499*** (0.463)
Existence at stake	−0.685 (0.743)	−1.518* (0.842)	−1.312 (1.047)	−0.278 (0.569)	−0.776 (0.492)	−0.675 (0.526)
Territorial conflict	1.400 (0.879)	1.675 (1.020)	1.461 (1.341)	1.461* (0.803)	1.303** (0.571)	1.194* (0.660)
Contiguity	−0.568 (0.891)	−0.605 (0.737)	−0.350 (0.633)	−0.433 (0.762)	−0.165 (0.602)	−0.135 (0.573)
Multilateral war	0.994 (0.848)	0.706 (0.886)	0.410 (1.034)	0.741 (0.876)	0.215 (0.799)	0.065 (0.771)
Balance of power	−1.982 (1.553)	−1.837 (1.911)	−1.444 (1.736)	−2.417 (1.392)	−1.804 (1.172)	−1.646 (1.229)
U.S. belligerent		7.063** (2.909)	7.550*** (2.538)		5.019*** (0.919)	5.203*** (1.001)
Constant				−3.278* (1.753)	1.626 (1.818)	2.445 (2.118)
N	48	48	48	48	48	48
R^2				0.329	0.512	0.520
Pseudo-R^2	0.155	0.277	0.302			
Log likelihood	−64.920	−55.502	−53.609			

Note: Cases are clustered by conflict.
* Statistically significant at the .10 level.
** Statistically significant at the .05 level.
*** Statistically significant at the .01 level.

Stronger agreements are also put in place after very deadly wars, although this relationship falls away when we control for U.S. involvement.[13] Belligerents with a more violent history tend to implement stronger agreements, significantly so when the United States is controlled for. While higher-stakes conflicts seem to yield weaker agreements, this relationship is not robust across different model specifications.[14] Wars over land are ended with stronger agreements, significantly so for the objective measure of agreements. Only two variables consistently support the counterargument over the rebuttal, and these only weakly. Neighbors tend to draft weaker agreements and balanced power relationships are associated with weaker agreements, but in neither case is the finding statistically significant. Consistent with both arguments, multilateral wars also yield stronger agreements, though again, this positive relationship might be simply an artifact of chance. In sum, table 4.3 provides moderate support for the functionalist argument, and virtually no support for the idea that agreements are merely epiphenomenal.

Effects of Situational Variables on Individual Agreement Mechanisms

We can explore the relationship between the baseline prospects for peace and the content of agreements more closely by breaking agreements into their component parts: withdrawal of forces, DMZs, peacekeeping, and so on. While the respective logics of the realist and functionalist arguments should apply to individual mechanisms, we might expect particular situational variables to affect some peace measures more than others. We might expect withdrawal from the cease-fire line to be especially unlikely in conflicts over territory or where the stakes are particularly high, while demilitarized zones might be most likely between neighbors. Similarly, whether third parties will get involved as guarantors or as peacekeepers might be determined by different factors than measures implemented by the belligerents themselves.

To examine such possibilities, I treated each mechanism in turn as a dependent variable, testing the relationship between each situational variable and each agreement component. Exploring the effects of eight situational variables on eleven aspects of agreements, checking for robustness to different measures and model specifications, produces much more output than can be displayed here. Table 4.4 summarizes the results, showing the relationships, positive or negative, between situational variables and

---

[13] The same is true for long wars.

[14] The coefficient is positive when Middle East cases are controlled for or when nonsignificant independent variables are dropped.

TABLE 4.4
Effects of Situational Variables on Individual Agreement Mechanisms

	Withdrawal	Demilitarized Zones	Arms Control	Peace-keeping Monitors	Peace-keeping Forces	External Involvement	Confidence-Building Measures	Dispute Resolution	Internal Control	Specificity	Formalism
Tie	+	+	+	+				**+**	+	+	+
Cost of war			+	+	—	+	**+**		—	**+**	**+**
History of Conflict		+	+	**+**	+	**+**		+	+	+	**+**
Existence at stake	—	+	+	**+**	—	—	+	**+**	**+**	+	
Territorial conflict	—	+	+	**+**	—			+	+	+	+
Contiguous	—	+	**+**	—	+ **+**	—				—	
Multilateral war		+	**+**	—	**+**	+			+	+	
Balance of power	+		—		—	+	—		—	—	—

+ or — Consistent, but not significant.
+ or — Consistent, but only rarely significant.
+ or — Consistent relationship, often significant.
+ or — Consistent relationship, almost always significant.
+ or — Strong, significant, robust relationship.

each agreement mechanism.[15] This table is arranged so that negative signs support the realist hypothesis that agreement mechanisms are more likely when the chances for renewed warfare are low, and positive signs support the opposite functionalist argument. The only exception to this is multilateral war, for which both arguments expect a positive relationship.

The size of the symbols signifies the amount of confidence we can have in the results. The largest symbols indicate relationships that are consistent across all statistical tests, and that are always significant. The next size down marks consistent relationships that are slightly less robust but almost always significant, and so on down to the smallest symbols, showing a consistently positive or negative relationship but one that never or almost never passes tests of statistical significance. So, for example, the positive relationship between wars that end in a military tie and the likelihood of dispute resolution procedures (shown with a large plus sign in the top row of the table) holds whether we use an ordinal or a dichotomous measure of dispute resolution, whether all of the situational variables in the model are included or various combinations of them, whether all but one of the "duplicate" cases (where several dyads shared a single cease-fire agreement, as after the Korean War) are dropped or all kept in, whether the duration of war or its cost in terms of lives lost is controlled for,[16] whether U.S. participation in the war is controlled for, and so on. On the other hand, the positive relationship between specific agreements and wars that end in a tie is marked with a very small plus sign because while the effect is consistently positive, it could be due to chance alone.

These smaller symbols denoting relationships that fail conventional tests of statistical significance are included in the table because we cannot be confident that *no* relationship exists; there is a preponderance of evidence in favor of a relationship in the direction shown, but it is certainly not beyond a reasonable doubt.[17] Where there is no consistent relationship between a situational variable and an agreement mechanism (that is, the sign of the coefficients flips across different tests), the cell is left blank.

The results in table 4.4 are mixed, with both positive and negative effects. The null hypothesis does fairly well: there are many empty cells and many small symbols indicating effects that cannot be statistically distinguished from zero with great confidence. The situational variables do not

---

[15] As explained in chapter 2, the type of regression used (ordinary least squares, ordered logit, logistic) depends on the form of the agreement variable under consideration (continuous, ordinal or dichotomous).

[16] These are too highly correlated to include together. The results are substantially the same for both.

[17] This is important since I am partly testing a counterargument to my own argument, and since there are relatively few cases in the data set.

explain most of the variation in agreement content.[18] On balance, however, the functionalist hypothesis about need does better than the realist argument about states' ability to implement strong agreements.

Let us look at each measure in turn, starting with troop withdrawal in the first column. We can see that while none of the relationships is very robust (hence relatively small symbols), withdrawal of forces from the cease-fire line appears to be less likely in high-stakes conflicts where letting down one's guard might be especially risky. Neighbors and those fighting over territory also seem less inclined to pull back their troops, but states that are evenly matched militarily are somewhat more likely to agree to this measure. More than any other mechanism examined here, withdrawal conforms to the realist counterargument, being more likely when peace is more likely to last in any case.

Demilitarized zones, on the other hand, are more likely when peace is harder to maintain. DMZs are particularly likely in territorial conflicts, such as the Football War, and also seem more likely in high-stakes conflicts such as the first Arab-Israeli war. They are more likely between neighbors, although this relationship is not as strong as we might expect. Sometimes even noncontiguous states create DMZs to separate troops, as in Korea.[19] DMZs are also more prevalent in multilateral wars, fights that end in a draw, and when belligerents have a more conflictual history, though these relationships are less robust and we should take them with a grain of salt.

The pattern for arms control measures also supports the functionalist argument. While arms control may be slightly less prevalent between states with evenly matched capabilities (the strongest arms restrictions in the cases examined here are those imposed on Iraq after the Gulf War), it is otherwise most likely when the situational variables make peace harder to keep; especially after high-stakes or territorial conflicts, or in multilateral wars.

International personnel are much more likely to be sent to monitor the cease-fire in high-stakes conflicts, in territorial conflicts, and when belligerents have frequently been at each others' throats in the past. They are also more likely after very deadly conflicts, and wars that end without a clear victor. They are less likely to be deployed to multilateral conflicts, and perhaps between neighbors. Here, however, armed peacekeepers (as opposed to unarmed monitors) are more likely. The international community appears to be more reluctant to send armed forces after very costly wars or fights over territory. A qualitative look at the cases reveals that peacekeeping, not surprisingly, is rare in wars involving a great power, as

---

[18] In most tests, the R^2 or pseudo-R^2 measures indicate that between 20% and 40% of the variation is explained by these models.

[19] Not coincidentally, this positive relationship between neighbors and DMZs is much stronger when a control for the United States as a belligerent is included.

any permanent member of the Security Council can veto a UN mission. But there are exceptions. The first ever armed peacekeeping force, the UN mission in the Sinai, was deployed to allow Britain and France a face-saving exit from the war, while non-UN peacekeepers were deployed in Vietnam and in Korea.[20]

Outsiders are less likely to get involved by mediating a cease-fire or guaranteeing the peace publicly when one side's existence is at stake. Note, however, that this measure does not pick up tacit guarantees of one side's safety such as that between the United States and Israel. Third parties are more likely to become involved when the belligerents have a history of conflict.

Confidence-building measures seem less likely when belligerents have roughly equal power, but are significantly more likely after very high cost wars, perhaps as a way of rebuilding trust after large-scale loss of life. Dispute resolution procedures, such as armistice commissions to resolve problems after the cease-fire goes into effect, are also more likely when the prospects for peace are less good; particularly after indecisive outcomes such as the Korean War, and high-stakes conflicts such as the first Arab-Israeli war. This is exactly the opposite of what the counterargument would predict.

Measures to deal with irregular forces or the possibility of involuntary defection are also generally more likely when peace is most precarious. The quantitative tests show that while internal control is somewhat less likely after high-cost wars and when belligerents are evenly matched militarily, it is more prevalent when one side's existence is threatened and after multilateral wars or those that end in a draw. It also appears more likely between belligerents with a history of conflict or those fighting over territory. While it is difficult to capture the danger of involuntary defection quantitatively, a qualitative examination further supports the functionalist hypotheses. Measures to deal with potential rogue forces were implemented in response to need. Irregular civilian forces in the border area between El Salvador and Honduras were disarmed after the Football War to prevent the kinds of incidents that had helped spark the war. Similarly, after the Sinai War, local inhabitants were prohibited near the armistice line to try to prevent *fedayeen* incursions in Gaza.

Looking at the last two columns in table 4.4, we can see that both the specificity and the formalism of agreements support the functionalist hypothesis more than the realist counterargument. Agreements tend

---

[20] Note that the UN coalition that fought in Korea is not coded as a peacekeeping mission. However, an ad hoc Neutral Nations Supervisory Commission, made up of representatives from Sweden, Switzerland, Poland, and Czechoslovakia, deployed to observe the cease-fire, and this is coded as a monitoring mission.

to be less formal and less specific when belligerents' military capabilities are relatively balanced, but the higher the death toll and the more the combatants have tangled in their history, the more specific and formal the cease-fire agreements they reach. Territorial conflicts and wars that end without a clear victory are also more likely to end with formal and specific agreements.[21]

The negotiating process that leads to cease-fire agreements is complex and is by no means fully captured in these quantitative tests. These tests do tell us something, however, about whether peace mechanisms are epiphenomenal, put in place only when peace would last in any case, or functional responses to precarious peace. In general, there is much more evidence that where situational variables have a consistent effect, it is to push those with a harder time maintaining peace to exert stronger efforts to do so. Given that this data set includes only states that have recently proven themselves deadly enemies and that this may bias the results in the opposite direction, we find stronger support than expected for the argument that when cooperation is more difficult, parties invest more heavily in measures to make it possible.

Predicted Baseline Prospects for Peace and Agreement Strength

A final quantitative cut at assessing the competing hypotheses involves comparing the overall prospects for peace and the overall strength of agreements. The index of agreement mechanisms used above provides a continuous measure of agreement strength. The indicator of the overall baseline prospects for peace is somewhat trickier. When a cease-fire occurs, if no deliberate effort to maintain peace is made, peace will last for some unknown amount of time. We can predict that duration, albeit imprecisely, using the situational variables and the hazard model described in the previous chapter. The predicted duration of peace from that analysis then serves as an indicator of the baseline ease or difficulty in maintaining peace. We can see whether cases in which peace is predicted to last longer are associated with stronger or weaker agreements.

However, a complication arises because efforts *are* usually made, through cease-fire agreements, to enhance the durability of peace. If these efforts work (a question I turn to in the chapters that follow), they will systematically cloud our predictions of how long peace would last in their absence, and thus our estimate of the baseline prospects for peace. This fact creates a bias that will tend to favor the realist hypothesis and work

---

[21] These findings generally support the hypothesis proposed by Abbott and Snidal 2000, 429 that states will opt for greater legalization when the benefits of cooperation are great but the potential for and costs of opportunism are high.

TABLE 4.5
Bias in Tests of Predicted Baseline Duration of Peace and Agreement Strength

If the Realist Logic is Correct		*If the Functionalist Logic Is Correct*	
Easy cases	Hard cases	Easy cases	Hard cases
⇓	⇓	⇓	⇓
Strong agreements	Weak agreements	Weak agreements	Strong agreements
⇓	⇓	⇓	⇓
Peace looks easier than it is	Peace looks harder than it is	Peace looks harder than it is	Peace looks easier than it is
⇓	⇓	⇓	⇓
Predicted duration longer than should be	Predicted duration shorter than should be	Predicted duration shorter than should be	Predicted duration longer than should be
⇓	⇓	⇓	⇓
Bias **exaggerates** positive relationship between baseline duration and strength hypothesized by **realist argument**		Bias **obscures** negative relationship between baseline duration and strength hypothesized by **functionalist argument**	

against the functionalist one. Table 4.5 shows how this works. Assume for the moment that strong agreements make peace more stable. If the logic of the realist argument is right, then in the easy cases, when peace is expected to last a long time, strong agreements will be more likely, and they will make peace last even longer. This will bias our estimates of the baseline duration of peace upwards; that is, we will predict it to last longer than we should. These cases will appear even easier than they are because we are attributing some of the effect of agreements to the situational variables. Conversely, in the hard cases, strong agreements will be unlikely, making these cases look relatively even harder than they are and biasing our estimates of the duration of peace downward. This will exaggerate the relationship predicted by the realist hypothesis because we will overestimate the baseline length of peace where there are strong agreements, and underestimate it where there are weak agreements.

If on the other hand the functionalist logic is right, weak agreements will be reached in the easy cases, and this will make peace fall apart more quickly relative to other cases. So in these cases peace will look harder to maintain than it really is and our baseline predictions will be shorter than they should be. In the truly harder cases, strong agreements will be put in place, and these will compensate somewhat for the baseline difficulty, making peace look easier to maintain than it really is and biasing the predicted baseline duration upward. This will mean that when we look at our biased estimates of the duration of peace and strength of agreements, the relationship hypothesized by the functionalist argument, that harder cases are associated with stronger agreements, will be obscured. We will underestimate the baseline length of peace when there are weak agreements and overestimate it when there are strong agreements.

In either case, then, ignoring the effects of any deliberate attempts to foster peace will bias our findings away from the functionalist hypothesis and toward the realist hypothesis. If there were many cases of cease-fires with no attempts to alter the prospects for peace, and if these cases were not otherwise atypical, we could clear this problem up easily enough. Without them, however, all we can do is be aware of the direction of the bias. This issue along with the selection of cases at the most acrimonious end of the spectrum means that this test is doubly biased in favor of the counterargument and against the functionalist rebuttal.

The easiest way to see the relationship between the overall baseline prospects for peace and overall strength of agreements is graphically. The scatterplots shown in figure 4.2 plot the index of agreement strength against the difficulty in achieving peace, as predicted in our analysis in chapter 3.[22] The realist counterargument would predict a downward slope in the plot, with stronger agreements at the easy end and weaker ones as peace gets harder to maintain. The functionalist rebuttal would predict a positive slope.

The top scatterplot shows two distinct clusters in the data. Further investigation reveals that all but one of the "outliers" in the upper left portion of the plot represent cases in which the United States was involved as a belligerent in the war. These are identified in the lower scatterplot. They are the United States and North Vietnam, the four dyads in the Korean War, and the three dyads in the Gulf War. (The remaining dot in this cluster is Israel and Egypt after the Sinai War.) Note that there is one case in which the United States was involved that is not in this cluster, near the origin of the plot. This represents North and South Vietnam in 1975. This is coded as a war in which the United States was a belligerent, but of course by the time of the "cease-fire" when the North overran the South, the United States had washed its hands of the situation.

---

[22] This is calculated as the natural log of the predicted duration of peace (in days), from the Weibull regression shown in column 1 of table 3.1. This is then inverted so that "easy" cases appear toward the left, "difficult" cases toward the right (to match figure 4.1).

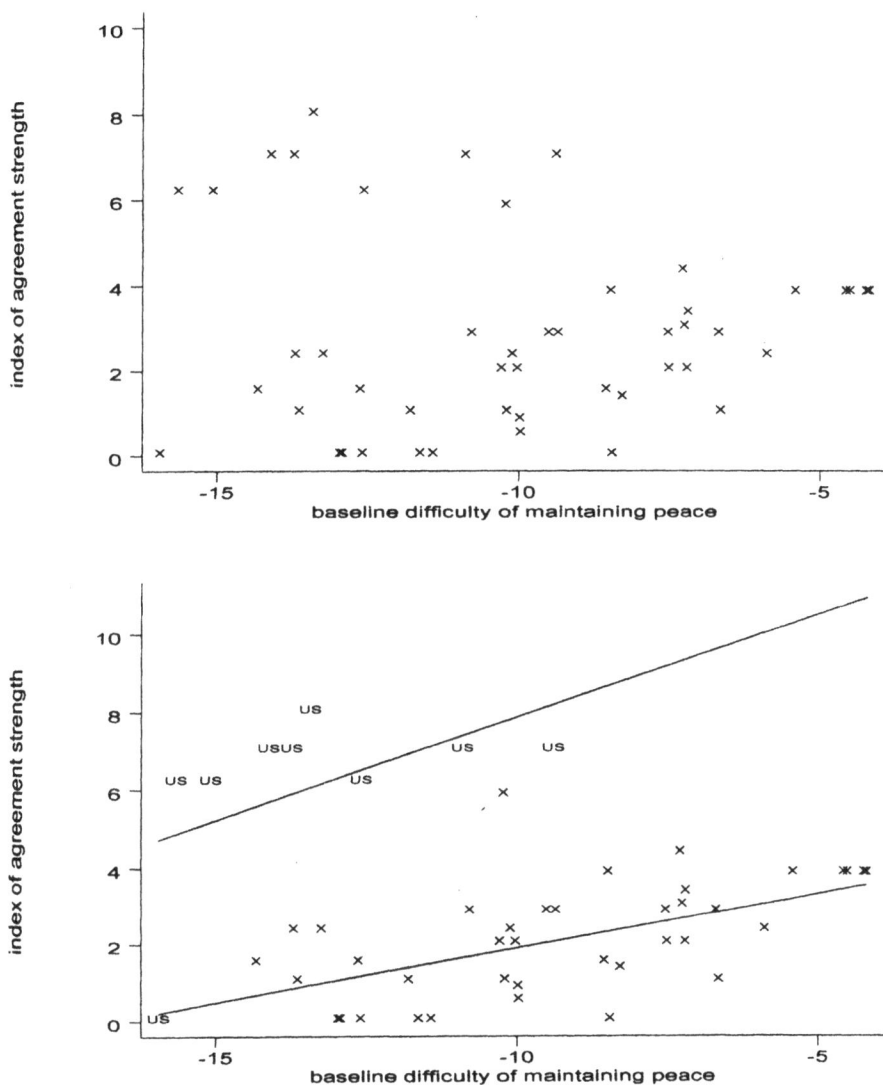

Figure 4.2 Baseline Predicted Peace and Agreement Strength

As we have noted before, there is clearly something different about the agreements the United States reaches after it fights; they are much stronger than those reached in other wars (this can also be seen in table 4.3). This is true when the United States is the overwhelmingly decisive victor, as in the Gulf, when it has fought to a draw, as in Korea, or when it has been badly bloodied, as in Vietnam. This is not simply the result of greater power, as other great powers reach much weaker agreements.[23] In the current political climate of the early twenty-first century, the United States appears to oppose strong international treaties, but at least when it comes to cease-fire agreements, the United States has tended to sign unusually strong agreements. This fits a general trend in American legal culture. International legal scholars have oft noted that Americans tend to draft much longer, more detailed, and better specified agreements than their counterparts in Europe.[24] The size of the legal profession in the United States may also help explain this tendency.[25]

Controlling for American exceptionalism, the generally upward-sloping nature of the data indicates a positive relationship between the baseline difficulty of maintaining peace and the strength of agreements.[26] As the baseline prospects for peace worsen, belligerents and the international community try to offset the obstacles to peace by drafting and implementing stronger agreements. Despite the double bias in favor of the realist hypothesis, we see no evidence that stronger agreements are reached when peace would be easy to maintain in any case. Rather we see rather clear evidence in favor of the functionalist rebuttal.

• • •

In sum, all three of the relatively large-N cuts at examining the relationship between the baseline prospects for peace and the strength of agreements suggest the same thing: agreements are more functional than epiphenomenal. We do not have a full explanation of agreement design; the situational variables do not perfectly predict agreement strength. But we can clearly dismiss the charge that strong agreements are reached only in the easy cases. To the extent that there is a relationship between the baseline prospects for peace and agreement strength, stronger agreements are generally reached not when peace would be likely to last

[23] On power and preferences for legalization, see Abbott and Snidal 2000, 433, 447ff.

[24] For example, American business contracts tend to be longer than those in Britain, which are in turn longer than those on the Continent. For one explanation, see Lundmark 2001. This American exceptionalism may be related to the tendency explained by Wolfers of those in the Anglo-American tradition to be more optimistic about the ability to shape international outcomes (what he calls a "philosophy of choice") and perhaps also to the trend noted by Lowi for liberal states to favor a rule-oriented foreign policy. Wolfers 1962, chap. 15; Lowi 1969, chap. 6. See also Merryman 1969.

[25] Abbott and Snidal 2000, 432, suggest this hypothesis.

[26] The lines show the OLS regression of the index of strength on the predicted baseline difficulty. The coefficient for the lower line (non-U.S. cases) is 0.28 with a robust standard error of 0.05 (therefore statistically significant at $p < .001$). The coefficient for U.S. cases is 0.53, but with so few cases it is not statistically significant.

in any case, as the counterargument would charge, but when peace is otherwise most fragile.

A more detailed, qualitative examination of the India-Pakistan and Israel-Syria cases supports this conclusion and reveals a more nuanced view of the relationship between the problems of agreement supply predicted by the realist counterargument and the functionalist logic of the rebuttal. In both cases implementation of measures to help maintain peace was hampered by enmity and conflict, but in both these cases obstacles to cooperation were most likely to be overcome when peace was most precarious.

III. CASE EVIDENCE

India and Pakistan

The first Kashmir war ended on January 1, 1949, with a cease-fire embodied in two UN resolutions.[27] The second Kashmir war ended with the cease-fire of September 23, 1965, also based on both sides' acceptance of a UN resolution.[28] The third war between India and Pakistan ended with the surrender of the Pakistani Eastern Command on December 16, 1971, conceding the secession of Bangladesh, and with India's unilateral cease-fire the next day.[29] In each case, the initial cease-fire was followed up soon after with a formal bilateral agreement: the Karachi Agreement of July 27, 1949, the Tashkent Declaration of January 10, 1966, and the Simla Agreement of July 2, 1972. What do these cases tell us about where strong agreements are reached?[30] Were the measures implemented in these agreements driven primarily by supply, by how much India and Pakistan could agree to, given the prospects for peace? Or were they driven more by demand, by the need to put measures in place to try to alleviate the danger of war?

These three cases support the functionalist hypothesis. After the first Kashmir war, the prospects for stable peace were bad but not terrible. Both sides had strong incentives to settle the Kashmir issue by force if necessary, linked as it was to each state's raison d'être. However, the relationship between Indians and Pakistanis had not yet hardened into deep enmity. Shared history and the mutual struggle for decolonization moderated the mistrust and hatred that would later develop. At the end of the war, the military aspects of the cease-fire were for the most part uncontroversial.[31] With one exception, there does not seem to have been a problem

[27] UNCIP Resolutions S/995, August 13, 1948, and S/1196, January 5, 1949.

[28] UN Security Council Resolution 211, September 20, 1965.

[29] Pakistan's instrument of surrender is reprinted in Jackson 1975, 233.

[30] I have not included the cease-fire reached after the Kargil war in this comparison as there is not yet enough information about what was agreed to and why.

[31] UNCIP 1949, 12.

of supply. The only measure considered that India and Pakistan could not agree to in 1949 because of their conflict was the withdrawal of forces from Kashmir (see below).

At the end of the second Kashmir war the baseline prospects for peace were significantly worse than they had been in 1949. When the cease-fire went into effect, the situation remained extremely tense. Reports of cease-fire violations were "continuous," according to UN military observers, and often involved serious fighting.[32] Soldiers were no more than 30 yards apart in some places, and both sides were attempting to shore up and improve their military positions. Moreover, prominent officials in both Pakistan and India were advocating another round of fighting to settle the Kashmir issue decisively.[33] But the agreement implemented by Pakistan and India was in many respects stronger than its predecessor. Relative to the temporary measures put in place in 1949, the 1965 cease-fire had more substance. For example, monitoring was beefed up, troops withdrew to the status quo ante, and a formal agreement was signed by the respective heads of state.

In 1971, the risk of renewed war was extremely low: Pakistan was thoroughly defeated, and India had gotten what it wanted on the battlefield. In terms of concrete mechanisms to prevent reinitiation of war, the 1971 cease-fire was very weak. It contained no new provisions for demilitarized zones, or arms control, the monitoring mechanism fell into disuse, and unlike its two predecessors, no concern was given to the issue of controlling irregular forces. This comparison across the three cease-fires in South Asia shows that stronger agreements were put in place when the prospects for peace were worst.

Detailed information on why India and Pakistan implemented the mechanisms they did, and why they did not implement others, is hard to come by. The available evidence, however, indicates that problems of supply did prohibit implementation of a few measures, that implementation was sometimes affected by exogenous factors, and that India and Pakistan were often motivated by need—that the mechanisms put in place were in response to particularly precarious situations.

Reluctance to withdraw forces from Kashmir provides perhaps the strongest support for the realist counterargument. Withdrawal of forces is extremely sensitive both politically and militarily. In 1949, Pakistan withdrew the Pathan tribesmen whose attack had triggered the war, but neither Pakistan nor India was willing to withdraw regular forces from the disputed territory, as called for in UN CIP Resolution 995. With-

---

[32] UN document S/6710 and addenda, 1965–66; Brines 1968.

[33] For example, Z. A. Bhutto, then foreign minister of Pakistan, was in favor of restarting the war. Lamb 1991, 268.

drawal would mean eschewing direct political control over territory in the run-up to the planned plebiscite that was to decide Kashmir's accession crisis. India in particular was unwilling to withdraw since its access to Kashmir is much more difficult than Pakistan's, making it very difficult to redeploy should Pakistan renege on a demilitarization agreement.[34]

In 1965, however, the instability caused by troops at very close range, frequently contesting the cease-fire line, motivated India and Pakistan to withdraw to the status quo ante (i.e., the pre-1965 cease-fire line).[35] This withdrawal was politically sensitive; India's withdrawal from the Haji Pir Pass was extremely unpopular domestically and within military circles, for example.[36] However, the danger of renewed warfare outweighed the political costs of withdrawal. Temporary demilitarized zones, first of one hundred yards, then of one thousand yards, were established to separate forces until the withdrawals agreed to at Tashkent were complete.[37] So while withdrawal and demilitarization of Kashmir was not feasible, limited withdrawals to mitigate the danger of accidental escalation were possible when the risk of renewed warfare was particularly acute.

The India-Pakistan case also suggests two exogenous factors that influence the content of agreements. One is the development of peacemaking and peacekeeping practices over time. The concept of confidence-building measures to increase military transparency so as to restrict activities likely to increase tension, and to improve communication in a crisis, had not yet been developed when India and Pakistan's conflict began.[38] Some of the arms control provisions negotiated between military commanders after the second Kashmir war regulated military activities (for example, there were very explicit rules governing mine clearance; mines could only be exploded between 3:00 and 5:00 P.M., and no military activity was permitted during the night).[39] These measures were intended to prevent misunderstandings and so would now be dubbed CBMs. A "hot line" communication link was established between military commanders after the 1971 war, and in the 1980s and 1990s India and Pakistan negotiated a number of CBMs. These later initiatives stemmed directly from moments of particularly risky conflict in 1986–87 and 1990.[40]

[34] Korbel 1954, 159.

[35] On the instability caused by forces on the "wrong" side of this line, see for example, the secretary-general's report, UN document S/6710/Add. 4, 1965, 2.

[36] Brines 1968, 403, 405. See also Das 1969, 397–98.

[37] UN document S/6719/Add. 1, 1965, 2. Military commanders could often be persuaded to agree to these pullbacks after local skirmishes. See for example, UN document S/6710/Add. 5, 7.

[38] The first "hot line" communication link was established between the United States and the USSR in 1963, but explicit CBMs were rare until the mid-1970s. See Krepon et al. 1993.

[39] Text of agreement reprinted in UN document S/6719/Add. 5, appendix, 1966.

[40] Bajpai 1996, 23.

The deployment of armed international troops (as opposed to monitors) for peacekeeping was also not available as a practice in 1949; it was not "invented" until 1956 after the Sinai War.[41] Pakistan did suggest a neutral force be deployed to Kashmir in 1949, but the UN commission replied that it had no such force at its disposal nor had the Security Council contemplated creating one.[42] Only later were peacekeepers deployed to South Asia. The development of new peace mechanisms represents an exogenous change in the options available to belligerents.

In later discussions over the possibility of international forces helping to keep peace or to administer a demilitarized Kashmir, we see a second exogenous factor. Newly independent states are understandably sensitive about sovereignty and are often hesitant to allow foreign troops to be stationed on their soil. There was certainly a political aspect especially to India's reluctance to allow armed peacekeepers to deploy, as UN control would undermine India's claim to Kashmir and would facilitate a plebiscite that India feared it would lose. As the stronger power, India has also generally sought to keep its dispute with Pakistan on a bilateral footing and out of multilateral arenas where its greater military strength would carry less weight. Nonetheless, much of India's reluctance to allow peacekeepers, especially in the 1950s and 1960s stemmed from genuine concerns over sovereignty and its ideology of nonalignment.[43] These concerns also precluded the use of external guarantees by great powers (particularly Britain, the obvious candidate) to help "enforce" the peace. Neither India nor Pakistan wished to invite their recent colonizers back to the subcontinent. Ideas thus affect the content of agreements to some extent. Ideas about sovereignty, ideological considerations of nonalignment, and especially the development of ideas about how peace might be maintained, the "state of the art," as it were, all exerted some influence on what mechanisms India and Pakistan included in their agreements.

We have seen some evidence that the conflict between India and Pakistan limited the strength of their agreements, and some indication that certain aspects of agreements were affected by exogenous factors. There is also considerable evidence that these two bitter enemies implemented the measures they did as a response to the precarious nature of peace. One promi-

---

[41] For an account of the invention, see Brian Urquhart's 1972 biography of Hammarskjold. Both the author and his subject were instrumental in creating this new practice at the UN.

[42] UN documents S/AC.12/44; and S/AC.12/55 in UNCIP 1949, 106–7, 111. In response to Pakistan's suggestion for a neutral force to guard against violations, UNCIP responded (whether naively or for political reasons) that the agreement would not be drawn up on the assumption that either side would violate it. Gupta 1966, 183.

[43] See Blinkenberg 1972, 153. Both UN and Commonwealth forces were discussed in this period.

nent example involves measures to control irregular forces and to deal with the problem of "involuntary defection." Internal control was a contentious political issue after the first Kashmir war because Pakistan claimed that it could not be held responsible for the Pathan attack that had started hostilities. Nonetheless, Pakistan arranged for the withdrawal of Pathan fighters in 1949. There was also concern that irregular Azad Kashmir forces might undermine the cease-fire. Interestingly, it was the Pakistani delegation to truce subcommittee meetings that stressed the need for Pakistan to be able to ensure Azad Kashmir compliance. Fearful of being dragged back to war by the actions of irregular troops, Pakistan moved Azad forces away from the cease-fire line.[44] Pakistan also suggested reorganizing and retraining the Azad Kashmir army and placing it under the Pakistani General Officer Commanding. According to the Pakistan delegation, "These arrangements are necessary to ensure that the Azad Kashmir Forces can be relied upon to observe the truce agreement."[45] Later agreements did not include specific measures to control irregular forces because the problem was no longer one of involuntary defection but of deliberate use of irregular forces to attack the other side (used by Pakistan against India in 1965 and by India against Pakistan in 1971).[46]

In the volatile months just after the 1965 cease-fire a number of modest arms control provisions were implemented. In October, the chief officer of UNIPOM, one of the UN's two observer missions (see below), got both sides to agree to ban test firing within 10,000 yards of the front lines.[47] In December, India and Pakistan agreed to limit air activity, banning light aircraft from within 1,600 meters of the lines of control, and high-performance aircraft from within 10,000 meters. They also agreed to issue no-firing orders to all formations as a way to curb the frequent and often serious violations and incidents along the cease-fire line in the months after the official cease-fire.[48] The UN put special effort into arranging these ad hoc arms control measures in response to the very precarious cease-fire. While guarded about agreeing to measures that would undermine

[44] Pakistan itself argued that "Azad Kashmir forces should be relieved in the forward areas by Pakistan regular forces and concentrated in the rear areas behind a minimum screen of regular Pakistan troops on the existing cease-fire line [because it is] better in the early stages at least of the truce period to have regular troops opposite each other in the forward areas." Statement by the Pakistan Delegation at the Meeting of the Truce Subcommittee held at Delhi March 9, 1949, UN document S/AC.12/TC.1, 1949, reprinted as Annex 10 in UNCIP 1949, 212.

[45] UNCIP 1949, 213.

[46] India insisted on the right to retaliate against Pakistan for guerrilla infiltrations after the second Kashmir war. See the foreign minister's speech to Parliament, quoted in Brines 1968, 406.

[47] UN document S/6710/Add. 6, 1965, 1.

[48] UN documents S/6710/Add. 14, 1965, 1; and S/6710/Add. 15, 1966, 1.

their ability to retaliate if under attack, the military commanders were also interested in keeping incidents under control. From the secretary-general's reports between the cease-fire in September and the Tashkent Declaration in January, it is clear that these arms control measures were put in place because the risk of renewed fighting was so high.[49] In contrast, in 1971 when peace appeared more stable, the cease-fire contained no provisions for arms control.

India and Pakistan also moved to formalize their cease-fire agreements in order to stabilize shaky cease-fires. The negotiation and signing of a formal agreement after a cease-fire was already in place may in some cases reflect the fact that states see this as the normal procedure—it is simply what states are supposed to do after they fight. However, at least in 1965 the conclusion of a formal agreement was explicitly a response to the danger of renewed warfare. Indian prime minister Lal Bahadur Shastri explained the importance of his meeting with Pakistan's Ayub Khan in Tashkent by saying the meetings were held "in order to see that there is no escalation of conflict between India and Pakistan. If there had been no agreement here, tension would have become more acute and it would have led to further conflagration."[50] Given domestic opposition to the Tashkent negotiations, their successful conclusion constituted a costly signal from the two leaders of their commitment to peace.

The United Nations also responded to variations in the prospects for peace in its provision of monitors. The United Nations Military Observer Group in India and Pakistan (UNMOGIP) was deployed in January 1949 "with the object of ensuring that the conditions of the truce are adhered to."[51] The number of military observers fluctuated between 35 and 67, "according to need."[52] The militaries of both sides cooperated extremely well with UNMOGIP in this period, granting free access to the cease-fire line and providing UNMOGIP with regular reports on classified military information. According to Wainhouse, "it seems clear that the military wished an effective cease-fire," and empowered UNMOGIP accordingly. The cordial relations between the Indian and Pakistani military authorities and the Chief Military Observer stood in contrast to the often tense relations at the negotiating table.[53]

When war broke out in 1965 the UN Security Council authorized a strengthening of UNMOGIP, from 45 just before the war to 102. Moreover, because the second war spilled out of Kashmir into India and Paki-

---

[49] UN document S/6710 and addenda, 1965–66.

[50] Quoted in Brines 1968, 405.

[51] Letter from UNCIP member Josef Korbel to Zafrullah Khan, August 27, 1948, reprinted in UNCIP 1949.

[52] UN 1996, 136.

[53] Wainhouse 1966, 370–71.

stan proper, the UN set up a separate mission to observe the cease-fire along the international border. The United Nations India-Pakistan Observation Mission (UNIPOM) was a temporary mission, consisting of 90 monitors; it was withdrawn in March 1966 once things had quieted down after the Tashkent Declaration's restoration of the status quo ante. UNMOGIP numbers were also reduced back to 45 after the tension subsided. The strengthening of the original monitoring mission and the addition of another was a direct response to the greater need for observers along a very tense 1,500-mile cease-fire line, as the functionalist argument would predict. The secretary-general's reports indicate a clear need for even more observers, but apparently France and Russia both objected to any marked increase in the UN's supervisory power.[54]

In the days preceding the outbreak of the 1971 war, Pakistan proposed a number of measures, including UN monitoring in East Pakistan, to try to prevent war. Pakistan evidently hoped that it could expose Indian aggression. However, the Security Council would not authorize observers for East Pakistan.[55] Once the war ended, there was no move to strengthen the UN's monitoring role in the area, and the operation of UNMOGIP has been undermined by Indian noncooperation since 1972.[56] India's opposition to involvement by outsiders in its dispute with Pakistan has prevented effective monitoring of the cease-fire, and UNMOGIP has been inactive for decades.[57] In general, the supply of UN observers has been largely demand driven: monitoring was beefed up in response to greater need. Moreover, while India's more recent opposition was political, it emerged when the prospects for peace were best, not when they were worst, as the counterargument would contend.

The India-Pakistan case suggests that there were a few mechanisms that could not be implemented because of the hostility between these states, as the counterargument would predict. However, some of the limits to supply were the result of exogenous factors—whether a measure had yet been developed, or the ideology and sensitivity about sovereignty of newly independent states. There is also ample evidence that those measures that were implemented were put in place in response to perceived threats to

---

[54] Brines 1968, 373.

[55] UN document S/10410 1971, 7, 14.

[56] India claimed that the 1971 war made the 1949 cease-fire line obsolete, and that the UN therefore no longer had standing in the dispute and UNMOGIP's mandate had lapsed. In January 1972, India stopped reporting complaints of cease-fire violations to the UN, though Pakistan continues to do so. UNMOGIP is still present in Kashmir, and India continues to provide accommodation and facilities but has restricted UNMOGIP's activities. UN 1996, 142.

[57] In the crisis over Kashmiri separatists infiltrating across the line of control in 2002 there were renewed calls for impartial monitoring.

the peace. Furthermore, a within-case comparison indicates clearly that India and Pakistan implemented stronger agreements when peace was most precarious, not when peace was most likely to last in any case.

Israel and Syria

The relationship between the baseline prospects for peace and the agreements concluded between Israel and Syria suggests a similar pattern. There have certainly been supply problems between these bitter enemies, but despite their mutual hatred, Israel and Syria have managed to implement a number of measures to offset the danger of war, and they have been most likely to do this when war seemed most likely.

There have been a series of cease-fires in the repeated wars between Israel and Syria since 1948, as well as one tacit agreement to avoid war before it began. In 1948, during the First Palestine War, Israel and the Arab states ceased fire on July 18, in accordance with UN Security Council Resolution 54 (1948). Fighting flared up again in October. Israel and Syria agreed to another cease-fire in April 1949, and signed a formal armistice agreement on July 20, 1949.[58] The Six-Day War ended for Israel and Syria on June 10, 1967, but no agreement was ever signed. The cease-fire ending the 1973 war was followed up by an agreement on disengagement signed May 31, 1974.[59] Israel and Syria reached a tacit preventive "Red Lines Agreement" to avert war in 1976 when Syria first intervened in Lebanon's civil war. After Israel's intervention in Lebanon, a cease-fire on June 11, 1982, halted most of the fighting between Israel and Syria in the Biqa' Valley in Lebanon, but the siege of Beirut ended only when Philip Habib arranged an agreement on the evacuation of Syrian and PLO forces from the city in August.

As in the India-Pakistan case, comparison across these cease-fires suggests that the strength of agreement corresponded to need. The July 1948 cease-fire was imposed by the UN when neither belligerent thought the war was fully over. It was a relatively weak agreement, containing no withdrawal of forces or demilitarized buffer zones, though it did contain a monitoring contingent (the UN Truce Supervision Organization or UNTSO). In 1949, one cease-fire had already failed, and while the war was now considered over, the threat of another round remained. Despite Syria's refusal to recognize the state of Israel, the belligerents signed a formal armistice agreement, demilitarized the contested areas between

---

[58] Separate but nearly identical cease-fire and armistice agreements were reached between Israel and each of the other Arab states.

[59] UN document S/11302/Add. 1, 1974.

them, and set up a forum for dispute resolution (the Israel-Syria Military Armistice Commission or ISMAC).

In 1967, in contrast, the immediate prospects for peace were fairly good. The dramatic and decisive defeat of the Arab armies left no threat of war in the immediate future. While this threat was soon to rise with Egypt's and Syria's military capabilities, at the time of the cease-fire there was little reason for Israel to withdraw its forces from or to demilitarize areas taken in the war, to allow UN peacekeepers or new monitors, or to revive the defunct procedures of ISMAC. Nor was a humiliated Syria in any mood to do anything that might imply recognition of Israel or to accommodate encroachment on its sovereignty. The Six-Day War thus ended with no document, not even a note spelling out the terms of the cease-fire, no withdrawal and no demilitarized zones. The monitors already there stayed on, but there was no possibility of an armed peacekeeping force, and ISMAC was rendered moot.

When the Yom Kippur War drew to a close, there was widespread feeling that another round of fighting would break out quickly if nothing were done to prevent it.[60] Syria had accepted a cease-fire only reluctantly after Egypt did so on its own, and Syria and Israel continued to wage a limited "war of attrition" along the cease-fire line during disengagement negotiations.[61] However, Israel and Syria reached a formal and specific accord, set up a demilitarized buffer along the full length of the cease-fire line, allowed a peacekeeping force, and limited military deployments so as to constrain their ability to attack each other. It is clear from the record that fear of renewed warfare is what made all this possible.

When Syria intervened in Lebanon in 1976, the threat of war with Israel was very high, but these two bitter enemies reached a tacit understanding in an effort to reduce the possibility of hostilities. The 1976 Red Lines Agreement was weak relative to many cease-fire agreements, but it was a preventive measure before war broke out, not an agreement to end hostilities. It was not politically feasible for either President Asad or Prime Minister Rabin to conclude a public or formal agreement. Public opinion at home would not have supported such collusion with the enemy, and internationally it would have appeared to be division of Lebanon into spheres of influence.[62] But given their history, even a tacit agreement between Israel and Syria to protect each other's interests and keep their forces apart is remarkable. The cease-fire in the Biqa' Valley in June 1982 was imposed by the United States and did not include explicit mechanisms to try to maintain peace. But the arrangement to allow the militarily risky evacua-

---

[60] See, for example, Kissinger 1982, 1038; UN 1996, 73.
[61] Ma'oz 1995, 132–33.
[62] Schiff 1984, 100.

tion of forces from Beirut was more robust; it was spelled out in greater detail and included a credible multinational peacekeeping force to ensure compliance. In short, Israel and Syria concluded their strongest agreements when observers at the time thought peace was most precarious (after the first war and the Yom Kippur War), and signed no agreement at all when renewed war seemed least likely (after the decisive Israeli victory in 1967).

This is not to say that these bitter enemies had an easy time implementing measures to maintain peace. No analysis of this case would lead to that conclusion. Supply problems were severe. This is especially clear on the issue of troop withdrawals. Given the incompatible territorial claims of Israel and Syria, the issue of withdrawing forces in the aftermath of war has been understandably contentious. As part of the armistice agreement in 1949, Syria removed its troops from land given to Israel under the UN partition plan. These areas were demilitarized (see map in chapter 2). The UN pushed for withdrawal back to the lines before the October resumption of hostilities, but Israel refused to withdraw from captured territory.[63] UN Security Council Resolution 242 (1967) calls for withdrawal from territories occupied in the Six-Day War in exchange for a political peace settlement; but this remains the heart of the political stalemate.[64]

Relinquishing territory is charged politically and has obvious distributional consequences. Israel and Syria were thus unable to achieve substantial withdrawals in 1948–49 or 1967. In 1973, however, instability along the cease-fire line and the high risk of renewed warfare led Israel and Syria, finally, to negotiate a disengagement agreement. Israel moved back to the status quo ante (the 1967 line) and gave up a small sliver of territory beyond the previous line.[65] The withdrawal agreement was anything but uncontroversial. The territory in question was deeply contested and Israel and Syria bargained hard over every meter, but the mutual threat of another round of fighting if no agreement was reached yielded a settlement.[66]

Efforts to specify agreements were also sometimes prevented by tension between Israel and Syria. For example, some provisions in the 1949 agreement, especially on the issue of civil administration within the demilitarized areas, were left blurry for the sake of reaching agreement, and demarcation of the cease-fire line was prevented by clashes in the mid-

---

[63] Bailey 1990, 49. Pelcovits 1993, 37, argues that while a retreat from the armistice lines and a solution to the refugee problem would have enabled a political settlement, Israel's security fears were too great to allow this.

[64] The UN generally tries to link cease-fires to withdrawal of forces to the status quo ante. Israel undertook considerable diplomatic effort to prevent this linkage in 1967. Bailey 1990, 231.

[65] Agreement on Disengagement between Israeli and Syrian Forces, May 31, 1974.

[66] Kissinger 1982, chap. 13.

1960s.[67] Dispute resolution procedures were also stymied by the conflict. The ISMAC procedures put in place in 1949 when political settlement seemed feasible later atrophied in an atmosphere of recrimination and repeated disputes. Israel objected to the body's competency to rule on civilian engineering projects in the demilitarized areas and by the late 1950s ceased participating in ISMAC except in "emergency and extraordinary" meetings when tensions along the armistice line were particularly acute.[68] At a more fundamental level, Syria's refusal to recognize the state of Israel made all negotiations and any formal or public agreement difficult.[69]

The supply of peacekeeping was constrained by sensitivities over sovereignty, as in South Asia, and by Israel's antipathy toward the UN. The practice of peacekeeping was developed to separate Israeli and Egyptian forces in the Sinai in 1956. However, Israel never allowed the UN Emergency Force (UNEF) on its own soil.[70] As tensions rose in late 1966, the United States considered a force similar to UNEF along the Israeli-Syrian and Israeli-Jordanian armistice lines, but in the face of Israeli opposition and concerns about UN budgets, the United States dropped the idea.[71] Peacekeeping forces were not considered in the aftermath of the 1967 war, presumably because as the victor, Israel would have none of it. In 1974, however, when Israel was negotiating withdrawal from its forward lines in Syrian territory, its opposition to UN peacekeeping disappeared. Now it wanted a strong UN contingent of forces, and it was Syria expressing concerns about sovereignty. Israel pushed for a force of at least 3,000 UN troops in the disengagement area, while Syria favored only a few hundred inspectors and wanted them to have a nonmilitary character; they settled on 1,250 UN troops. Because the symbolism of the sovereignty issue was important in the domestic politics of both sides, even the name of the operation was an issue. The compromise was to include both "observer" and "force" in the mission's title, hence the UN Disen-

[67] However, demarcation of Jewish and Arab cultivation areas took place under the 1949 armistice regime in direct response to violent incidents among farmers. Bar-Yaacov 1967, 56–57; Kinsolving 1967, 20.

[68] Bailey 1990, 189; Bull 1976, 51; Khouri 1985, 238; Kinsolving 1967, 22, 85; Pelcovits 1993, chap. 3, 164, 204–6. After the Six-Day War, ISMAC ceased to operate altogether. Kissinger's account of the negotiations after the Yom Kippur War makes no mention of dispute resolution. Kissinger 1982, chap. 23. It is unclear whether it was ruled out because of Israel's unfavorable experience with it after 1949, whether it was not considered necessary, or was not even considered.

[69] Israel's reluctance to legitimize or give any credibility to the PLO also affected negotiations in Lebanon. Thakur 1987.

[70] Egypt was also sensitive to UNEF's infringement on its sovereignty. One of Nasser's motives for requesting UNEF's withdrawal just before the 1967 war was the criticism he faced for hiding behind UN protection. Khouri 1985, 245.

[71] Khouri 1985, 237.

gagement Observer Force (UNDOF).[72] The evacuation of Syrian and PLO forces from besieged Beirut also required the presence of peacekeeping forces. While the UN had a force in Lebanon already, its credibility had been strained by continued fighting, so a non-UN force was created. The multinational force (MNF I) consisted of approximately 2,600 troops from France, Italy, and the United States.[73]

Provision of external guarantees of the peace was also affected by Israel's relationship with the UN, and more importantly by the Cold War. Because of its history and its strategic location, the Middle East conflict has been a concern of the international community and the great powers from the beginning. Indeed, the first cease-fires in the Palestine War were to be enforced not through reciprocity but by the United Nations. The international community was to deal with aggressors by applying unspecified sanctions under Article 40 of the Charter.[74] The 1949 armistice included no explicit guarantees of the peace by third parties, though Bernadotte had believed these would be necessary to allay both sides' fears.[75] As Israel became increasingly wary of the UN and votes against it in the General Assembly,[76] and as Cold War rivalries hamstrung the international organization, the role of peacemaker and guarantor of the peace fell increasingly to the superpowers. The protection offered to Israel and Syria by the United States and the Soviet Union, respectively, provided assurance, not of peace but of safety from complete defeat for either side. Sometimes the United States and the Soviet Union acted to restrain Israel and Syria when the threat of war got too high, but often the response of the superpowers to aggressive moves was muted.[77] Still, the superpowers'

[72] Kissinger 1982, 1044, 1094. There had been talk of U.S. and Soviet forces being sent to observe and enforce the cease-fire, but because the United States objected vehemently to the introduction of Soviet forces in the Middle East, it pushed instead for an enlarged UN mission. Bailey 1990, 330–32.

[73] Mackinlay 1989, 76. Israel originally suggested a non-UN force in June 1982, then backed away from the idea for fear that should peacekeeping prove unreliable, Israel would be faced with the unappealing prospect of unilateral action against U.S. (rather than UN) forces. Thakur 1987, 35. In the end though, the credibility of U.S. forces was necessary to secure agreement.

[74] The UN cease-fires explicitly prohibited reciprocal action in response to violations. Not surprisingly, neither side abided by this notion of enforcement, nor were sanctions ever applied.

[75] The UN staked its "honour and effectiveness" on the workings of the armistice regime. Bailey 1990, 42.

[76] For an analysis of the deteriorating relationship between Israel and the UN after 1949, see Pelcovits 1993, 19. See also Bar-Yaacov 1967, 57.

[77] For examples of both see Bailey 1990, 227; Khouri 1985, 254, 258–59; and Ma'oz 1995, 100–101. The United States was particularly reluctant to assess blame after the 1967 war. Bailey 1990, 247.

desire to avoid being dragged into war over the Middle East helped to ensure that efforts would be taken to prevent escalation.

In the 1974 disengagement agreement, the United States provided assurances on several points that Israel and Syria were unable to declare publicly for political reasons.[78] And through its role as mediator in Lebanon, the United States was able to pressure Israel to cease fire in the Biqa' in 1982, and to arrange an end to the siege of Beirut. American participation in the peacekeeping force in Beirut also implied a U.S. guarantee of the withdrawal arrangements, though the United States vowed to leave if the plan collapsed.[79]

It is clear from this description of the agreements Israel and Syria implemented that the logic of supply was often at work: in many instances it was impossible or very difficult for the adversaries to put in place strong mechanisms to maintain peace. Some of the reluctance to institute stronger measures was due to Israeli and Syrian sensitivity to anything that might infringe on their sovereignty. But some of the supply problem had to do with their conflict itself. Israel and Syria were wary of measures that would adversely affect the eventual political settlement of their conflict. They also balked at mechanisms that required concessions on symbolic issues important to their domestic populations. And they bargained especially hard over measures that had distributional consequences for their military contest or for the territorial dispute between them.

These pressures limiting agreements were more or less constant, however, and Israel and Syria were more likely to overcome these obstacles when the threat of renewed warfare was highest. In other words, the logic of supply was operating throughout this case, but when the risk of war was particularly high, it was offset by the logic of need.

Syria's refusal to recognize Israel was an obstacle throughout, yet the two signed a formal agreement in 1949 and again in 1974.[80] Withdrawal of forces in 1974 was no more politically or militarily palatable than previously, but took place nonetheless. Arms control provisions in 1974 were also very sensitive, for obvious military reasons, but also politically because they limited Syrian forces very near Damascus, raising prickly sovereignty issues. However, Israel and Syria reached agreements to keep heavy

---

[78] These included Israel's agreement not to position weapons on the crests of hills where they could reach Quneitra, and Syria's assurance that it would prevent Palestinian raids from the Golan, something it was already doing but could never admit to publicly. Kissinger 1982, 1088, 1104.

[79] Thakur 1987.

[80] Syria had pushed at first for the 1949 armistice to be signed on behalf of the armed forces, not the respective governments. Azcarate 1966, 119; Pelcovits 1993, 43. That it was signed by the two governments was significant politically, and gave it greater legal force. See Kissinger 1982, 1074, on the perceived need for a bilateral agreement in 1974.

artillery out of range of the opponent.[81] Israel and Syria also tacitly agreed to keep their forces away from each other in Lebanon when the danger of war was high in 1976, and again in the mid 1980s.[82]

Likewise, Israel and Syria established demilitarized zones in response to friction and the danger of clashes between their forces. In 1949, they demilitarized the area between the cease-fire line and the international border, though this was in part a way to skirt the issue of whose land it was.[83] In 1967, when the danger of war was much lower, no DMZ was established. General Odd Bull, the UN truce supervisor at the time, had hoped for a two-kilometer buffer zone between the Israeli and Syrian lines, "but in this we were not successful."[84] The 1974 agreement to separate forces and create a demilitarized zone is the clearest example of belligerents instituting measures in response to need. The effort to draft such an agreement was a direct response to the instability along the cease-fire line in the immediate aftermath of the war. Both the parties and the mediator were operating on the assumption that failure to reach a disengagement agreement would lead quickly to the resumption of hostilities.[85]

As in Kashmir, the supply of international monitors fluctuated according to perceived need. There were 572 UNTSO monitors deployed at the time of the 1949 cease-fire, but their numbers were reduced when the armistice agreements were signed and were kept low in the first few years when the armistice was working well.[86] The operation's size has fluctuated between about 30 and 140 observers in the years since, depending on need. UNTSO is still present in the Middle East, but since 1967, Israeli noncooperation with its investigations has rendered it ineffective.[87] However, monitoring between Israel and Syria was taken up by UNDOF after the Yom Kippur War.

Overall, then, we see that the bitter adversarial relationship between Israel and Syria has limited the strength of the agreements they could conclude, as the realist counterargument would contend. But Israel and

[81] Kissinger 1982, 1092, 1099.

[82] Evron 1987, 170–74; Pelcovits 1984, 64.

[83] Azcarate 1966, 117; Bailey 1990, 66; Bar-Yaacov 1967, 39–41, 49, 53; Kinsolving 1967, 35–36.

[84] He does not elaborate why, but presumably neither side was willing to yield any territory. Bull 1976, 123. See also Bailey 1990, 273–74.

[85] While a larger disengagement zone would have been even better, there was not enough space between locations with domestic political salience (for example, Israeli settlements and the Syrian town of Quneitra) to create a wider buffer. The demilitarized zone is three to six kilometers across and is flanked by staged limited forces zones to further increase the physical buffer between the two sides. Kissinger 1982, esp. 1099; UN 1996, 73.

[86] The UN also pushed to have a patrol boat on Lake Tiberias (Galilee) to reduce fishing incidents and clashes involving Israel's patrol boats, but Israel refused on sovereignty grounds. Bailey 1990, 71; Bull 1976, 45; Khouri 1985, 196; Kinsolving 1967, 24.

[87] Khouri 1985, 275–76.

Syria were also able to overcome significant differences of opinion, as well as military and political obstacles, to put in place mechanisms that might enhance the durability of peace. And they were most likely to do so when the prospects for peace were otherwise most dim. That Israel and Syria implemented the strongest agreements when peace was most precarious supports the functionalist hypothesis.

CONCLUSION

The central argument of this study is that cease-fire agreements can influence the durability of peace. The counterargument to this theory is that agreements are epiphenomenal—belligerents can only achieve strong cease-fire agreements in those situations where the agreements are irrelevant because peace would last in any case. This counterargument does not hold up empirically. In the quantitative analysis we see some support for the null hypothesis that the two competing dynamics cancel each other out or that agreements are exogenous to the baseline prospects for peace. But the large-N analysis also indicates clearly that to the extent there is a systematic relationship, it runs directly against the counterargument that agreements are epiphenomenal. Despite tests biased away from the functionalist argument and in favor of the realist hypothesis, we see much more support for the former than the latter. Stronger agreements are a functional response to more precarious peace.

The case studies suggest a slightly more nuanced relationship between the dynamics of supply and demand. Factors other than the baseline prospects for peace sometimes affect the content of agreements. The development of new peace-maintaining practices shapes the options available over time—peacekeepers can only be deployed once peacekeeping has been invented as a practice.[88] Concerns about sovereignty also shape agreements in a way that is often exogenous to the prospects for peace. Recently independent states are particularly reluctant to allow outsiders an important role that might infringe on their newfound independence. These factors help explain why states do not always "get it right" when they design agreements. They do not always draft exactly the measures needed to maintain peace.

As in the quantitative analysis, however, to the extent that agreements are endogenous to the baseline prospects for peace, we find much more

---

[88] For an account of the historical evolution of arms control, see Croft 1996, chap. 1. Another example of the evolution of peace practices has taken place recently in civil war settlements with the creation of truth and reconciliation commissions and war crimes trials. Holding anyone accountable for crimes committed during internal conflicts was rare before the mid-1990s but has now become something of a standard. Tepperman 2002.

support for the functionalist hypothesis than for the realist counterargument. Obstacles to supply do indeed exist among deadly enemies, however even such staunch adversaries as India and Pakistan, and Israel and Syria manage to implement measures to help stabilize peace. And they are most likely to do so when peace is otherwise most fragile. In both cases when peace was most likely to last (Israel and Syria in 1967 and India and Pakistan in 1971), only a week agreement, or no agreement at all, was put in place, while these adversaries overcame their reluctance to cooperate and drafted stronger agreements when the danger of renewed warfare was highest.

Stronger mechanisms are implemented not when peace would be easy to maintain, but in the hardest cases. Despite tests and case selection that should favor the realist counterargument, we see evidence that belligerents anticipate the obstacles to maintaining peace and act to overcome them. Measures to alter incentives, reduce uncertainty, and prevent accidents are at least in part a functional response to otherwise fragile peace, implemented because they are expected to help maintain peace. Agreements are functional, not epiphenomenal. It remains to be seen, however, empirically just how effective these agreements are.

CHAPTER FIVE

AGREEMENTS AND THE DURABILITY OF PEACE

ARE CEASE-FIRE AGREEMENTS just "scraps of paper" with no ability to affect the behavior of states, or do stronger agreements lead to more stable peace? This chapter presents evidence that cease-fire agreements matter in the construction of durable peace. They are an effective way to enhance the chances of lasting peace; strong agreements help prevent the resumption of war.

The theory outlined in chapter 1 suggested that such mechanisms as the withdrawal of forces, demilitarized zones, dispute-resolution procedures, and peacekeeping improve the prospects for lasting peace by making it more costly to reinitiate conflict, reducing uncertainty about compliance, and preventing accidents from spiraling out of control. I use the term *agreement strength* to refer to the number and extent of these measures implemented as part of a cease-fire. By this definition, the Iranian-brokered cease-fire between Armenia and Azerbaijan in 1992 was very weak. It contained no efforts to separate troops, to bring in outsiders as peacekeepers or guarantors of the peace, to set up measures to deal with disputes, or to prevent rogue groups from igniting another war. The cease-fire that ended the Falklands War contained no mechanisms to keep peace. At the other end of the spectrum, both the armistice agreement that ended the Korean War in 1953 and the agreements reached after the Yom Kippur War were much stronger, involving demilitarized zones, international peacekeepers, and joint commissions to implement the cease-fire and resolve disputes as they arose. Falling somewhere in between are agreements such as those reached after the Sino-Indian War (with a demilitarized zone, but no peacekeeping) and the first Kashmir war (with a small contingent of UN monitors and only a narrow area separating forces). The main hypothesis of this study is that stronger agreements foster more durable peace than weaker ones, all else being equal. To test this hypothesis, the present chapter examines the cease-fires of the last half century first qualitatively, then quantitatively.

I. A QUALITATIVE SURVEY OF AGREEMENTS AND THE DURABILITY OF PEACE

Because agreements are related to the baseline prospects for peace, we cannot tell whether strong agreements improve the chances for peace simply by looking at agreement strength and durability alone. Just as more police are assigned to beats where crime is more likely, we have seen that strong agreements are more likely to be implemented when peace is more difficult to keep. And just as it would be unfair to judge the effectiveness of policing by simply comparing crime rates in heavily policed neighborhoods with those in less patrolled areas, we would get a skewed view of how cease-fire agreements work if we did not take the baseline prospects for peace into account. The quantitative evaluation presented below controls for the degree of difficulty of maintaining peace by including the situational factors discussed in chapter 3 in multivariate hazard analysis. To get a qualitative sense of whether stronger agreements are better for peace, we need to compare cases of similar baseline prospects.

Table 5.1 groups cases into five levels of difficulty, based on the results of the duration analysis used in chapter 3. To recap briefly, in that analysis we found five aspects of the situation at the time of the cease-fire to be important determinants of the prospects for peace: the decisiveness of victory, the cost of the war, the belligerents' history of conflict, whether they are neighbors, and whether the war threatened one side's existence as a state.[1] Wars that end without a clear victor, with relatively few casualties, between neighbors with a highly contentious shared history, in which one or both sides' existence was at stake are at the most difficult end of the spectrum. The first cease-fire in the 1948 Arab-Israeli war is a good example of such a doomed peace. At the opposite end is the United States and Iraq in the Gulf War: a very decisive victory with high casualties overall, among noncontiguous states with relatively little prior conflict. Other cases range between these extremes based on their combination of these situational variables. Because it relies on quantitative measures, the ranking in table 5.1 is somewhat crude; for example, it distinguishes between ties and victories but not among gradations of decisiveness. But it does allow a single objective measure of the baseline prospects for peace, so that we can examine roughly commensurate cases.

While there are some exceptions to the rule, table 5.1 indicates that among comparable cases, stronger agreements tend to last longer than weaker ones.[2] Not surprisingly, all of the cease-fires in the hardest category (very difficult) eventually fail. But with one exception those with stronger agreements tend to last longer than others in this ill-fated group. The very weak agreement between Armenia and Azerbaijan in 1992 im-

---

[1] Table 5.1 ranks cases by the predicted duration of peace based on these five variables in a Weibull regression.

[2] The variation in strength of agreement within each category underlines the point that the baseline prospects for peace do not perfectly determine agreement strength. While the previous chapter showed a general tendency for stronger agreements in harder cases, agreement strength is to some extent exogenous to the difficulty of the case.

TABLE 5.1
Agreements and the Durability of Peace, by Difficulty Category

Baseline Difficulty of Maintaining Peace	War	Strength of Agreement	Fight Again?	Peace (months)
Very Difficult	Palestine 1 (all 5 cases) 1948	Weak	Yes	3
	Six-Day (Israel-Syria) 1967	Very weak	Yes	76
	Azeri-Armenian 1 1992	Very weak	Yes	0.7
	Kashmir 1 1949	Moderate	Yes	199
	Palestine 2 (Israel-Lebanon) 1949	Moderate	Yes	402
	Kashmir 2 1965	Moderate	Yes	74
	Palestine 2 (Israel–Jordan & Syria) 1949	Moderate	Yes	223
Difficult	Turco-Cypriot 1 1974	Weak	Yes	0.5
	Palestine 2 (Israel-Egypt) 1949	Moderate	Yes	94
	Football (El Salvador-Honduras) 1969	Moderate	No	
	Football (El Salvador-Honduras) (F) 1980	Strong	No	
	Lebanon (Israel-Syria) 1982	Weak	No	
	Six-Day (Israel-Egypt) 1967	Very weak	Yes	21
	Sino-Vietnamese 2 1987	None	No	
	Sino-Vietnamese 2 (F) 1993/1996	Very weak/weak	No	
	Korean (South Korea–North Korea) 1953	Strong	No	
Moderate	Sinai (U.K. & France–Egypt) 1956	Weak	No	
	Palestine 2 (Israel-Iraq) 1949	Moderate	Yes	299
	Six-Day (Israel-Jordan) 1967	Very weak	Yes	76
	Yom Kippur (Israel-Syria) 1973	Strong	Yes	103
	Israeli-Egyptian War of Attrition 1970	Very weak	Yes	38
	Sino-Vietnamese 1 1979	None	Yes	94
	Sinai (Israel-Egypt) 1956	Weak	Yes	127
	Turco-Cypriot 2 1974	Very weak	No	
	Yom Kippur (Israel-Egypt) 1973	Strong	No	
	Korean (South Korea–China) 1953	Strong	No	
Easy	Yom Kippur (Israel-Jordan) 1973	None	No	
	Yom Kippur (Israel-Jordan) (F) 1994	Strong	No	
	Sino-Indian 1962	Weak	No	
	Sino-Indian (F) 1996	Moderate	No	
	Bangladesh (India-Pakistan) 1971	Weak	Yes	329
	Gulf War (Kuwait-Iraq) 1991	Strong	No	
	Uganda-Tanzania 1979	None	No	
	Ethiopian-Somalian 1978	Very weak	No	
	Ethiopian-Somalian (F) 1988	Moderate	No	
	Falklands (U.K.-Argentina) 1982	None	No	
	Falklands (F) 1989	Weak	No	

Note: (F) = follow-up agreements reached after the initial cease-fire (listed if substantially different in strength).

TABLE 5.1 (cont'd)
Agreements and the Durability of Peace, by Difficulty Category

Baseline Difficulty of Maintaining Peace	War	Strength of Agreement	Fight Again?	Peace (months)
Very Easy	Russo-Hungarian 1956	None	No	
	Russo-Hungarian (F) 1957	Very weak	No	
	Azeri-Armenian 2 1994	Very weak	No	
	Uganda-Tanzania (Libya) 1979	None	No	
	Iran-Iraq 1988	Moderate	No	
	Vietnam (U.S.–North Vietnam) 1973	Strong	No	
	Korean (U.S.–China & North Korea) 1953	Strong	No	
	Ethiopian-Somalian (Cuba-Somalia) 1978	Very weak	No	
	Vietnam (North-South Vietnam) 1975	None	No	
	Gulf War (U.S. & Saudi Arabia–Iraq) 1991	Strong	Yes[a]	143

Note: (F) = follow-up agreements reached after the initial cease-fire (listed if substantially different in strength).
[a] Peace failed as this study went to press.

plemented virtually nothing in the way of measures to cement peace. It fell apart in less than a month. The cease-fire agreement in Palestine in July 1948 was also relatively weak. It was monitored by the UN, but was only tacitly agreed to by Israel and the Arab states. It was also quite vague and put in place nothing to increase the cost of restarting the war. Israel broke the cease-fire three months later.

The substantially stronger armistice agreements between Israel and Jordan, Lebanon, and Syria in 1949 and the agreements reached between India and Pakistan after their first two wars over Kashmir fared much better. A relatively long stretch of peace in the Middle East, almost 19 years, is attributable at least in part to the military armistice commission, defensive forces zones, and other measures spelled out in the formal armistice agreements in 1949. Both Kashmir wars ended with formal bilateral cease-fire accords, both entailed pulling troops back to create at least a narrow space between opposing forces along the cease-fire line, and both were monitored by UN peacekeeping missions. The first involved concrete action to prevent the Pathan tribesmen whose actions had started the war from starting another (by moving them behind regular Pakistani forces), and the second set up a joint commission of border personnel and military-to-military contacts to try to prevent and, if necessary, deal with minor cease-fire infractions. These efforts did not work indefinitely, but given the dire prospects for peace in South Asia, it is remarkable that war took as long as it did (about seventeen and six years, respectively) to resume.

The exceptional case in this category is the cease-fire between Israel and Syria in the Six-Day War in 1967. Peace lasted for over six years despite a very weak agreement. Our rather blunt dichotomous measure of military decisiveness means that the baseline difficulty of this case is probably overrated. Given the very lopsided military outcome, this cease-fire should probably be classified along with the Israeli-Jordanian or Israeli-Egyptian dyads as "moderately difficult" or "difficult" rather than "very difficult."[3] In the immediate aftermath of the war, the prospects for peace were relatively good, certainly much better than they had been in 1948 or 1949. The surprise here, to the world and especially to Israel, was that war came again as quickly as it did despite Israel's trouncing of its neighbors in 1967. Overall, then, within this category peace lasts longer when stronger agreements are in place.

In the second category in table 5.1 (difficult), the pattern is much the same, with stronger agreements leading to more durable peace. But again there is one exception: the second Sino-Vietnamese war. The long-standing border war between China and Vietnam quieted down over the course of 1987 with no public cease-fire agreement. Peace has lasted to date. Some reports have suggested that secret agreements were reached in 1988 and 1989, so perhaps the strength of this case has been coded too low.[4] But peace in this case probably had more to do with the waning of Cambodia's civil war than with the content of these alleged agreements. The antagonism between China and Vietnam was very much connected to their involvement in Cambodia, and as that conflict wound down, the interstate war also eased. In November 1991, after the Paris Peace Agreement on Cambodia, China and Vietnam reached a trade agreement and a provisional agreement on border issues. This was followed by another agreement in 1993 and a treaty settling the outstanding border disputes in December 1999.[5] The stability of peace between China and Vietnam between 1987 and the settling of the border dispute is not well explained by my argument. The stability of peace between Israel and Syria since their fight in Lebanon in 1982 is less problematic because the main cease-fire line between Israel and Syria in the Golan has the benefit of the very strong agreement implemented after the 1973 war (more on this case below).

[3] In the model used here, the Syrian case is predicted to be harder than these other dyads in part because the death toll on this front was lower than elsewhere. A model using total deaths for the war would group these dyads closer together.

[4] See Daniel Southerland, "Beijing, Hanoi Avoid Annual Hostilities: Truce Is Reported in Border Battles," *Washington Post*, January 22, 1988; and Andrew Higgins, "Hanoi and Peking End Stand-off with 'Back-Door' Talks," *Independent*, January 21, 1989.

[5] "Vietnam and China Sign Landmark Border Treaty," Agence France Presse, December 30, 1999.

The other cases in this category are consistent with my theory. Other than China and Vietnam in 1987, the only very weak agreement in this category of cases is the Israeli-Egypt cease-fire in 1967, which despite Israel's decisive victory, faltered less than two years later with the War of Attrition. The much stronger armistice agreement between Israel and Egypt in 1949 led to a much longer stretch without war. The first cease-fire in the Turco-Cypriot War was fairly weak and quickly failed. It was a formal agreement, and peacekeepers were present on the island, but they had deployed to deal only with the intercommunal conflict in Cyprus, not with an interstate war. The Geneva Declaration on which the cease-fire was based discussed the need for a buffer zone between forces and for arms reductions, but none of these measures was implemented before peace broke down two weeks into the cease-fire. Meanwhile, the strong agreements in this category have lasted. Despite ongoing animosity and tension, North and South Korea have not fought since 1953. While this is no doubt mostly due to mutual superpower deterrence, the very strong measures implemented as part of the armistice agreement—particularly the demilitarized zone, but also monitoring by neutral nations, a military armistice commission, joint observation by the belligerents themselves, and specific rules on announcing troop rotations—have helped to bolster peace in one of the most dangerous spots on the globe.

The history of the troubled peace between El Salvador and Honduras provides a better example (less overdetermined than Korea) of the effects of measures to keep peace. The Football War is so called because in the midst of serious provocations by both sides, World Cup elimination matches drew violently rowdy crowds in both countries, adding to the tensions that erupted in full-scale border fighting in July 1969.[6] A cease-fire reached on July 18 was initially rather weak. The OAS sent a small team of monitors, but the cease-fire contained little else in the way of efforts to maintain peace. The border remained tense, and fighting broke out in early 1970. A stronger agreement, the Pact of San José, was reached in June, creating a six-kilometer demilitarized "security zone" and restricting flights and naval patrols near this zone and in the Gulf of Fonseca. It also called for the disarming of "irregular civilian forces" and specified Guatemala, Nicaragua, and Costa Rica as guarantors of the agreement under the auspices of the OAS. Once these measures were in place, the border quieted down considerably and stayed calm until serious clashes erupted in 1976. OAS observers who had withdrawn earlier were redeployed, and an even stronger formal and bilateral agreement restored the cease-fire.

[6] The provocations included border crossings by Salvadoran army personnel and civilian vigilantes, and on Honduras's part, mass evictions of Salvadoran immigrants, with the press calling for Salvadorans to be "cleansed" from Honduran towns. Anderson 1981, 80–105.

The August 1976 Act of Managua entailed the withdrawal of troops and paramilitary forces and the demilitarization of all disputed border areas and a much more detailed system for disarming civilians in disputed regions. This agreement helped keep relations calm enough for shuttle diplomacy between the two countries to settle the border dispute. In October 1980 a peace treaty was signed setting up a commission to negotiate the border and mandating that the dispute be sent to the International Court of Justice (ICJ) if a bilateral agreement could not be reached. It was so submitted in 1986, and in 1992 the ICJ awarded approximately two-thirds of the disputed territory to Honduras, a decision that both sides accepted.

None of the fighting between El Salvador and Honduras after 1969 qualifies as a full-scale war, but in these lower-level clashes we can see clearly the effect of the two states' efforts to prevent the resumption of war. The initial relatively weak agreement was not effective and so was bolstered in 1970, restoring calm. Those measures weakened over time, particularly with the withdrawal of the observer mission, and serious fighting broke out again. But an even stronger agreement was then implemented that put an end to the skirmishes and eventually allowed a peace process to settle the territorial issue.

In the moderately difficult category in table 5.1 the same general pattern holds. A few weak agreements have lasted, notably after Turkey's unilateral partition of Cyprus and after France and Britain's embarrassment in the Sinai War. While in both of these cases the cease-fire agreements were relatively weak overall, both involved peacekeeping forces that deserve at least partial credit for helping solidify the peace. The UN force in Cyprus has been criticized for failing to foster a political solution to that conflict, but virtually all observers give it credit for preventing intercommunal bloodshed that would almost certainly set off a wider war. The UN Emergency Force (UNEF) in the Sinai in 1956 was the first armed international peacekeeping force and allowed the peaceful withdrawal of British, French, and Israeli forces. But when Egypt asked UNEF to leave in 1967, there was nothing it could do to prevent the Six-Day War (more on this case in chapter 6) and there was little else to maintain peace once the UN left.

The other wars in this category demonstrate that peace is more likely to last when strong agreements are in place. The first Sino-Vietnamese war ended with China's withdrawal to the border in 1979 but with no cease-fire agreement. Border clashes continued with particularly heavy fighting in 1983 and escalation back to full-scale war in the late 1980s. A stronger agreement might well have controlled these clashes and prevented a spiral to full-scale war. The agreement that ended the War of Attrition between Egypt and Israel in 1970 was also very weak. The cease-fire negotiated by U.S. Secretary of State William Rogers implemented no concrete mechanisms to separate forces, reestablish the long-defunct dispute-resolution procedures set up in 1949, or bring in new peacekeepers. There was little in it to alter incentives, provide reassurance, or prevent accidents. The two rivals slid back to war only a few years later. In contrast, the much stronger measures put in place between these same enemies after the Yom Kippur War have led to lasting peace. Egypt and Israel agreed to the staged withdrawal of forces and a large peacekeeping force within a few months of the war. A follow-up agreement in 1975 widened the disengagement zones and established a joint commission for dispute resolution and an early-warning verification system operated by the United States. In 1979 after Sadat's historic visit to Jerusalem and the Camp David peace process, Israel and Egypt signed a peace treaty with even stronger verification and arms control measures accompanying the formal end of their state of war.[7] While the agreement reached between Israel and Syria in 1973 did not prevent them from fighting in Lebanon in 1982, it has held in the Golan (more on this case below). The remaining three Middle East cases in this category fit the general pattern: the weakest agreement, between Israel-Jordan in 1967, fell apart most quickly; the stronger agreement with Egypt in 1956 lasted a bit longer; while the strongest, with Iraq in 1949, lasted the longest of the three.

The last two categories in table 5.1 tell us less about the effectiveness of strong agreements because almost none of these cases failed. Both the strong agreements and the weak ones last when maintaining peace is this easy. It is worth noting, however, that there are two very different kinds of cases in the "easy" and "very easy" categories: very decisive victories and very costly wars. Most of the weak agreements followed overwhelmingly lopsided military outcomes: the Soviet suppression of Hungary, North Vietnam's elimination of South Vietnam, India's dissection of Pakistan in 1971, Tanzania's ouster of Uganda's government, China's swift defeat of India, Britain's overpowering Argentina, and Armenia's occupation of Nagorno-Karabakh in 1994. After the very costly wars, however, belligerents have tended to implement strong agreements: the Korean armistice agreement, the Paris Peace Agreement between the United States and North Vietnam, and the cease-fire that ended the Iran-Iraq War. So there appear to be two routes to stable peace—overwhelming victory, or strong mechanisms to maintain peace after costly wars.[8]

---

[7] The UN peacekeeping force was withdrawn because of Soviet opposition to the peace treaty, but was replaced by a 2,500-strong multinational force. The Multinational Force and Observers (MFO) is led by the United States. Other currently participating states are Australia, Canada, Colombia, Fiji, France, Hungary, Italy, New Zealand, and Uruguay. <www.iaw.on.ca/~awoolley/mfo.html>.

[8] The Gulf War ended with both, but peace faltered with the American preventive war in 2003.

The one exception to this pattern is the war between Ethiopia and Somalia, which ended neither with an overwhelming victory, nor a strong agreement.[9] In response to a U.S. proposal, Somalia withdrew its troops from the disputed Ogaden region in March 1978. The cease-fire agreement was extremely weak, only a tacit agreement with no measures to prevent the resumption of war. While escalation to full-scale fighting was avoided, guerilla warfare continued along with raids by regular army personnel. The war had not really ended, only changed its form.[10] But in April 1988, the two rivals reached a much stronger agreement, withdrawing their forces 10–15 kilometers from the border, setting up a joint military committee to supervise the disengagement, promising to cease interference in each other's internal affairs (i.e., supporting rebel armies), and restoring diplomatic relations. The agreement was politically costly particularly for Somalia's Siad Barre. Ogadenis, the dominant clan in the Somali army, felt that Barre had renounced Somalia's claim to their homeland, and this contributed to his downfall in 1991.[11] The relatively strong agreement between Ethiopia and Somalia may thus have had the perverse effect of contributing to the civil war in Somalia that followed Barre's ouster, but was also fairly effective at keeping the two states from each other's throats.

In sum, in cases where it is difficult to maintain peace we can see that strong agreements improve stability. Among cases of similar baseline prospects, peace tends to be more durable the stronger the agreement in place. In the easiest cases, peace almost always lasts, because of either overwhelming victory or strong efforts to bolster peace. This qualitative survey of cases, then, suggests that the content of agreements does matter. Mechanisms implemented to improve the chances for peace are effective.

II. The Case Studies

India and Pakistan

Comparisons both among the India-Pakistan cease-fires and the Israeli-Syria truces also indicate that agreements affect stability. A very superficial glance at the cease-fires in South Asia would lead us to conclude that strong agreements are in fact detrimental to peace. The strongest agreement, the one reached after the second Kashmir war, failed most quickly, while the weakest, after the Bangladesh War, lasted longest. But superficial glances are misleading. As we saw in chapter 4, India and Pakistan implemented the strongest agreement after the second war in 1965,

---

[9] Ethiopia had the military upper hand, but not decisively so.
[10] Zartman 1989, 107.
[11] Makinda 1992, 27. See also Lefebvre 1991.

when peace was most precarious, and the weakest agreement after the 1971 war, when peace needed little help, at least initially. How then can we tell whether stronger agreements helped bolster the chances for peace? Direct evidence is hard to come by. It is difficult enough to know why war occurred when it did, even harder to know why it did not at other times. We can, however, get glimpses of the effect of stronger agreements by looking more closely at the course of the Indo-Pakistani conflict.

When the first war in Kashmir stopped on January 1, 1949, the initial cease-fire arrangements were not very strong. The fighting ended on the basis of each side's informal acceptance of a UN proposal. A small UN monitoring team arrived, establishing the core of the UNMOGIP, and a few other mechanisms were put in place relatively quickly. But it was not until the formal agreement reached at Karachi on July 27 that troops were pulled back slightly to create a separation zone between them, that Pakistan redeployed Azad Kashmir forces behind regular Pakistani troops, and that the cease-fire line was clearly demarcated. There were a number of incidents between Indian and Pakistani soldiers along the cease-fire line in the seven months leading up to the Karachi agreement. The observer teams acted along with military authorities on both sides to keep these from becoming more serious breaches of the cease-fire. But more tellingly, the number and seriousness of these incidents subsided markedly with the strengthening of the cease-fire mechanisms in July.[12]

Over the next decade or so, as India and Pakistan tried to negotiate a solution to the Kashmiri problem, conditions were a bit more stable, though not without risk of renewed warfare. According to Josef Korbel, "There were moments when the truce was in real danger," particularly when the negotiations were not going well, but these dangers "subsided again, thanks partly to the calming presence and the tireless work of [UN] observers."[13] As a former member of UNCIP, Korbel is perhaps a biased observer, but even the historian Russell Brines, a classical realist generally skeptical of the UN's role in South Asia, gives credit to the military agreements reached after the first Kashmir war and to the UN observers for eliminating military suspicions and reducing the possibility of surprise attack.[14]

When more than 10 years of negotiations did not yield a Kashmir settlement, Pakistan began to consider military options. In 1965, as skirmishes and shooting incidents escalated along the border, Pakistan tested the military waters in the Rann of Kutch. Meanwhile, infiltration into Indian-held Kashmir by *mujahedin* increased. In August, Pakistan instigated an attack by over a thousand guerillas crossing the cease-fire line from Pakistani-

---

[12] UNCIP 1949, see especially the Third Interim Report, UN document S/1196 1949.

[13] Korbel 1954, 162.

[14] Brines 1968, 239.

controlled Kashmir in the hope of triggering a revolt on the Indian side. India retaliated by crossing the cease-fire line to cut off the *mujahedin*. By September regular Pakistani and Indian forces were again at war.

The Karachi agreement, then, was not strong enough to stop Pakistan's deliberate instigation of war, but it did affect the way Pakistan carried it out. Rather than attack openly in violation of the cease-fire agreement, Pakistan provoked India into crossing the cease-fire line with regular forces, bringing international condemnation down on India rather than Pakistan.

In the immediate aftermath of this second Kashmir war, the effect of stronger agreement mechanisms is even clearer. India and Pakistan reached a cease-fire under strong diplomatic pressure. Once again, the initial cease-fire agreement was rather weak, consisting only of each side's acceptance of the brief UN resolution and the creation of a new peacekeeping force for the part of the cease-fire line not already monitored by UNMOGIP. The cease-fire line in Kashmir was extremely volatile in the first few months until a much stronger agreement was reached at Tashkent on January 10, 1966. There, Prime Minister Lal Bahadur Shastri and President Ayub Khan agreed to withdraw to the prewar lines[15] and to keep their forces at least two thousand yards apart, to establish a joint border commission and a hot line, and to abide by detailed rules for mine clearance.

The before and after pictures that emerge from reading the UN secretary-general's reports on Kashmir are dramatically different.[16] Between the cease-fire in September and the implementation of the Tashkent mechanisms in January, the documents are thick with reports of serious fighting, often with substantial casualties. Indian and Pakistani soldiers were within 30 yards of each other in some places, and both sides were trying to improve their positions by edging forward. The cease-fire was barely holding. In some places local arrangements were made to restore the cease-fire and separate troops, but skirmishes continued to break out. But in the UN reports filed after the strengthening of the cease-fire arrangements at Tashkent the cease-fire line is quiet.[17] Again, we see clear evidence that implementing peace mechanisms stabilized the cease-fire line.

The Simla Agreement reached after the Bangladesh War was quite weak. But in the immediate aftermath of India's thorough military victory, the risk of renewed warfare in South Asia was minimal and the cease-fire line was relatively calm, despite the lack of strong mechanisms to keep peace.

---

[15] When the fighting stopped, both sides held territory on the "wrong" side of the line.

[16] These reports are filed periodically to keep the Security Council apprised of UN peacekeeping missions. They are based on the observations and reports of UN monitors on the ground.

[17] UN documents S/6710 and Add. 1–17, 1965–66; and S/6719 and addenda, 1965–66.

Over time, however, Kashmir became increasingly unstable. From 1980 on there were clashes along the line of control. In 1984 and 1985 India and Pakistan fought on the Siachen Glacier, where the cease-fire line is not demarcated. Relations were particularly tense, and both sides mobilized for war during India's "Brass Tacks" military exercises, in 1986.[18]

The Kashmiri situation has meanwhile been complicated by the rise of a much stronger indigenous separatist movement and by both states' nuclear tests in May 1998. A number of confidence-building measures were reached in the 1990s, requiring advance notice of military exercises, among other things.[19] But the mechanisms set up to prevent war in Kashmir in 1949 and again in 1965 have all fallen into disuse. The dispute-resolution procedures are defunct, and the UN observer mission, while still in place, has been discredited by the intervening wars. India has pushed for the Kashmir issue to be dealt with bilaterally and no longer cooperates with UN investigations. While the nuclear threat might deter escalation to total war, neither it nor the pacifying effects of joint democracy have maintained peace. In the summer of 1999 India and Pakistan fought their fourth war in the Kargil region of Kashmir. A stronger agreement, particularly one with better monitoring or higher costs for the deliberate use of irregular forces, might have prevented this war.[20]

Over the course of the 50-year conflict between India and Pakistan we can see evidence that agreement mechanisms affect the durability of peace. In 1949 and especially in 1965 moves to strengthen cease-fire agreements clearly helped stabilize the cease-fire lines. The decisiveness of India's victory in 1971 kept peace for a time. But the weak arrangements in Kashmir have since allowed almost daily skirmishing, serious fighting in Siachen in the mid-1980s, and yet another war in 1999.

Israel and Syria

The relationship between the strength of agreements and the durability of peace is even easier to see in comparing the cease-fires reached between Israel and Syria. The weakest ones fell apart most quickly and the strongest ones lasted longest. That Israel and Syria generally implemented stronger measures when the prospects for peace were most dim makes this finding all the more significant.

The very first cease-fire between Israel and the Arab states was the intentionally temporary four-week truce that went into effect on June 11, 1948. While this agreement was not strong compared to cease-fire

---

[18] Wirsing 1994, 198.
[19] See Krepon and Sevak 1995.
[20] Ganguly 2001, 121–26.

agreements that are meant to last permanently, it was not insubstantial. Ninety-three Belgian, French, and American observers making up UNTSO deployed to monitor the cease-fire.[21] The truce agreement froze the number and position of troops.[22] And since the actions of irregular forces, particularly Jewish terrorist organizations, were a concern, the agreement held all sides responsible for violations coming from territory under their control, although it did nothing concrete to restrain such forces. It also demilitarized some areas of Jerusalem, although this was intended to provide safe havens for civilians, not to separate troops from one another.[23] Despite the fact that an attack in the days before this truce was to expire would have been militarily advantageous, both sides waited dutifully for midnight of the final day before resuming hostilities.[24] While this first agreement did not last long, and probably would not have prevented another eventual round of fighting even if it had not been explicitly temporary, it clearly affected the behavior of the belligerents.

A second relatively weak cease-fire was reached soon after. It was ordered by the United Nations in Security Council Resolution 54 (July 15, 1948) and went into effect on July 18. While this cease-fire was meant to keep the peace permanently, its mechanisms were not much stronger than the June 11 agreement; the only significant difference was that more UN monitors were deployed. The resulting pause in the fighting lasted only three months, ending with an Israeli offensive first into the Negev on October 15 and then into western Galilee. As this phase of the war wound down, Syria was the most reluctant Arab state to negotiate with Israel, but a cease-fire came into effect on April 13, 1949, and Israel and Syria signed a formal armistice agreement on July 20.

The Israeli-Syrian armistice agreement of 1949 set up what was initially a fairly strong cease-fire arrangement. It established demilitarized zones in the contested areas between the cease-fire line and the international border between Syria and Israel[25] and limited forces in areas on either side of the line. UNTSO observers continued to monitor the cease-fire and to investigate allegations of cease-fire violations. The agreement set up a military

---

[21] UNTSO was the first UN mission to monitor a cease-fire.

[22] It also called for an arms embargo, though this was not complied with; Czechoslovakia sold arms to both sides. Shimon Peres recalled later that Israel procured some arms by setting up a film company in England as a front. They filmed planes taking off that flew on to Israel. Bailey 1990, 27.

[23] Bailey 1990, 17.

[24] Bailey 1990, 33. Their restraint until the end belies game theory's implication that a short and finite agreement should unravel well before the final period because reciprocity relies on the promise of future rewards and the threat of future retaliation.

[25] Technically the international border between Syria and what had been the British mandate of Palestine.

armistice commission (ISMAC) consisting of two Israelis, two Syrians, and a UN representative as chair. The agreement was fairly specific in its terms compared to many cease-fires, but a particular combination of ambiguity and rigidity would serve to undermine the entire armistice regime.

The demilitarization of contested territory was a compromise meant to sidestep the issue of borders, but the agreement was ambiguous on sovereignty over these areas. Israel claimed sovereign rights to conduct engineering projects, mostly to irrigate farmland, and Syria contested this right. In the first years after the war there were numerous incidents, sometimes violent ones, between Arab farmers and fishermen and Israeli settlers. These were contained and managed by the UN observers and ISMAC. Disputes over Israel's right to drain marshes, build bridges, and divert waters within the demilitarized areas proved still more contentious.[26] Israel refused to attend ISMAC meetings that dealt with these issues, as discussing them would mean accepting that its rights were open to question. By the mid-1950s the formal system of dispute resolution was largely hamstrung, and there was no flexibility in the armistice agreement to adopt new procedures. Since UNTSO investigations were closely tied to ISMAC, the effectiveness of the observers was also eroded. The armistice regime can thus be credited with providing stability in the immediate aftermath of the war, but participants and historians agree that its effectiveness had mostly disappeared by the late 1950s.[27]

Britain, France, and Israel attacked Egypt in October 1956, but despite its alliance commitment to Egypt, Syria did not join the fray. The armistice regime, however, deserves no credit for this stability along the Israeli-Syrian front. Syria was deterred by the threat of British attack. It is fair to say, however, that the weakness of what was left of the armistice mechanisms by the 1960s deserves at least part of the blame for the outbreak of the Six-Day War.

The 1967 war was the result of a classic security dilemma spiral. The year began with serious clashes along the Israel-Syria armistice line. In April, Palestinian guerilla attacks from within Syria and Israeli reprisals for them escalated to tank battles and clashes between the Israeli and Syrian air forces. Six Syrian planes were shot down, and Israeli planes swept over the suburbs of Damascus.[28] Arab leaders interpreted Israeli rhetoric about overthrowing the Syrian regime, along with Soviet misinformation that Israel was massing troops on Syria's border, as evidence

---

[26] For detailed accounts of the disputes between civilians and over engineering projects, see Bar-Yaacov 1967; Kinsolving 1967; and Khouri 1963.

[27] See, for example, Azcarate 1966; Khouri 1963; Pelcovits 1993, 47–48; and Shebtai 1990.

[28] Ovendale 1984, 178.

of an imminent Israeli attack. Egyptian President Nasser put troops on alert, requested the withdrawal of UNEF, and closed the Gulf of Aqaba to Israeli shipping.

Israel interpreted these moves, along with hostile Arab rhetoric, as evidence that war was imminent and launched a preemptive attack on June 5, 1967. Of course it is impossible to know whether stronger agreement mechanisms between either Israel and Egypt or Israel and Syria could have prevented this war. What is clear is that by 1967 there was almost nothing to constrain attack, to clarify misunderstandings about either side's intentions, or to control the sorts of clashes that increased tensions immediately before the war.

To head off the possibility of Soviet intervention, the United States pressured Israel to halt its advance on June 10, 1967. The cease-fire implemented nothing in the way of mechanisms to prevent another war. UNTSO observers were still stationed in the Middle East, but they were by now completely discredited. Neither the humiliated Arabs nor the victorious Israelis were in a mood to negotiate any measures to bolster peace. But despite the fact that peace should have been quite durable after Israel's trouncing of its neighbors in 1967, Israel and Egypt fought again in 1969, and the whole region was back at war in 1973. Again, we will never know whether a strong peace agreement in 1967 might have helped avoid these wars, but it is likely that monitoring would at least have prevented the surprise attack by Egypt and Syria on October 6 (Yom Kippur), 1973.

After the Yom Kippur War, Egypt and Israel embarked on a series of disengagement agreements and eventually signed a peace treaty. Disengagement negotiations between Israel and Syria were much more difficult. Nevertheless, after shuttle diplomacy by Henry Kissinger, these two bitter enemies reached an agreement to stabilize the cease-fire on May 31, 1974. They proceeded to implement a very strong set of measures, not to establish formal peace, but to prevent another war. Israel withdrew to the 1967 lines, and from a sliver of territory, including the town of Quneitra, occupied in the Six-Day War.[29] The agreement established a demilitarized zone ranging from three to six kilometers wide, and the UN sent an armed peacekeeping force of 1,250 troops, UNDOF, to serve as a buffer between Israeli and Syrian forces. The agreement limited armaments on either side of the DMZ, particularly those that could reach Israeli settlements or Syrian towns. Syria also agreed privately that the cease-fire applied to Palestinian guerillas, though for political reasons it could not proclaim this publicly.[30]

---

[29] That Asad manage to regain at least a sliver of occupied territory was extremely important symbolically. See Kissinger 1982, 1042–43.

[30] For a detailed and firsthand account of the negotiations, see Kissinger 1982, chap. 23.

The 1974 disengagement agreement has been extremely successful. Despite the deep hatred and mutual suspicion between Israel and Syria, their ongoing dispute over the Golan Heights and the Palestinian issue as well, their border has remained peaceful. The cease-fire held in the Golan even as Israeli and Syrian forces fought outright next door in Lebanon in 1982. In the quantitative study below, this case is penalized for the fighting in Lebanon because peace is measured as lasting until the belligerents fight again anywhere. If anything, however, the fact that the cease-fire line in the Golan remained peaceful during the 1980s despite the war in Lebanon is testament to the effectiveness of the strong mechanisms put in place in 1974. Outright hatred on both sides notwithstanding, and despite the serious escalation of the Palestinian conflict during the first Intifada and again more recently, peace has held between Israel and Syria. Whether war would have occurred in the meantime we will never know, but the fact that Israeli and Syrian troops are separated by a DMZ, with peacekeeping forces between them, rather than eyeball-to-eyeball in the politically charged and strategically important Golan Heights, has certainly prevented clashes and accidents that could easily have sparked heavier fighting.

The effects of the agreements reached in Lebanon are harder to assess, because the situation there is so complex. When Syria first intervened in Lebanon's civil war in 1976, it did so with the blessing of the United States and the acquiescence of Israel. Israel and Syria respected a tacit arrangement, known as the Red Lines Agreement. This agreement helped Israel and Syria avoid direct confrontation when Israel invaded Lebanon in 1978. In April 1981, however, the agreement collapsed when Phalangist forces provoked a clash between Israel and Syria in which Israel attacked Syrian helicopters.[31] Syria moved surface-to-air missiles into Lebanon, and Israel responded by annexing the Golan Heights, signaling its refusal to consider handing the territory back to Syria. Israel launched a full-scale invasion of Lebanon in June 1982, with Defense Minister Sharon planning, unbeknownst to the Israeli cabinet, to push Syria out of Lebanon. Fearing Soviet involvement, the United States quickly pressured Israel to cease fire in eastern and central Lebanon, but fighting continued around Beirut. In August, the American Philip Habib mediated a cease-fire, the evacuation of PLO and Syrian troops from Beirut, and the deployment of a multinational force (MNF I) to supervise the withdrawal. Israel withdrew from most of Lebanon in 1985. Because of the indirect nature of most of the fighting between Syria and Israel in Lebanon, it is difficult to compare the 1982 cease-fire to those reached after the Arab-Israeli wars. Out of context, it ranks as a relatively weak agreement (and is coded

---

[31] The Phalangists hoped Israel would drive Syria out of Lebanon altogether. Schiff 1984, 102. See also Ma'oz 1995, 169.

as such in the Cease-Fires data set), but for its purposes it was fairly strong. It separated Syrian and Israel forces effectively and was backed up by a strong ad hoc peacekeeping force. U.S. mediation and involvement in the peacekeeping implied a U.S. guarantee of the withdrawal arrangements, although the United States vowed to pull out if the plan went sour.[32] The withdrawal went smoothly, and Israel and Syria have managed to avoid direct confrontation in Lebanon since.

The prospects for lasting peace between Israel and Syria have never been very good and will not be until the fundamental issues of territory, recognition, and a Palestinian state have been resolved. When nothing has been done to prevent it, repeated war has been the outcome. But this review of their history makes clear that when these two deadly enemies have implemented measures to increase the chances for peace, they have managed to avoid the quick resumption of war. Even these bitter enemies have been able to foster durable peace.

III. A QUANTITATIVE LOOK AT AGREEMENTS AND THE DURABILITY OF PEACE

The quantitative evidence also strongly supports the conclusion that agreements affect the durability of peace. Tables 5.2 and 5.3 show the results of hazard analysis of cease-fires since 1946. Results are shown for both measures of agreements described in chapter 2: the subjective coding of strength in table 5.2 and the more objective index of agreement mechanisms in table 5.3. These tables report hazard ratios and robust standard errors from a sample of the statistical tests run on the duration of peace. As explained in chapter 3, variables with hazard ratios greater than 1.0 increase the risk of another war. Variables with hazard ratios less than 1.0 make peace more stable. And variables with hazard ratios of 1.0 have no impact on the likelihood of war resuming. Hazard ratios that are statistically distinguishable from 1.0 are marked with asterisks.

By either the objective or the subjective measure, agreement strength reduces the hazard rate. Stronger agreements are associated with a lower risk of renewed warfare. For neither measure is this effect statistically significant when the variable is tested by itself (see column 1 of each table). Once the situational variables are controlled for, however, it becomes

---

[32] Thakur 1987. The U.S. attempt to keep peace in Lebanon's civil war with a second peacekeeping deployment (MNF II) went very sour when 241 U.S. Marines and almost 60 French troops were killed on October 23, 1983, but that was a separate effort altogether from the agreement to evacuate the PLO and Syrian troops from Beirut. MNF II was a dismal failure, but the oft-forgotten MNF I was a great success.

TABLE 5.2
Agreement Strength and the Durability of Peace

	Weibull Hazard Ratios (robust standard errors)		
Agreement strength	0.862 (0.148)	0.605*** (0.055)	0.724*** (0.077)	
None				1.004 [js] (0.571)
Very weak				1.310 [js] (0.456)
Moderate				0.363*** [js] (0.071)
Strong				0.131** [js] (0.134)
Tie		34.823*** (11.551)	42.448*** (17.386)	29.009*** (13.814)
Cost of war		0.533*** (0.089)	0.926 (0.231)	0.619*** (0.085)
History of conflict		2.569*** (0.658)	2.348*** (0.426)	2.434*** (0.577)
Existence at stake		7.849*** (3.273)	13.120*** (9.495)	6.413*** (2.319)
Contiguous		3.296*** (0.848)	3.146*** (0.941)	4.298*** (1.497)
Change in relative capabilities		2.435*** (0.464)	2.364*** (0.502)	
U.S. belligerent			0.000*** (0.000)	
P	0.504*** (0.083)	0.817 (0.114)	0.864 (0.164)	0.838 (0.101)
N	876	770	770	876
No. of subjects	48	48	48	48
Log likelihood	−70.023	−45.502	−43.095	−46.489

Note: Cases are clustered by conflict.
 * Statistically significant at the .10 level
 ** Statistically significant at the .05 level
 *** Statistically significant at the .01 level
 [js] Jointly significant at the .001 level.

clear that stronger cease-fire agreements significantly reduce the risk of another war. If the counterargument that agreements are merely epiphenomenal were correct, we would see exactly the opposite pattern. Agreement strength would have a significant effect in the bivariate model, but not once we controlled for the difficulty of the case.

The second column of table 5.2 shows that, controlling for the baseline prospects for peace, increasing agreement strength reduces the risk of renewed warfare. The hazard ratio (about 0.6) means that an increase in strength is associated with a decrease in the risk of another war, all else equal. The robust standard errors indicate that this is a statistically significant finding, very unlikely to be simply an artifact of chance in the data.

Because we have seen that the United States tends to draft particularly strong agreements when it is involved in a war, and since none of the wars the United States fought in were repeated (before these data were censored), we might think this result is spurious, driven by the U.S. cases. However, the finding holds up even when we control for U.S. participation in the war (column 3).[33] This finding also holds up when other situational variables tested in chapter 3 (multilateral war, territorial conflict, measures of the expected utility for war, etc.) are added to the model, when cases of joint democracy are dropped to control for the democratic peace, when duplicate agreement cases or cases that might not be considered principal belligerents are dropped, or when a control is added for the Arab-Israel wars (results not shown). The results are also substantially the same whether we use a parametric Weibull specification or the semiparametric Cox method. In other words, any way you slice the data, the results stay the same; stronger agreements yield more durable peace.

Agreement strength is coded as a categorical variable (none, very weak, weak, etc.). Column 4 of table 5.2 shows the hazard ratios of each category as compared to the middle of the range ("weak" agreements are the omitted, comparison category). As my theory would predict, hazard ratios are greater than 1.0 for agreements at the weaker end of the spectrum, and less than 1.0 for stronger agreements, with the smallest hazard ratio appearing for the strongest agreements. This means that weaker than average agreements are more likely to fall apart, while stronger than average agreements reduce the risk of renewed fighting. While the individual hazard ratios are not all significant, these effects are jointly significant at $p \leq .001$ (in Wald tests). The risk of failure for a moderately strong agreement is 36% that of a weak agreement. The risk of a strong agreement failing is only 13% that of a weak agreement. Again, this finding is robust to differ-

---

[33] The size of the effect drops slightly, but remains statistically significant. The hazard of another war if the United States was involved is predicted to be essentially zero—the model predicts that peace will last forever, because that is what is observed so far in this time period.

TABLE 5.3
Agreement Index and the Durability of Peace

	Weibull Hazard Ratios (robust standard errors)			
Index of agreement strength	0.967 (0.090)	0.808*** (0.054)	0.809*** (0.053)	0.867** (0.054)
Tie		29.877*** (6.469)	32.804*** (6.855)	44.297*** (19.299)
Cost of war		0.524*** (0.087)	0.522*** (0.087)	0.930 (0.219)
History of conflict		2.613*** (0.580)	2.584*** (0.560)	2.410*** (0.388)
Existence at stake		7.542*** (3.094)	7.777*** (3.345)	13.188*** (9.340)
Contiguous		3.124*** (0.822)	3.130*** (0.795)	3.150*** (0.889)
Change in relative capabilities			2.332*** (0.441)	2.333*** (0.521)
U.S. belligerent				0.000*** (0.000)
P	0.497*** (0.082)	0.808 (0.125)	0.810 (0.123)	0.871 (0.169)
N	876	876	770	770
No. of subjects	48	48	48	48
Log likelihood	−70.386	−48.089	−46.382	−43.375

Note: Cases are clustered by conflict.
* Statistically significant at the .10 level.
** Statistically significant at the .05 level.
*** Statistically significant at the .01 level.

ent model specifications and controls. Having no agreement at all is a bit more stable than a very weak one, but very weak agreements are about 30% more likely to falter than those at the next strength level.[34]

Table 5.3 points to the same conclusion with a different, more objective measure of agreement strength. Agreements that implement more mechanisms to keep peace significantly reduce the risk of another war, all else equal. This finding is very robust, and there is very little chance that we

---

[34] When U.S. cases are controlled for, no agreements are more stable than the weakest agreements, and the effect of strong agreements is somewhat smaller, but the pattern remains substantially the same.

would see such a strong relationship in the data if none truly existed. The results hold up when we control for changes in relative capability over time, and for U.S. cases (columns 3 and 4, respectively), and with other specifications and controls.[35] Again, the conclusions remain the same whether a Weibull or Cox regression is used. In all of these tests, a unit increase in the index of agreement strength (the equivalent of adding one mechanism) decreases the hazard rate by about 15–20%.

What both tables show quite clearly is that, controlling for the baseline prospects of peace, stronger agreements reduce the risk of renewed warfare. Any way you run the tests, the hypothesis holds up: stronger agreements yield more durable peace.

Duration Dependence

In chapter 2, I noted that one of the advantages of a Weibull model is that it allows us to investigate duration dependence, that is, whether the risk of another war changes over time. Intuitively, we would probably expect that peace is most fragile in the immediate aftermath of war, but gets consolidated over time as the dust settles, trust is reestablished at least minimally, and the war recedes in public memory. On the other hand, informational arguments about war might lead us to predict the opposite. In this perspective, war is caused in part by private information about capabilities and resolve. This private information (and the fact that states have incentives to misrepresent it) prevents states from finding bargains both would prefer to war.[36] Actually fighting the war reveals this information; it publicizes states' capabilities and resolve. Following this logic, war should be least likely right after the fighting ends and should become more likely over time as private information about changes in capabilities and resolve accumulates.

The shape parameter P indicates whether the risk of another war increases, decreases, or remains constant as time goes by. Values of P greater than 1.0 indicate an increasing hazard, P equal to 1.0 reveals a constant hazard, and P less than 1.0 means the hazard declines. In almost every duration model run for this study, P is less than 1.0 (see tables 3.1, 3.2, 5.2, 5.3, and 6.1–6.4).[37] P is not always statistically significant, so we cannot reject the null hypothesis that the hazard remains flat, but we can

[35] That is, the results are the same when years in which both states are democratic are dropped from the analysis, when the other situational variables that were not found to be significant in chapter 3 are included, when duplicate agreement cases are dropped, when states that might not be considered principal belligerents are dropped, or when a control is added for the Middle East cases.

[36] Fearon 1995.

[37] The few tests in which P is greater than 1.0 are affected by missing data bias, with cease-fires that fail most quickly omitted.

172 · Chapter Five

clearly reject the hypothesis derived from the information perspective. If there is a change in the risk of war, our intuition about it is the right one. Peace is most fragile early on and gets more stable as it survives.

Conclusion

The evidence from three very different research methods (a survey of cases, in-depth case studies, and quantitative analysis) all points in the same direction: agreements matter. Peace is harder to maintain in some cases than others, and is likely hardest in the immediate aftermath of war, but the obstacles to peace can be overcome through deliberate efforts on the part of belligerents and the international community. When peace is relatively hard to keep, stronger agreements help it last longer, and when it is somewhat easier, strong agreements give it a better chance of becoming permanent. In short, cease-fire agreements matter; strong agreements make it easier to maintain peace.

CHAPTER SIX

PEACE MECHANISMS: WHAT WORKS AND WHAT DOESN'T?

CHAPTER 1 SPELLED OUT a number of specific mechanisms that might help belligerents maintain peace. The previous chapter showed that agreements that are stronger in the aggregate, that is, those that include more of these mechanisms, yield more durable peace. But to answer the practical question of how best to give peace a chance, we need to know which measures are most effective, which are less relevant or irrelevant, and whether any of them are actually counterproductive. We need to disaggregate "strength" into its component parts. This chapter therefore looks at each individual measure in turn to see empirically whether and how it contributes to durable peace.

There are several strategies belligerents might employ to overcome the obstacles to peace. These include raising the cost of breaking the cease-fire, either physically or politically, reducing uncertainty about actions and intentions, and preventing or managing accidents and skirmishes that might escalate back to war. As noted in the theoretical discussion of specific mechanisms in chapter 1, many measures serve several purposes at once: creating a demilitarized zone both makes it physically harder to launch an attack and helps prevent tussles along the cease-fire line. International peacekeepers can provide something of a physical buffer, but they are probably more effective as monitors of the cease-fire, reducing uncertainty, and as mediators on the ground to help restore local cease-fires and avoid escalation when clashes occur, thus dampening accidental spirals. Willingness to implement physical constraints or measures to prevent accidents simultaneously serves to signal belligerents' intent, since those planning to break a cease-fire will be less willing to agree to such measures. It is therefore virtually impossible to distinguish these strategies empirically. We cannot test whether some strategies work better than others. We can, however, test whether specific mechanisms work better than others. We can observe whether peace lasts longer when demilitarized zones are in place, say, or when peacekeepers are present.

The first part of this chapter examines the empirical effectiveness of mechanisms that physically separate or impose limits on military forces. Does the withdrawal of forces back from the cease-fire line contribute to peace? Are demilitarized zones effective conflict management tools? Does arms control work between recent belligerents? How effective are measures to prevent rogue groups from violating the cease-fire? The second section looks at what outsiders can do to bolster peace. Does peacekeeping keep peace? How important is it to have a third party provide a formal guarantee of the peace? The third section investigates measures that provide information or open channels of communication. Do confidence-building measures to exchange information about military activities help stabilize peace? Are dispute resolution mechanisms effective? Are more specific agreements more durable than vaguer ones? Do audience costs and international opinion affect the stability of peace? Does having a formal rather than tacit agreement make any difference? Does it matter whether an agreement is technically a cease-fire agreement or a peace agreement? The final section discusses the importance of settling the issues over which the war was fought in the first place, comparing wars that end with an imposed settlement, those that end with an agreement on the basic issues, and those that end with the issues still very much in dispute.

As in the other empirical chapters in this book, I draw on three sorts of evidence to answer these questions. I test whether each mechanism contributes to the durability of peace statistically, I look at all of the cases qualitatively to look for patterns, and I draw on the in-depth case studies to help us understand if these mechanisms work, and if so, how. The quantitative results are presented in tables 6.1–6.4. To save space, only a sample of the statistical tests is shown here. For each mechanism I checked whether the results were robust to various model specifications.[1] Because some agreement mechanisms are correlated with others, I also tested whether the results held when these other measures were included. In most cases none of this affected the results in important ways. Where it did I mention this in the discussion that follows. As in chapters 3 and 5, hazard ratios are reported. If they work, agreement mechanisms should have hazard ratios less than 1.0, reducing the hazard of another war.

One caveat is in order. Because the universe of cases is small, and because agreement mechanisms are not implemented in isolation from each other as in a controlled lab experiment, it is difficult to say with precision which mechanisms work better than others. The findings here should be taken with a grain of salt. However, even if definitive answers about the relative merits of different measures cannot be had, a systematic look at 50 years of experience with the maintenance of peace is worth taking, for some measures have a much better record than others.

---

[1] Robustness checks included using dichotomous or categorical measures, adding or omitting each of the situational variables examined in chapter 3, controlling for U.S. cases, and for Middle East cases, dropping cases of duplicate agreements, and cases in which one

I. Physical Separation and Constraints

Troop Withdrawal

One of the most contentious issues in cease-fire negotiations is whether combatants will withdraw from territory captured during the war. Chapter 1 hypothesized that withdrawing troops might contribute to stability by making it harder for either side to attack, by preventing skirmishes along the cease-fire line, and by providing a costly, and therefore credible, signal of intentions to keep peace. However, we saw in chapter 4 that withdrawing troops in the aftermath of war is more likely when the prospects for peace are relatively good (see table 4.3 and the case studies). It is therefore particularly important to control for the baseline prospects of peace in assessing the effects of withdrawal on the durability of peace.

The Cease-Fires data set records for each period whether troops have withdrawn partially, to the status quo antebellum, or beyond this (or not at all, the omitted category in the statistical analysis shown here). As we can see in table 6.1, partial withdrawal is associated with particularly stable peace. There are very few cases in this category, however, and in almost all of them partial withdrawal is a very temporary state preceding further withdrawals at least to the status quo ante, so the fact that peace does not fail in these periods does not tell us very much.

Troops withdraw to the status quo antebellum in about one-third of all the cases examined here. This suggests that the norm against taking territory by force is fairly strong. This is especially noteworthy given that many of the "no withdrawal" cases did not involve territorial gain, either because they were not fought over territory (the Uganda-Tanzania War, for example) or because they ended at the territorial status quo ante (the Falklands War and the War of Attrition between Israel and Egypt are two examples). Where one side took territory and kept it after the war, peace has not generally been stable. The repeated and ongoing strife over territories occupied by Israel in the Six-Day War in 1967 is the clearest example.

However, returning to the territorial status quo ante does not necessarily lead to durable peace. Israel and Egypt fought again after Israel's withdrawal from the Sinai in 1956, India and Pakistan fought again after returning to pre-1965 cease-fire lines, and China and Vietnam fought again after China's withdrawal to the "historic borderline" in 1979.[2] Statistically, withdrawal to the status quo ante is associated with unstable peace (the hazard ratio is greater than 1.0), though not significantly so.

---

side might not qualify as a principal belligerent. I also ran tests with both Weibull and Cox specifications to see if this made a significant difference.

[2] Allcock 1992, 467.

TABLE 6.1
Physical Constraints

	Weibull Hazard Ratios (robust standard errors)			
Withdrawal				
Partial	0.000***			
	(0.000)			
Status quo ante	2.205			
	(1.552)			
Beyond status quo ante	0.000***			
	(0.000)			
Demilitarized zones				
Partial		0.618		
		(0.275)		
Full		0.129**		
		(0.137)		
Arms control			0.995	
			(0.435)	
Internal control				
Responsible				1.475
				(0.504)
Concrete				0.494
				(0.406)
Tie	26.322***	30.030***	27.376***	33.005***
	(5.943)	(9.383)	(4.768)	(10.078)
Cost of war	0.476***	0.625**	0.513***	0.473***
	(0.085)	(0.121)	(0.093)	(0.109)
History of conflict	2.946***	2.713***	2.894***	3.090***
	(0.472)	(0.445)	(0.504)	(0.527)
Existence at stake	5.765**	7.756***	5.719***	3.959***
	(4.119)	(2.795)	(2.231)	(1.856)
Contiguous	3.919**	2.979***	2.087**	2.593***
	(2.159)	(0.963)	(0.767)	(0.916)
Change in relative capabilities	6.553***	2.740***	2.419***	2.238***
	(3.532)	(0.650)	(0.567)	(0.520)
P	0.719**	0.763*	0.732*	0.780**
	(0.121)	(0.110)	(0.118)	(0.091)
N	770	770	770	770
No. of subjects	48	48	48	48
Log likelihood	−44.054	−46.320	−47.547	−46.428

Note: Cases clustered by conflict.
* Statistically significant at the .10 level.
** Statistically significant at the .05 level.
*** Statistically significant at the .01 level.

There have been a handful of cases in which belligerents have withdrawn forces beyond the status quo ante, giving up territory they held when the war began. China withdrew 20 kilometers back from the previous line of control after its war with India in 1962. Both Honduras and El Salvador withdrew from disputed border areas in 1976 after serious clashes threatened the peace between them. In a series of staged disengagement agreements with Egypt after the Yom Kippur War, Israel gave up territory it had taken not in that war but in 1967. And in 1988, a decade after their initial cease-fire, Ethiopia and Somalia withdrew 10–15 kilometers from the international border.[3] In all of these cases, peace has lasted to date. The hazard of another war is thus estimated to be zero. Willingness to remove one's forces from territory controlled even before the war would seem from these cases to provide a strong signal of commitment to peace. In each of these cases withdrawals were accompanied by the creation of a significant demilitarized zone along the border (see below). It is possible that we are just seeing the stabilizing effects of demilitarized zones, and that it does not particularly matter where the zone is relative to the prewar status quo. The symbolism and domestic political import of territory lost in war makes this unlikely, however. There is no room for a 20–40 kilometer DMZ between Israel and Egypt anywhere other than in the Sinai, but even if there was, it is hard to imagine that any old territory would do.

The case studies also suggest the importance of withdrawal of forces, more by its absence than by its presence. Given the territorial disputes at the heart of both the South Asian and the Middle Eastern conflicts, in neither case has it been possible to withdraw troops from wide swaths of land, and in both cases failure to withdraw has led to the resumption of war.

As the first Kashmir war ended, India and Pakistan agreed in principle to the phased withdrawal of troops from Kashmir. Pakistan and the tribesmen who started the first Kashmir war were to withdraw first, and then India would withdraw the "bulk of [its] forces" in stages.[4] Pakistan withdrew the Pathan tribesmen, but none of the other withdrawals ever took place. Failure to implement this part of the 1949 agreement left the Kashmir issue to simmer, boiling over into warfare again and again over the next 50 years.

When the second round of fighting stopped in 1965, both India and Pakistan occupied some territory on the other's side (that is, on the wrong side of the 1949 cease-fire line in Kashmir, or of the international border

---

[3] Zartman 1989, 123. Ethiopia also gave back a strip of land it had held since 1983.

[4] Pakistan was to withdraw first, as India had insisted that Pakistan's introduction of regular forces into the conflict be treated as an act of aggression. On the politics of synchronizing withdrawals, see Bailey 1982, 114ff.

between the two countries proper), and this caused a great deal of tension in the first months of the cease-fire.[5] Withdrawal of forces from areas taken in the war was certainly not politically uncontroversial. But at Tashkent both sides agreed to return to the status quo antebellum. Later that month, military commanders worked out a plan for the phased withdrawal of troops.[6] The cease-fire lines stabilized almost immediately.[7] The Simla Agreement reached after the Bangladesh War also called for withdrawal of forces to the border between India and West Pakistan, and established the "line of actual control" as of December 17, 1971, as the cease-fire line in Kashmir.[8] The agreements at Tashkent and at Simla to return at least to the status quo antebellum were politically important signals that both sides considered the war over. Willingness to move troops to the status quo ante helps to communicate the absence of aggressive intent or territorial designs, just as unwillingness to do so indicates the opposite.

Given the incompatible territorial claims of Israel and Syria, the issue of troop withdrawal in the aftermath of war has been equally contentious. In the first two cease-fires in 1948, hostilities resumed before any withdrawal could be worked out. As part of the armistice agreement in 1949, Syria withdrew its troops from land given to Israel under the UN partition plan and these areas were demilitarized. It is unlikely that Israel would have maintained the cease-fire, or perhaps even agreed to it in the first place, had Syria not relinquished this territory.

After the Six-Day War, Israel held on to the territory it captured in the Sinai, the West Bank, and the Golan Heights. UN Security Council Resolution 242 calls for withdrawal from occupied territories in exchange for a political peace settlement; but this has unfortunately proved much easier said than done. Israel's refusal to return land occupied in 1967 prompted Syria and Egypt to try to take it back by force in 1973.[9] This territory remains the heart of the conflict between Israel and Syria. But the agreement reached in 1974 after the Yom Kippur War to return at least to the 1967 lines (the new status quo ante), and for Israel to give back Quneitra, was crucial for maintaining peace in the Golan.[10]

The fight between Israel and Syria in Lebanon ended with an agreement on the evacuation of Syrian (and PLO) forces from Beirut. Israel hoped

---

[5] See the secretary-general's report, UN document S/6710/Add. 4, 1965, 2.

[6] For the timetables, see UN document S/6719/Add. 5, 1966, 3–4.

[7] Very few incidents took place along the cease-fire line after withdrawal was implemented in February 1966. Blinkenberg 1972, 284.

[8] India insisted that the 1949 cease-fire line was obsolete, but the line of control only deviated from the old line in minor ways. UN 1996, 142.

[9] Khouri 1985, 335.

[10] Kissinger 1982, chap. 23.

to negotiate the complete mutual withdrawal of Israeli and Syrian forces from Lebanon, but in the end withdrew unilaterally when the costs of remaining in the Lebanese quagmire became prohibitive. Syria agreed tacitly not to move forward into the areas evacuated by Israel.[11]

It is extremely difficult for bitter enemies to agree to yield territory. Failure to withdraw from contested territory sows the seeds for more war, but often such a withdrawal is inseparable from political settlement of the underlying dispute. It is not a mechanism that deadly enemies can easily use to prevent war while they continue to disagree over the fundamentals. Withdrawal at least to previous cease-fire lines did help stabilize the situation between India and Pakistan in 1965 and 1971, and between Israel and Syria in 1973. But returning to prewar lines certainly does not guarantee peace. Failure to withdraw from territory conquered in war makes another fight likely, but withdrawal to the status quo ante is not enough to make peace last. Removing forces from territory held even before the war, however, sends a credible signal of commitment to peace.

Demilitarized Zones

While they are clearly connected, we can distinguish the effects of withdrawal from territory taken by force from the effects of separating troops with a demilitarized zone. There is strong evidence that demilitarized zones help promote stable peace. In over half of the cease-fires and follow-up agreements examined for this study, combatants agreed to separate their forces to some extent. Sometimes the DMZ was very narrow (one thousand yards or less on either side) or only applied to particular areas. In other cases anywhere from one to 20 kilometers on either side of the entire cease-fire line was put off limits. Partial and full DMZs are examined in turn.

Surprisingly, peace breaks down eventually in every case with a limited or partial DMZ. But this is a particularly difficult set of cases, including the three wars between India and Pakistan, the first wars between Israel and the Arab states, the Sinai War, and the 1967 cease-fire between Israel and Syria. As table 6.1 indicates, once the baseline prospects for peace are taken into account in the statistical analysis, the hazard ratio for partial DMZs is less than 1.0 (though it is not statistically significant). Partial DMZs may have helped prolong peace in these particularly precarious cases, even though they eventually failed, but we cannot be sure of this effect.

[11] Evron 1987, 170–74; Pelcovits 1984, 64.

The case studies suggest that the creation of even narrow demilitarized zones can help stabilize troubled cease-fires, but that in some cases demilitarizing contested areas can be counterproductive. After both Kashmir wars, India and Pakistan established a narrow buffer area between soldiers. When the second cease-fire went into effect in 1965, troops were in some places less than 30 yards apart. In response to the clashes inevitable when forces are this close, local military representatives agreed initially to pull back about one hundred yards.[12] Then at Tashkent, India and Pakistan agreed to demilitarize one thousand yards on either side of the cease-fire line. These narrow demilitarized zones did not provide much of a physical constraint to raise the cost of an attack. But in both cases, by separating forces even slightly, they helped defuse tension and prevent accidents and clashes. The effect of creating a buffer space between troops is clear in the record of day-to-day incidents along the cease-fire line.[13]

The experience of Israel and Syria with the demilitarized areas created in the armistice agreement in 1949 suggests some caution, however. In the first Arab-Israeli war, Syria occupied some Israeli land (i.e., land designated for Israel under the UN partition plan). During the armistice negotiations, both sides claimed this territory. As a compromise, the armistice agreement demilitarized the areas between the cease-fire line and the international border. Part of the rationale for this was to minimize friction and the likelihood of clashes between the opposing armies. But the more important reason to demilitarize this territory was to skirt the issue of whose land it was.[14]

These zones failed to prevent clashes between Syrians and Israelis along the armistice line. Worse, the ambiguity over sovereignty made them a serious bone of contention. Most of the incidents that took place between 1949 and 1967 were the result of the dispute over the demilitarized territory. Israel acted aggressively to exert its sovereignty over the areas. Meanwhile, Syria claimed the territorial issue remained unsettled and contested Israel's actions, often by force. Fishing and farming rights in the areas were violently contested as well.[15] Attacks and reprisals over these issues intensified the animosity between Israel and Syria considerably, and contributed to the atmosphere of fear and distrust that spiraled into the Six-Day War.[16] Rather than providing a buffer, these areas created a power vacuum.

---

[12] UN documents S/6719/Add. 1, 1965, 2; and S/6710/Add. 5, 7.

[13] See UNCIP 1949, and UN document S/6710 and addenda, 1965–66.

[14] Azcarate 1966, 117; Bailey 1990, 66; Bar-Yaacov 1967, 39–41, 49, 53; Kinsolving 1967, 35–36.

[15] Khouri 1963, 1985; Ma'oz 1995. For detailed accounts of these incidents see Bar-Yaacov 1967; and Kinsolving 1967. (Bar-Yaacov has a useful list of the UN documents covering the incidents between 1950 and 1966 on p. 354.).

[16] Of course, if these areas had not been demilitarized, the violence in these contested areas might have been even worse.

The 1967 war ended with Israeli and Syrian forces separated by no more than three to four hundred yards in some places.[17] A more substantial buffer zone would not in itself have prevented Syrian and Egyptian aggression in 1973, but its absence certainly made their surprise attack easier. These cases suggest that even narrow buffer areas to separate troops can help prevent skirmishes between troops left "eyeball to eyeball" when the fighting ends, but that demilitarizing contested territory may not work well as a substitute for settling land disputes.

While partial DMZs may have somewhat mixed effects, it is clear that wider DMZs are an effective means of avoiding war. Both the quantitative and qualitative evidence supports this conclusion. Hazard analysis indicates that, all else equal, the risk of another war drops dramatically and significantly when a full DMZ is in place (see table 6.1).[18] In fact when belligerents separate their forces by at least two kilometers, peace almost always lasts. This is true in both the relatively easy cases (such as the Sino-Indian War) and much more difficult cases (the Football War and the Korean War). The success of the Korean case is overdetermined, though the DMZ has likely helped. The demilitarized areas between El Salvador and Honduras helped to prevent war until the border was settled in 1992. In fact the only case of war resuming between combatants whose forces were separated by a DMZ is Israel and Syria's war in 1982. The 1974 disengagement agreement set up a three- to six-kilometer DMZ flanked by staged limited forces zones to further increase the physical buffer between the two sides.[19] This buffer has successfully kept Syrian and Israeli troops from each other's throats. That fighting broke out between Israel and Syria in Lebanon, but not across the DMZ in the Golan in 1982, is testament not to the failure of the DMZ, but arguably to its success.

Arms Control

In theory, arms control measures ought to be another way that belligerents can affect the ease of returning to war. Evidence from the cases sur-

---

[17] Bull 1976, 123–24.

[18] Wider DMZs are associated with more durable peace than narrower ones, but the effect of width is not statistically significant. The effect of DMZs is muted when U.S. cases are controlled for.

[19] Under the Red Lines Agreement, Israel and Syria tacitly agreed to keep their forces separate to avoid confrontation, though this was more a by-product of the agreement to stay out of each other's spheres of influence than the primary motivation. Pelcovits 1984, 63–65, notes that after the war in 1982, there was discussion of a formal disengagement agreement to separate Israeli and Syrian forces in the Biqa' Valley, but Israel's decision to withdraw unilaterally (and Syria's tacit agreement not to move forward as Israel did so), made this unnecessary.

veyed here does not suggest that this is a particularly effective way to maintain peace, however. Analyzed out of context, arms control measures actually appear to be detrimental to peace (they raise the hazard rate in statistical tests if nothing else is controlled for). Once the baseline prospects for peace are taken into account, this negative effect drops away, but arms control measures are not associated with more stable peace (see table 6.1, column 3).[20] Nor is a clear pattern apparent in a qualitative look at the cases. Limited forces areas might have helped keep peace in some difficult cases, between El Salvador and Honduras, for example, or after the Yom Kippur War, but these were established in conjunction with demilitarized zones, making it hard to distinguish the effects of arms control itself. Very strong arms control measures are rare in the aftermath of war. The only case of extensive prohibitions on weapons is the ban imposed on Iraqi weapons of mass destruction after the Gulf War. This is of course a very lopsided arms control regime, and one could argue that while it may have helped stabilize the region, it has also been a cause of ongoing conflict.[21] Whatever one's opinion of the record of arms control in Iraq, it is not an easily generalizable case.

Modest restrictions on arms and troop levels have been employed on occasion between India and Pakistan and between Israel and Syria. In the volatile months after the 1965 cease-fire went into effect, India and Pakistan agreed to ban test firing within 10,000 yards of the cease-fire, to keep light aircraft at least 1,600 meters and high performance aircraft 10,000 meters from the front lines.[22] This helped reduce tension and prevent accidents and misunderstandings. These measures operated more as confidence-building measures than as constraints on military capability. They had a negligible effect on either side's ability to launch an attack, but they did help control activities near the cease-fire line that were likely to cause tension.

The ill-fated cease-fire during the first Palestine War in 1948 called for an arms embargo and a ban on introducing new fighting personnel to the area (i.e., through Jewish immigration), but these were widely ignored. The 1949 armistice agreement also limited forces to numbers sufficient for defense, but this does not seem to have had much effect.[23] The limited-forces areas and restrictions created in the 1974 disengagement negotia-

---

[20] The hazard ratio fluctuates from slightly less than 1.0 to slightly more than 1.0 depending on the model specification, and is never even close to significant.

[21] According to Towle 1997, this pattern is typical for attempts at enforced disarmament.

[22] UN document S/6710/Add. 6, 1965, 1; and Add. 15, 1966, 1.

[23] For details, see Annex III and IV, Israel and Syria, General Armistice Agreement, July 20, 1949, United Nations Treaty Series 42 no. 657.

tions were more important.[24] They were controversial, particularly because they limited Syrian forces very near Damascus, thus raising prickly sovereignty issues. But by requiring both sides to keep heavy artillery where it could not reach the opponent's forces, the restrictions limited Israel and Syria's ability to strike each other.

One example from Kashmir suggests a possible downside to arms control, however. The first Kashmir cease-fire prohibited the introduction of new military personnel into Kashmir. Unlike many provisions of the UNCIP resolution, this was respected by both sides. In a minor way it affected the outbreak of the next war. Pakistan's offensive in 1965 took advantage of its much easier access to Kashmir:

> While Pakistan could assemble a striking force without legal complications in its own nearby territory, the battle area was in Kashmir, where the disposition of Indian troops was curtailed by the [1949] Cease-Fire Agreement.[25]

This is a minor example, and Pakistan might have gone to war even without this advantage, but it suggests that arms control measures might sometimes contribute to war by creating imbalances in military capability.

While this says nothing about the effects of arms control in other contexts (such as managing arms races between the superpowers), the arms control implemented in the aftermath of war cannot be said to be an effective mechanism to prevent war's recurrence. While limits on arms might help keep peace in some cases, they may also sometimes be counterproductive.

Internal Control

Measures implemented to guard against rogue groups breaking the cease-fire fare only slightly better than arms control measures. In many cases, cease-fire agreements state that each side is responsible for any hostile acts emanating from territory under its control. Such statements have not been effective; if anything they are associated with particularly short-lived peace.[26] In a few cases, belligerents have implemented concrete measures to control potential spoilers. These have been helpful, all else equal, though their positive effect is not statistically significant (see table 6.1,

[24] Bands of territory 10 kilometers wide on either side of the DMZ were limited to 75 tanks, 36 short-range guns, and six thousand soldiers, further 10-kilometer bands were limited to 450 tanks, and surface-to-air missiles were not to be deployed closer than 25 kilometers from the DMZ. Kissinger 1982, 1092, 1099. See map in Shalev 1994.

[25] Brines 1968, 320.

[26] This association is neither statistically significant nor robust to different model specifications, however.

column 4). In the aftermath of the Football War, El Salvador and Honduras moved to disarm irregular civilian forces who had contributed to the disturbances setting off the war. This seems to have helped quiet things down along the border, especially after 1976 when more specific measures to disarm civilians in the demilitarized zone were implemented. When UNEF was stationed in the Sinai after the 1956 war, it was mandated to prevent infiltration across the border by *fedayeen* from the Gaza Strip. It was quite effective, reducing the number of raids considerably, especially in comparison with ongoing raids along Israel's borders with Jordan and Lebanon.[27]

Both the Kashmir conflict and the Middle East conflict have been plagued by problems with irregular forces and troops each side could at least claim not to control. The Kashmir dispute began when Pathan tribesmen invaded Kashmir. When the dust settled, Pakistan agreed to arrange for their withdrawal despite claims that it was not responsible for their actions. As noted in chapter 4, Pakistan also suggested measures to control Azad Kashmir forces in 1949. These moves were effective in preventing serious violations of the cease-fire by Pathan or Azad Kashmir fighters.

In 1965 and 1971, however, the problem in Kashmir was not possible violations by rogue groups, but deliberate state policies to use such groups to launch covert aggression. Pakistan was guilty of this strategy in 1965, India in 1971. Tensions in the early 2000s also centered on this issue of Pakistan's support for Kashmiri militants.[28] Interestingly, the effectiveness of other measures for preventing war, especially those relying on reputation and the reaction of the international community (discussed below), have exacerbated the problem of "irregular" forces, as they provide a way to act aggressively without taking the full brunt of international condemnation.[29]

The problem of "involuntary defection" was also a concern in the early years of the Arab-Israeli conflict, as it continues to be today. Israel's control over the Irgun and the Stern Gang and the Arab states' control over Palestinian fighters was often shaky. The problem proved to be fatal for the UN's first mediator to the region, Count Folke Bernadotte: he was killed by a Jewish terrorist group, the Stern Gang, in September 1948. But no concrete measures were implemented to control rogue groups.[30] By 1967, the problem of guerilla attacks was less involuntary defection than a deliberate policy allowing *fedayeen* raids against Israel. Unlike Leb-

[27] Ghali 1993b, 123.

[28] See Ganguly 2001.

[29] This may shift with the new focus on terrorism after September 11, 2001, if a stronger norm develops against support for irregular forces that employ terrorism.

[30] Syria insisted that it could not police or resist the "people's liberation struggle against Israel," and the Soviet Union vetoed a Security Council resolution calling for measures to prevent guerilla activity against Israel. Bailey 1990, 187; Khouri 1985, 92.

anon and Jordan, both Syria and Egypt effectively controlled the guerillas operating from their territory.[31]

For the most part, Israel relied on a policy of reprisals, often disproportionate to the harm inflicted by the terrorists, to deter guerila raids. This policy was controversial and won Israel no friends internationally. It also tended to increase popular Arab hatred against the Jewish state. So while it was often very effective in the short-term, leading Syria to rein in the *fedayeen*, it also made it more difficult to keep peace, and to negotiate a political solution. During the 1974 disengagement negotiations, Asad agreed privately to stop *fedayeen* raids, though he would not commit to this publicly. A public move against the Palestinian cause would have been political suicide, but Asad lived up to his private agreement.[32]

These cases suggest that when the problem is truly one of involuntary defection, states are often able to implement effective measures to control rogue groups. But when the problem is the use of allegedly rogue groups to pursue "voluntary" aggression, much less can be (or at least has been) done.

II. EXTERNAL GUARANTEES AND PEACEKEEPING: WHAT OUTSIDERS CAN DO

In the last half century, the international community has been heavily involved in helping to settle conflicts and maintain peace, both under the auspices of the United Nations and through unilateral efforts by regional or great powers. Third parties have sent mediators, attempted to restrain client states, and have sometimes explicitly stated their willingness to guarantee peace. The UN, regional organizations like the OAS, and on occasion ad hoc international groups (such as the Neutral Nations Supervisory Commission in Korea) have attempted to keep peace by deploying international observers or armed peacekeepers to monitor and manage cease-fires or provide a buffer between opposing forces. How effective have these efforts been? To what extent, and by what means, can outsiders help recent combatants maintain peace?

Third-Party Involvement

Outside states often have a strong interest in peace. In many wars, an interested third party sends a mediator to help negotiate a cease-fire, or puts pressure on a client state to stop fighting. Iran mediated the 1992

---

[31] Khouri 1985, 359; Ma'oz 1995, 118.
[32] Kissinger 1982, 1090–91; Ma'oz 1995, 141; Schiff 1984, 97.

cease-fire in the Armenian-Azerbaijani war, for example. U.S. pressure in response to a Soviet threat helped end the Sinai War, and in a more cooperative vein, both superpowers pushed for an end to the Iran-Iraq War in the late 1980s. This level of involvement may be effective at stopping the fighting, but it does not make peace any easier to keep once a cease-fire is in place. Peace lasts no longer when an outsider has gotten involved in this way than when no third state has tried to help make peace (see table 6.2).[33] On the contrary, this level of external involvement seems to lead to significantly less durable peace, although this negative finding is not very robust.[34]

The case studies suggest that while involvement in mediating an end to war implies a certain level of commitment, this level is often very low. The Soviet Union mediated between India and Pakistan after the second Kashmir war, and while this was important for reaching an agreement,[35] the Soviets explicitly refused to get involved in keeping the peace or providing guarantees. Kosygin made it quite clear that responsibility for the agreement lay with India and Pakistan themselves.[36] Britain would have been the most logical candidate to provide a guarantee, either in 1949 or in 1965, but having just shed British rule, neither side was willing to invite the colonialists back.

In the Middle East the role of outsiders, particularly the superpowers, has been extremely important, but mixed in its effects. In 1949 the UN mediator, Bernadotte, felt that a third-party (i.e., non-UN) guarantee of the peace would be necessary.[37] No such guarantees were forthcoming, however. As the Cold War developed, the Soviet Union and the United States took on the role of patrons to Syria and Israel respectively. The superpowers clearly played a role in restraining their client states at various points, and their own desire to avoid being pulled into war over the Middle East ensured that they would prevent fighting from escalating too badly, but they did not prevent war from breaking out. Their security assurances were a double-edged sword, preventing things from getting out of hand, but by doing so also making it safer to risk limited war.

---

[33] Note that I do not include cases of UN mediation in this category of third-party involvement, only cases in which another sovereign state has taken a particular interest in making peace. Including cases of UN mediation, such as the cease-fires in the first Arab-Israeli war, would not improve the record for maintaining peace.

[34] This apparently detrimental effect drops away when duplicate agreement cases are excluded, or when situational control variables are added or dropped (e.g. when stakes are not controlled for, or when multilateral wars are).

[35] For example, India's agreement to withdraw from Haji Pir, a sticking point in the negotiations, was influenced by the Soviet (and UN) role in the negotiations. Das 1969, 397.

[36] Brines 1968, 411.

[37] Bailey 1990, 42.

TABLE 6.2
Role of Outsiders

	Weibull Hazard Ratios (robust standard errors)		
Third party			
Mediate cease-fire	3.299***		
	(1.489)		
Guarantee peace	0.000***		
	(0.000)		
Peacekeeping			
Monitoring		0.333*	0.001***
		(0.197)	(0.003)
Armed forces		0.807	0.001*
		(0.646)	(0.003)
Tie	32.028***	44.239***	70898.33**
	(6.847)	(20.977)	(319366.3)
Cost of war	0.425***	0.496***	0.159*
	(0.088)	(0.091)	(0.175)
History of conflict	1.625**	3.556***	1605.81**
	(0.363)	(1.038)	(6055.881)
Existence at stake	12.440***	10.502***	2124.884*
	(7.433)	(2.428)	(9081.03)
Contiguous	7.351***	2.628**	4.171**
	(3.041)	(1.053)	(2.878)
Change in relative capabilities	2.045***	2.228***	0.853
	(0.393)	(0.511)	(0.317)
P	0.844	0.755*	1.825
	(0.122)	(0.109)	(1.180)
N	770	770	593
No. of subjects	48	48	37
Log likelihood	−44.920	−46.781	−16.669

Notes: In the rightmost column, cases with previously established peacekeeping missions (and no new mission) are dropped. Cases clustered by conflict.
  * Statistically significant at the .10 level.
  ** Statistically significant at the .05 level.
  *** Statistically significant at the .01 level.

U.S. mediation in the negotiations to end Syrian and Israeli fighting in Lebanon, and American involvement in the peacekeeping force deployed to Beirut, implied commitment to the peace. Once again, this was important for reaching a cease-fire; the United States pressured Israel to cease fire in the Biqa' valley, for example. But the United States also made it clear that it would not explicitly guarantee the peace, vowing to withdraw if fighting broke out.[38] Assurances from Kissinger about certain details of the 1974 disengagement agreement were also important for reaching the accord, but it is not clear to what extent those assurances later affected decisions to uphold promises.

Involvement of outside states as mediators, or as patron states restraining clients, implies a level of interest in peace. Such implicit guarantees may well help belligerents negotiate a cease-fire, but they are not effective at maintaining peace over the longer haul. Explicit guarantees of the peace are much more effective. In fact, peace has never fallen apart when outside states explicitly ensure a cease-fire agreement (the estimated hazard in table 6.2 therefore drops to zero).

Explicit guarantees are rather rare, so it is hard to know how much weight we should give to this finding, but it is quite robust.[39] That outsiders (including the United Kingdom, the USSR, Canada, China, France, Hungary, Indonesia, and Poland) signed an act "contributing to and guaranteeing peace in Indochina" cannot be said to have been important for peace in Vietnam.[40] These states did nothing to enforce the provisions of the Paris Peace Agreement once the United States had withdrawn. On the other hand, after the Football War, the commitment of Guatemala, Nicaragua, and Costa Rica to guarantee the peace does seem to have been important. When fighting flared up in 1976, these three were an important part of the effort to reinstate a cease-fire, redeploy OAS monitors, and strengthen the peace agreement. American security guarantees were also clearly a crucial part of the success of the Israeli-Egyptian peace agreement in 1979.

Unlike in civil wars, a guarantee of the peace is not essential for peace in interstate wars. There are plenty of cases of lasting peace without a third-party guarantee.[41] And while third-party involvement short of an explicit commitment may help belligerents reach a cease-fire, it does not help them keep it.[42] Explicit guarantees of the peace by an outside state, however, do have an excellent track record for helping peace last.

---

[38] Thakur 1987.

[39] For example, it is not merely an artifact of other agreement measures that happen to be correlated with guarantees.

[40] Act of the International Conference on Vietnam, signed in Paris, March 2, 1973.

[41] On the importance of security guarantees in civil wars, see Walter 2001.

[42] In a similar vein, Hampson 1996, 207, argues that durable peace after civil wars requires nurturing by "unified and sustained third-party involvement in both the negotiation and implementation of the agreement."

Peacekeeping

International peacekeeping may be the most important innovation in conflict resolution in the last half-century. The international community has sent monitors or armed forces to observe the cease-fire, investigate and mediate complaints of violations, or provide a buffer between opposing forces in about two-thirds of the interstate cease-fires since World War II. Have peacekeepers helped keep the peace? The evidence suggests that they have, but that their effectiveness is easily undermined.

That having peacekeepers present helps keep peace is not self-evident from a quick look at the numbers. Peace fell apart eventually in about 60% of the cases in which unarmed monitoring missions were present, and in almost 40% of the cases with armed peacekeeping forces, as compared to only about 20% of cease-fires with no peacekeeping. At first glance, then, peacekeeping appears to be detrimental to peace. But peacekeepers, and especially monitors, are more likely to be deployed when peace is most precarious. In particular, peacekeepers are not sent after wars that end in very lopsided military outcomes. The "no peacekeeping" category includes the only cases of the complete elimination of one side by the other (South Vietnam by North Vietnam), or of a government deposed by the enemy (Uganda's by Tanzania and Hungary's by the Soviet Union). It also includes such clear victories as the United Kingdom's over Argentina and China's over India. After two other very decisive defeats, the Six-Day War and the Bangladesh War, peacekeepers were present because a mission had been deployed after a previous war, but no new peacekeeping mission was sent (more on these cases below).

Not surprisingly, then, once the degree of difficulty of maintaining peace is taken into account, the negative relationship between peace-keeping and peace falls away. In quantitative tests controlling for the situational variables that shape the baseline prospects for peace, the hazard ratios for both monitoring and armed peacekeeping drop below 1.0 (see table 6.2). This means that the risk of war is lower when peacekeepers are present than when they are not. For armed peacekeepers, however, this relationship is not statistically significant. With so few cases in this category, we cannot be certain that this finding does not arise by chance alone.[43]

A closer look at peacekeeping's record suggests an important distinction between new peacekeeping missions deployed to help keep peace at, or immediately after, a cease-fire, and those that were already in place before the war broke out. Over half of the cases of war breaking out again when peacekeepers were present are attributable to missions that had been de-

[43] Armed peacekeeping is more prevalent in civil wars after the Cold War, where it, along with other types of UN missions, has a statistically significant effect on the duration of peace. Fortna 2002.

ployed for a previous cease-fire and had already failed at least once (hence there was another cease-fire). Two of these missions, UNTSO in the Middle East and UNMOGIP in Kashmir, are discussed in more detail below. The third, the UN Force in Cyprus (UNFICYP) was originally deployed in 1964 to keep peace between Turkish and Greek Cypriots after an eruption of fighting over attempts to change the power-sharing constitution. While the UN force was sent in part to forestall unilateral action by Turkey (by treaty Turkey, Greece, and Great Britain each held the right to intervene military if the three of them together could not guarantee peace and security on the island), the force was designed to maintain a cease-fire in a civil war. It was in no position to prevent military action by Turkey in 1974 after a coup inspired by Greece against the Cypriot government of Archbishop Makarios. And having failed to stop the outbreak of the war, there was nothing it could do to stop Turkey from occupying northern Cyprus two weeks after the first cease-fire went into effect.[44]

The experience of the various peacekeeping missions sent to the Middle East and to South Asia support the conclusion that "new" peacekeeping can help maintain peace, but that having failed once, missions are discredited and no longer serve much purpose. Armed peacekeepers have never been deployed to India and Pakistan, at first because the practice of sending international troops had not yet been invented, and later because India objected on ideological (anticolonialist) and sovereignty grounds. India did not object to unarmed monitors, however, and the UN Military Observer Group in India and Pakistan (UNMOGIP) deployed in January 1949. The observers collected information on troops, "orders of battle," and other classified military information, and are credited with alleviating both sides' fears and the possibility of surprise attack.[45] But the mission's most important role was not preventing undetected breaches of the cease-fire; in fact, most of the observers' day-to-day operations consisted of responding to the parties' own complaints of violations. Rather, it was to serve as referee, adjudicating between valid charges of cease-fire violations and disingenuous allegations. By investigating accusations and issuing findings on what had happened and who had started it, the peacekeepers were able to keep a lid on the cycle of retaliation and dispel rumors of atrocities that might otherwise have incited violence among local Kashmiris.[46]

The observers' referee function is important locally, but it can also play a role internationally by helping the international community distinguish between aggression and legitimate retaliation or trumped-up

---

[44] UNFICYP has done a very effective job of preventing intercommunal violence in Cyprus, however.

[45] Wainhouse 1966, 371; Brines 1968, 239, 320.

[46] Korbel 1954, e.g., 162–63; UNCIP 1949; see also Brines 1968; and Lamb 1991.

charges. In this regard, however, UNMOGIP fell short in 1965, undermining its own credibility. When infiltrators supported by Pakistan crossed the cease-fire line from Azad Kashmir into Indian-controlled territory, Secretary-General U Thant decided not to publicize monitors' reports from Kashmir. He drafted a report, but when Pakistan objected to it, he shelved it. He writes,

> Weighing carefully all considerations, I came to the conclusion that a public statement by the Secretary-General at that time would serve no constructive purpose and might well do more harm than good. My first and primary objective had to be to see the fighting end rather than indicting or denouncing any party for starting and continuing it.[47]

While the secretary-general may have had good political reasons to avoid alienating Pakistan, his policy undermined the effectiveness of monitors as international referees and discredited UNMOGIP, especially in India's eyes.

After the 1965 war, the UN sent a new mission, not to Kashmir, but to the international border between India and Pakistan proper. This mission, the UN India-Pakistan Observer Mission (UNIPOM) successfully helped maintain calm until Indian and Pakistani forces withdrew to their own side of the border after the Tashkent Declaration, and then UNIPOM withdrew. UNMOGIP is still deployed in Kashmir, but after the 1965 war, and especially after 1971, India refuses to cooperate with UN observers, and the mission is largely inactive.

In the early years of the Arab-Israeli conflict, UNTSO monitors also played an important role in providing information, investigating, and adjudicating alleged violations and negotiating local cease-fires when clashes broke out.[48] As the armistice regime and the military armistice commission machinery broke down, however, UNTSO's effectiveness also declined.

In 1956 the UN developed the practice of deploying armed international forces ("blue helmets," as opposed to unarmed monitors, or "blue berets") as peacekeepers. An international force was needed to allow the withdrawal of Israeli troops and a face-saving exit for Britain and France after the Sinai War. The first armed peacekeeping mission, UNEF, originally six thousand strong, created a buffer between withdrawing Israeli troops and Egyptian forces. Israel refused to let UNEF deploy on its side of the border, but the force remained in Egypt until 1967. The UNEF case demonstrates both the limits and the effects of peacekeeping. As tensions

---

[47] UN document S/6651, 1965, 7.

[48] Azcarate 1966, 100; Bull 1976, 41; Pelcovits 1993, 209–19. For details of specific examples of UNTSO's work, see Bar-Yaacov 1967; Khouri 1963, 21; and Kinsolving 1967.

mounted toward war in 1967, Nasser requested UNEF's withdrawal. He did so partly for political reasons, to respond to the accusation that he needed UN protection from Israel, but also because he was well aware that should he desire to fight Israel, the UN peacekeepers presented a significant obstacle. Whether he intended to strike Israel unprovoked or only in response to an offensive by Israel against Syria, Israel saw Nasser's move as a signal of impending attack and launched a preemptive strike.[49] The UNEF experience thus indicates that peacekeeping provides both a real constraint against attack and an important signal of intentions. Peacekeepers operate only with the consent of the host country, and therefore can be expelled.[50] Agreeing to peacekeepers ties the hands of belligerents, but they retain the ability to untie the knot. Of course, had Israel agreed to accept UN peacekeepers on its soil, either in 1956 or in 1967, Nasser would not have been able unilaterally to remove the buffer force, and the "course of history could have been different."[51] Moreover, the act of tying or untying one's hands with peacekeeping is a clear signal of intent; the untying cannot be done in secret.

The original UNTSO monitors remained in the Middle East after the 1967 war and seem to have helped manage low-level friction to some extent: things were calmer along the Israel-Syria and Israel-Lebanon fronts, where UNTSO was stationed, than along the Israeli-Jordanian front, where there was no monitoring, or in the Suez, until UNTSO redeployed there.[52] But UNTSO could not prevent the War of Attrition in 1969, and in 1973 observers were not even able to tell which side had started the Yom Kippur War.[53] UNTSO remains in the Middle East to this day, but after repeated warfare, and given largely antagonistic relations between the UN and Israel, it is not an effective peacekeeping tool.

On the other hand, the peacekeeping force sent to monitor and provide a buffer between Israel and Syria in the Golan after 1973 has been very successful. UNDOF deployed in 1974 to supervise Israel's withdrawal from areas east of the 1967 lines and to keep Israeli and Syrian troops apart during the disengagement. UNDOF continues to monitor the buffer zone from observation posts and mobile patrols. UN personnel also play a diplomatic role, resolving disputes over alleged violations or "unauthorized crossings" into the demilitarized zone. For both sides, the presence

[49] Up to this point, Israel had viewed aggressive posturing in Egypt as merely political maneuvering. Khouri 1985, 245–48.

[50] Peacekeeping missions authorized under Chapter VII of the UN Charter do not require the consent of the "peacekept" and are increasingly being used to enforce peace in civil conflicts.

[51] Secretary-General U Thant, quoted in Bailey 1990, 195.

[52] Khouri 1985, 291.

[53] Bailey 1990, 308; Ma'oz 1995, 99.

of UNDOF provides some security by serving as an alarm should either side try to seize the Golan.[54] The fact that both sides continue to cooperate with UNDOF investigations also serves as a signaling device, indicating (relatively) benign intentions. The ad hoc multinational force sent to Lebanon in 1982 (MNF I, not to be confused with MNF II) was deployed only for a short time, but was one of the few peacekeeping successes in Lebanon. MNF I provided the security necessary for the evacuation of Syrian and PLO forces from Beirut. Similarly, the Multinational Force and Observers (MFO) deployed in the Sinai in 1982 after the Egypt-Israeli Peace Agreement has played an instrumental verification role reassuring both sides of the other's compliance.

The mixed results in South Asia and the Middle East suggest that peacekeeping can work, but that once it fails, leaving a mission in place indefinitely is ineffective. If we remove "old" peacekeeping cases from the quantitative analysis, we can see the effects of peacekeeping clearly. If we drop cases in which peacekeepers were present from a previous war, but no new mission was deployed, the effect of both monitoring and armed peacekeeping is dramatic and statistically significant (table 6.2, column 3). The hazard rate when either monitors or armed peacekeepers are present is only a tiny fraction of that of cease-fires with no peacekeeping.[55] The UN often leaves missions in place for decades even after they have failed as a way to signal ongoing international interest (it would be politically difficult to withdraw UNTSO, for example), but these peacekeeping operations have no positive effect on peace.

Peacekeeping is clearly not a magic bullet. Its effects are limited by the belligerents' consent, and it sometimes fails to keep peace. Once it fails, the peacekeeping mission is discredited and can do little to prevent another outbreak of fighting. New peacekeeping missions, however, help keep peace. Peace is much more likely to last when international monitors or soldiers are sent than when belligerents are left to their own devices.

III. COMMUNICATION AND SIGNALING

Confidence-Building Measures

Confidence-building measures provide information about or regulate military activities (such as mine clearance or troop maneuvers) that are likely

---

[54] For an assessment of UNDOF, see Ghali 1993a.

[55] Note that dropping these cases makes the hazard ratios of several situational variables skyrocket, in part due to selection bias. Recoding peacekeeping to reflect only new missions (rather than dropping cases) also indicates that both monitoring and armed peacekeepers reduce the risk of another war substantially, though the hazard ratio for monitors is only significant when Middle East conflicts are controlled for.

to cause tension between deadly enemies. Communication hot lines to allow leaders to contact each other in a crisis are also considered CBMs. The concept of confidence-building measures as a peacemaking tool was not developed until the mid-1970s, but provisions that we would now dub CBMs were sometimes implemented before that. Nonetheless, CBMs have been relatively rare in cease-fire agreements: only about one in four contained any mechanism for exchanging information to reduce military friction. There is some evidence that these measures help states maintain peace, but with so few cases it is hard to know how effective CBMs are in the aftermath of war.

The Korean armistice agreement called for advance notification of troop rotations. There were detailed provisions governing mine clearance after the second Kashmir war and in the Paris Peace Agreement in Vietnam, and Iran and Iraq shared information on minefields in 1991. Hot lines between military commanders were established after the 1965 and 1971 wars between India and Pakistan, and in a follow-up agreement after the Falklands War. The Israeli-Egyptian peace agreement included a hot line and an elaborate verification system run by the United States involving aerial and electronic surveillance in the Sinai.[56] With the exception of the India-Pakistan cases, these measures are associated with lasting peace.

The hazard of renewed war is lower when CBMs are implemented than when they are not, but the relationship is not statistically significant (see table 6.3). With so few cases, it is possible that this is just a coincidence in our data. The Israel-Syria case study does not help us evaluate the effect of CBMs since they have never been implemented between these two states. The India-Pakistan case is certainly not a showcase of CBM success. Arms control provisions that limited military activity near the cease-fire line in Kashmir (discussed above) seem to have reduced tensions, but communication links have not prevented war. Motivated by the risk of a nuclear exchange, India and Pakistan agreed to a number of confidence-building measures in the late 1980s and early 1990s. These may have helped prevent nuclear war when very small arsenals gave India and Pakistan a strong incentive for a preventive or preemptive strike.[57] But these measures did not prevent conventional fighting in 1999.

[56] There was extensive verification of Iraq after the Gulf War, though the one-sidedness of this case cuts against the idea of mutual confidence-building.

[57] Experts on nuclear weapons in South Asia viewed such an attack as frighteningly likely in the days and weeks after nuclear tests in May 1998. Roundtable on the India-Pakistan Nuclear Tests, Center for International Security and Arms Control, Stanford University, May 28, 1998.

In short, the jury is still out on CBMs as a tool for helping maintain peace in the aftermath of war. The evidence we have suggests that they may be useful, but we do not have enough of it to make a strong case for their effectiveness.

Dispute Resolution

Diplomatic relations are often severed during war, making communication and accurate signaling of intentions all the more difficult. Chapter 1 hypothesized that dispute resolution procedures established in a cease-fire agreement might ameliorate this problem. I coded two types of communication channels: ongoing third-party mediation after a cease-fire has been reached (not to be confused with mediation to reach the cease-fire, which was discussed above), and joint commissions consisting of representatives of the combatant states.[58] The former is apparently not an effective tool for maintaining peace, but the latter has been very successful.

In table 6.3 we can see that ongoing mediation is actually associated with a higher risk of another war. Mediation and negotiations continued after the first cease-fire in the Turco-Cypriot War, after the first cease-fire in Palestine (first by Count Bernadotte and then, after his assassination, by Ralph Bunche) and during the first cease-fire in the Armenian-Azerbaijani war. All of these flared up again quickly. Informal meetings between Indian and Pakistani sector commanders after the 1965 Kashmir war were mediated by UN special representative General Marambio. These meetings were generally more successful than public high-level meetings at reaching agreement on local disputes and problems and helping to prevent an immediate resumption of the war, but they were not well institutionalized. It is possible that ongoing third-party mediation and the rapid breakdown of peace are associated because these cease-fires were considered quite temporary even at the time, and outsiders were hoping to make them permanent. This is a post hoc explanation, however. In any case, we cannot conclude that communication through a third-party mediator is an effective tool for dispute resolution.

Joint commissions made up of the belligerents themselves are much more successful. Peace has rarely failed after cease-fires that set up joint commissions to work out disputes as they arise. The hazard of another war drops to almost zero when a joint commission is created (see table 6.3, column 2). The Korean armistice agreement set up a military armistice commission and joint observer teams to work out violations of the agreement. Egypt and Israel set up a joint commission of representatives

[58] Note that I do not include the work of peacekeepers in day-to-day dispute resolution in this coding.

TABLE 6.3
Communication and Signaling

	Weibull Hazard Ratios (robust standard errors)			
Confidence-building measures	0.136 (0.426)			
Dispute resolution				
Ongoing mediation		4.867*** (1.394)		
Joint commission		0.000*** (0.000)		
Specificity			0.963*** (0.007)	
Formal agreement				0.416* (0.220)
Tie	30.666*** (9.103)	10.150*** (1.861)	35.289*** (12.308)	24.511*** (6.518)
Cost of war	0.699 (0.307)	0.712** (0.119)	0.763** (0.091)	0.521*** (0.088)
History of conflict	2.874*** (0.656)	2.126*** (0.352)	1.682*** (0.262)	2.392*** (0.725)
Existence at stake	5.768*** (3.025)	7.022*** (3.000)	25.907*** (13.513)	6.651*** (3.776)
Contiguous	2.442* (1.240)	2.573*** (0.604)	6.955*** (2.151)	3.337*** (1.358)
Change in relative capabilities	2.324 *** (0.492)	3.283*** (0.725)	4.570*** (0.749)	2.321*** (0.391)
P	0.747 (0.151)	0.933 (0.150)	1.081 (0.165)	0.853 (0.203)
N	770	770	757	770
No. of subjects	48	48	47	48
Log likelihood	−46.769	−38.002	−37.644	−46.407

Note: Cases clustered by conflict.
 * Statistically significant at the .10 level.
 ** Statistically significant at the .05 level.
 *** Statistically significant at the .01 level.

as part of their peace treaty in 1979, and Ethiopia and Somalia established a joint military committee to supervise disengagement in 1988. In 1980, Honduras and El Salvador agreed to very specific details on a joint commission to settle their boundary dispute. One would not want to attribute lasting peace in all of these cases only to the dispute resolution procedures established. The mixed commission to settle disputes arising from the stationing of Soviet troops in Hungary set up in 1957 was not a major factor contributing to peace, for example. But in other cases, Honduras and El Salvador especially, but also Ethiopia and Somalia, Egypt and Israel, and perhaps China and Vietnam after 1993, the work of joint commissions was arguably quite important for sustaining peace.

The military armistice commissions (MACs) set up bilaterally between Israel and its opponents in the first Arab-Israeli war provide an interesting example. They worked quite well in the first years after the war to handle disputes over land use, fishing and farming rights, small incidents between soldiers, and accidental border crossings.[59] But they broke down as animosities hardened in the mid-1950s. Unresolved sovereignty issues led to Israel's refusal to participate in the Israeli-Syrian MAC, and Syria also began obstructing the commission. Israel withdrew from its commission with Jordan in 1953 and refused to allow Egyptian representatives to attend meetings in the El Auja demilitarized zone in 1956. The MACs were largely defunct before the Sinai War, and had been inoperative for years before the 1967 war.

One could argue that joint commissions only work with the "political will" of the combatants and that they are therefore unimportant in their own right. That political will is crucial is clearly true; commissions can easily be obstructed and fall into disuse as they did in the Middle East. But to argue that they are therefore irrelevant misses their role as an important signal of intentions. When Israel and later Syria stopped cooperating with the MACs, this fact sent a signal that there would no longer be a good-faith effort to resolve problems and avoid war. The breakdown of the MAC regime was in part caused by rising hostility, but it also contributed to this hostility and the tensions that eventually led back to war. Conversely, the willingness of El Salvador and Honduras or Ethiopia and Somalia to cooperate with a joint commission and abide by its decisions on disputes signaled a commitment to making peace work. Joint dispute resolution procedures are therefore an important mechanism enabling states who want to avoid war to do so.

[59] See, for example, Kinsolving 1967, 24.

Specificity

Chapter 1 hypothesized that more specific agreements would be more likely to last than vaguer ones because spelling out the terms of a cease-fire more precisely helps to avoid misunderstandings about what constitutes compliance. There is at least circumstantial support for this hypothesis. The more specific and detailed the agreement, the lower the hazard of another round of fighting, all else equal (see table 6.3, column 3). More specific agreements are more likely to include other measures to help keep peace, but the effect of specificity holds up even when these other measures are controlled for. The most detailed agreements (e.g., the Israeli-Egyptian agreements reached after 1973) have been followed by lasting peace. Cases of medium detail have been moderately successful. Examples in this category include the agreements reached after the Sino-Indian War, the Gulf War, the first and second Kashmir wars, and the armistice agreements reached after the first Arab-Israeli war. Much shorter and less detailed agreements such as those reached after the Sinai War, the Six-Day War, the 1948 cease-fire in the first Arab-Israeli war, and first Turco-Cypriot cease-fire, have tended to fail much more quickly.

In both the India-Pakistan and Israel-Syria cases, the most important aspect of specifying a cease-fire is the clear demarcation of the cease-fire line and clarification of who owns what land. Efforts by both India and Pakistan to push the line to their advantage led to very tense situations, particularly in 1965, but to some extent in all three cease-fires. Many of the incidents that took place between the cease-fire and the withdrawal to a demarcated cease-fire line were attempts by both sides to improve their territorial position as much as possible.[60] Formal demarcation of the line solved the problem in all three cases, with the number of skirmishes falling noticeably once the line was fixed and marked. Demarcation of the line removes uncertainty about where it lies, and also removes the incentive to try to whittle away some territorial advantage. Since a small advance will not change the legal location of the line once it has been demarcated, there is much less to be gained by fighting to push it forward.[61]

Most of the disputes and clashes between Israel and Syria between 1949 and 1967 took place over issues that were not clearly worked out in the armistice agreement, particularly the matter of sovereignty and administration in the demilitarized areas. Because the matter of control of the land was not settled, both sides had an incentive to push the point in order to establish precedent. The clashes arising from ambiguities in the

[60] UN document S/6710 and addenda, 1965–66. For a specific example, see Add. 9, 7.
[61] Demarcation of the line provides a focal point in the distributional game over the division of territory.

agreement and unsettled sovereignty contributed to the exacerbation of hostile relations that led eventually to the 1967 war. Conversely, the very specific disengagement agreement reached after the Yom Kippur War contributed to the absence of incidents in the Golan. In Lebanon, the well-worked-out details of the Beirut agreement are credited with allowing a smooth and incident-free evacuation of PLO and Syrian forces.[62] The unspecified nature of the cease-fire in the Biqa' Valley, on the other hand, seems to have contributed to clashes and violations until Israel withdrew from Lebanon in 1983.

Of course, specifying the cease-fire line and who owns what will not prevent war altogether. Even though the terms of the 1967 cease-fire were not well specified, it would be absurd to argue that uncertainty or vagueness about what exactly constituted compliance was responsible for the Arab attack in 1973. And while the inherently ambiguous nature of the tacit agreement reached in 1976 over Lebanon did contribute to the arrangement's deterioration and to serious clashes, Israel's decision to attack Syrian forces was made with clear knowledge that this violated the understanding.[63] Deliberate attacks can not be forestalled by specifying the terms of compliance, but defining compliance can help prevent skirmishing as both sides try to improve their positions. Empirically, more specific agreements yield more durable peace.

Formal Agreement and Audience Costs

I hypothesized that formal agreements might be more stable because they invoke international law and induce domestic and especially international audience costs, providing a credible signal of intentions. All else equal, peace does tend to last longer after formal agreements than after tacit or unilaterally declared cease-fires. The hazard of another war after a formal cease-fire is less than half that of an informal one (see table 6.3, column 4). The difference is only marginally significant and not terribly robust, however, so we should treat this quantitative finding with some caution.

Cases with no agreement or a unilaterally declared cease-fire that is tacitly accepted by the other side tend to be fairly stable, though this is largely the result of lopsided military outcomes (the Ugandan-Tanzanian, Russo-Hungarian, and Falklands wars, for example). Tacit or informal agreement to a cease-fire proposal put forth by the UN or a third-party mediator tends to be quite unstable (e.g., the 1948 cease-fire in Palestine, the Six-Day War, and the first cease-fire between Armenia and Azerbaijan), though in some cases even informal agreements can last (the Sinai

[62] Thakur 1987, 95.
[63] Evron 1987, 95.

War ended with no formal agreement between Britain or France and Egypt). Formally accepted cease-fire proposals (as in the War of Attrition between Egypt and Israel or the Iran-Iraq war), and formal bilateral or multilateral agreements (the Korean and Arab-Israeli armistice agreements, the formal agreements signed at Karachi, Tashkent, and Simla between India and Pakistan, and the agreements reached between Israel and both Syria and Egypt after the Yom Kippur War), tend to fare better than tacit ones. Both the quantitative and the large-N qualitative evidence suggest that formal agreements are more durable that informal ones, but in neither is the finding definitive.

The case studies show that international reactions were frequently an important concern in decisions about war and peace.[64] The general norm against aggression makes the role of formal agreements difficult to observe. That is, it is hard to distinguish the international reaction to a state reneging on a cease-fire agreement from the opprobrium directed against any aggression whether a formal agreement was made or not. But the cases also provide at least some evidence that formal agreements create lines that states are reluctant to cross.

States are unlikely to trust in the effects of international reputation alone to keep peace. When Korbel, one of the UNCIP mediators, assured Nehru that should Pakistan violate the 1949 truce, "the whole weight of the UN would be turned against Pakistan," he reports, "the Prime Minister merely raised his eyes and smiled with gentle but obvious skepticism." Korbel had no greater luck convincing Pakistan's Zafrullah Khan.[65] Nonetheless, it is clear that in both South Asia and the Middle East, great care has been taken to avoid being seen as the aggressor by the international community. In both cases, formal agreements have been broken, but it is not the case that states simply disregarded their formal commitments or international reactions to their behavior.

India and Pakistan were extremely careful to avoid overtly breaching the cease-fire and being labeled the aggressor by the international community. As tensions were growing both in 1965 and 1971, each side went to great diplomatic effort to blame the other for starting the hostilities.[66] Even after the wars were over, India and Pakistan continued their debate

[64] The role of domestic audiences is less clear, although in some cases domestic opposition to peace can make willingness to commit formally to an agreement a costly signal of intent. Anwar Sadat's politically very expensive overture to Israel and the peace agreement reached in 1979 is a good example.

[65] Korbel 1954, 142–43.

[66] See, for example, communications to UN secretary-general U Thant from Prime Minister Shastri and from President Ayub Khan, September 12 and 13, respectively, in UN document S/6683, 1965; see also Brines 1968, 302–3, 323. On mutual recriminations over who turned a dangerous situation into open war in 1971, see Blinkenberg 1972, 322.

over who started it, each claiming defensive and legitimate reaction to the other's aggression. If the belligerents did not care about world opinion, they would not have insisted so vehemently on their innocence.

These rhetorical debates may have been merely words, but there is more concrete evidence of the operation of audience costs. The way in which India and Pakistan chose to carry out aggression indicates their concern not to be labeled the aggressor. When Pakistan chose to challenge the status quo over Kashmir in 1965 and again in 1999, and when India chose to intervene in Pakistan's civil war and to split Pakistan apart, neither could simply and openly invade. Rather, Pakistan sent Kashmiri forces across the cease-fire line, and India sponsored the Mukti Bahini insurgency. They hid violation of their agreement under the cover of indigenous insurgencies, only intervening openly once the other had been provoked into conflict. In 1965 Pakistan's use of raiders rather than regular military units undermined the attack's effectiveness.[67] The ploy of avoiding open attack by regular forces was clearly for international consumption—they were not fooling each other, as the predictable retaliations showed. It was an attempt to legitimate aggression so as to avoid paying international audience costs. In 1965 at least, this artifice worked. While historians have laid the blame for the outbreak of the 1965 war on Pakistan's official and deliberate use of raiders to invade Kashmir, at the time most of the international blame fell on India for its decision to cross the cease-fire line to cut off the raiders.[68] India appears to have learned from this and employed the tactic of instigating guerrilla attacks in 1971. In 1999, Pakistan seems to have believed it could get away with seizing the heights in Kargil by claiming it was Kashmiri separatists, not regular Pakistani troops, who had crossed the line of control.[69]

More direct evidence can also be seen in the historical record that the prospect of adverse international reactions helped maintain peace. As we have seen, in the aftermath of the second Kashmir war, there was considerable pressure within Pakistan, both in popular opinion and from decision makers such as Bhutto, to restart the war and press for a more decisive victory. President Ayub was deterred in part by the anticipated international reaction, especially the prospect of losing international aid.[70] India put off an overt military response to the conflict in East Pakistan in March or April 1971, in part because of the international reaction if diplomatic means of resolving the conflict were not first exhausted. This was only one of several reasons, and of course it did not prevent the eventual out-

[67] Brines 1968, 310.
[68] Brines 1968, 333.
[69] Ganguly 2001, 115.
[70] Blinkenberg 1972, 275.

break of war. However, international costs, both diplomatic and economic, have also helped deter India from intervening again in Pakistani domestic politics since 1971. Weakening Pakistan was not worth "the possible alienation of India's crucial Middle Eastern oil suppliers, international disapproval, and a further erosion of India's position in the nonaligned movement."[71]

India and Pakistan were clearly concerned about audience costs, that is, about international reactions to violations of the cease-fire. But audience costs could have been more effectively applied. They depend on the ability of the international community to determine aggression and on world reaction. As we have seen, in the run-up to the 1965 war, the role of monitors as referees to distinguish unprovoked aggression from legitimate retaliation was undermined by the UN secretary-general's decision not to assess blame or announce "who started it." Even before this, the international community's failure to react strongly to fighting in the Rann of Kutch in 1965 sent the signal that the world would not react strongly to the outbreak of hostilities. This encouraged Pakistani aggression later that year.[72] The UN's reluctance to offend India and Pakistan and the unwillingness of the superpowers to criticize their allies limited the effectiveness of audience costs as a deterrent to war. India and Pakistan were clearly thinking about audience costs and were restrained by them, but the international community could have done more to make it clear that aggression, even covert aggression using insurgents, would be condemned.

The seriousness with which the belligerents took the international audience can be seen in their efforts to circumvent the agreements and to publicly blame each other for aggression. But, as noted above, it is hard to know whether the formal nature of agreements played a role in this. There was a clear stabilizing effect along the cease-fire line after the signing of both the Karachi and Tashkent agreements, suggesting that these public and formal agreements sent an important signal. But because these agreements implemented a number of other concrete measures, it is difficult to separate the effect of the formal agreement from these other mechanisms. After the second Kashmir war, participants at the time certainly felt that reaching a formal agreement was important symbolically, and bilateral relations warmed up considerably in the "Spirit of Tashkent" after the agreement was signed in January 1966.[73]

The importance of formal agreements themselves can sometimes be observed in the breach. The hostilities on the Siachen Glacier in the early

---

[71] Ganguly 1986, 12, 120.

[72] Brines 1968, 290. Pakistan's probe may have been an attempt to gauge the international community's response as much as India's.

[73] Brines 1968, 405.

1980s provides one example. The cease-fire line of 1971, the "line of actual control," was demarcated through most of Kashmir, but it fades away into the glaciers of the Karakoram mountains. No one had bothered to define the exact line up in this inhospitable territory, partly because such a definition would have required agreement on where the border with China lay, and this was in dispute. Specifying the terminus of the cease-fire line would require either India to grant China's territorial claim, or Pakistan to renounce it. The lack of a defined cease-fire line amounted to a loophole in the international law. The "glacier offered a route by which the cease-fire line could be outflanked without a technical violation of the 1972 Simla Agreement."[74] By 1982, Indian and Pakistani patrols were vying for control of the glacier, and in the mid-1980s they were skirmishing at altitudes of 20,000 feet.[75] In the Siachen dispute India and Pakistan were going to extraordinary lengths, or more literally heights, to press for advantage without breaking the formal cease-fire line agreed to in 1972. The taboo against crossing the line set in the 1972 Simla Agreement remains. In 1999, India ruled out crossing the line of control to cut off the infiltrators in Kargil, resorting to air power rather than risk being accused of violating the line.[76] Having been blamed for the 1965 war because it was provoked into crossing the formal cease-fire line, India avoided this political mistake in Kargil.

The importance of international reactions has been equally important in the Middle East. Peace has lasted longest on the two occasions when Israel and Syria reached formal, public agreements. And there is ample evidence that while it did not always keep peace, concern for the international reaction to their behavior affected the belligerents' behavior. That Israel and the Arab states adhered scrupulously to the temporary cease-fire called for by the UN Security Council in June 1948 demonstrates the authority the UN was then given. Concern for international opinion delayed, but did not prevent, Israel's offensive three months into the next cease-fire. Israel postponed its attack in the wake of Bernadotte's assassination and the international outcry it caused. Israeli foreign minister Sharett opposed the offensive altogether on the grounds that it would harm Israel's international reputation.[77] Israel also went to some lengths (by some reports even firing on one of its own vehicles) to make it appear that its attack was in response to an Egyptian violation.[78]

Israel tended to be condemned much more heavily for its retaliatory attacks than the Arab states were for the guerilla raids coming from their

[74] Lamb 1991, 325–26.
[75] More soldiers are said to have died from altitude sickness than from unfriendly fire.
[76] Ganguly 2001, 117.
[77] Khouri 1985, 86.
[78] Bailey 1990, 46; Khouri 1985, 87.

territory because the former were more obvious in nature and were clearly official policy. Some policymakers were sensitive to this international opprobrium, but Israel did not abandon its reprisal policy.[79] Israel's perception that the international condemnation was unfair contributed to the deterioration of its relations with the UN, and Israel soon came to exhibit much more concern for U.S. opinion than for that of the world body. Israel's reprisal policy may have delayed development of its favorable relationship with the United States, but given U.S. domestic political considerations and the Cold War context, it did not do lasting harm.[80]

In 1967, the operation of audience costs is seen in part by their absence. The international community had reacted mildly to Israeli retaliatory raids earlier in the year. More important, the United States eased its restraint on Israel and provided a "yellow light" for preemptive action. Israel could thus proceed without fear of undue international costs.[81] Nonetheless, Israel was wary of upsetting its relationship with Washington as it contemplated its offensive, and was careful not to appear to attack before diplomacy had been given a chance, lest it be blamed for starting the war.[82] Both sides claimed the other had started the war, and the Security Council decided not to get bogged down in deciding who was the aggressor.[83]

On the morning of October 6, 1973, Israel learned of the impending attack from Syria and Egypt. Israel decided against another preemptive strike because, as Golda Meir put it, "there is always the possibility that we will need help, and if we strike first, we will get nothing from anyone."[84] Syria, on the other hand, was likely to gain international standing within the Arab world for taking on Israel boldly and attempting to reclaim Arab lands.

There is also some evidence that formal commitments induce audience costs more than tacit ones; international opinion did not come into play substantially to uphold the tacit Red Lines Agreement. Once the strategic reasons to avoid war in Lebanon fell away, it was relatively easy to ignore the informal arrangement.[85] A mild response from the United States to Israeli provocations (to Israel's declaring Jerusalem its capital and annexing the Golan Heights) contributed to the Israeli decision to attack Syrian forces in 1982, albeit with a wary eye on Washington's reaction.

---

[79] Israel was on its best behavior while it awaited membership in the UN. Khouri 1985, 187; Ma'oz 1995, 52, 74; Pelcovits 1993, 45, 53.

[80] Khouri 1985, 187; Pelcovits 1993, 12.

[81] Khouri 1985, 244; Ma'oz 1995, 100–101.

[82] Foreign Minister Abba Eban reminded the Israeli cabinet of the harm done in 1956 when Israel was seen as the aggressor. Khouri 1985, 254.

[83] Bailey 1990, 225–27; Khouri 1985, 259.

[84] Quoted in Bailey 1990, 307.

[85] Ma'oz 1995, 169–70.

And once again, Israel waited for a fig leaf, deliberately provoking Syria into firing the first shot.[86] As in South Asia, formal agreements were important symbolically, if nothing else. In a conflict in which recognition of one side as a legitimate state is an issue, a formal agreement carries political weight as a signal.[87]

The existence of the cease-fire agreement reached in June 1982 between Israel and Syria also constrained (though it did not stop) Israeli military moves in Lebanon. This agreement prevented Israeli forces from launching a full attack on Syrian positions and from taking the Beirut-Damascus highway. As Zeev Schiff and Ehud Ya'ari explain: "To order an outright attack on the road would be too flagrant a violation of the cease-fire with Syria, and would moreover require cabinet approval." Instead, Sharon urged his officers to "creep" forward to improve their positions in response to alleged Palestinian and Syrian fire. "But there was a price for this skulking around in the hills: the army could not concentrate reinforcements or use their air force at full strength to aid the ground forces." What became known as the "creeping cease-fire" also eroded Sharon's standing within the Israeli cabinet.[88] This agreement apparently induced both international audience costs, particularly with the United States, and domestic ones with the Israeli cabinet.

International opinion often failed to prevent war between Israel and Syria, but this was not because it was completely disregarded by the belligerents. Indeed there is ample evidence that Israel was concerned particularly with U.S. reactions, while Syria paid attention to Soviet opinion and the reaction of the Arab world. Rather, Cold War considerations stunted the ability of the international community to condemn aggression consistently.

In sum, international reactions and concern with the cost of being labeled the aggressor clearly affect decisions regarding war and peace. There is also some evidence that formal agreements invoke these international costs more than informal or tacit cease-fires, though the general norm against aggression means some costs will be paid for breaking even an informal truce. The cases also suggest that the effects of international audience costs are often limited, either by the UN's desire to maintain neutrality or by great powers turning a blind eye for strategic reasons. Nonetheless, peace lasts longer when formal agreements are in place, suggesting that they serve as an important signal to the other side and to the international audience.

[86] Evron 1987, 118, 127; Ma'oz 1995, 171–74.

[87] See Azcarate 1966 and Pelcovits 1993 on the importance of the 1949 armistice agreements being signed by government representatives rather than military ones. And see Kissinger 1982 on this issue for the disengagement agreements reached in 1974.

[88] Schiff and Ya'ari 1984, 203.

SETTLING THE ISSUES

This study has focused on mechanisms that adversaries can use to maintain peace even if they continue to disagree fundamentally and even if
they are still formally in a state of war. It is a study of cease-fires more
than peace agreements. But no treatment of agreements and the durability
of peace would be complete without a discussion of peace settlements.

We would certainly expect that war will be less likely to re-erupt when
belligerents reach a peace agreement than when they merely agree to
cease-fire. When fighting stops, it is not necessarily self-evident which is
the case, however. One way to distinguish cases a priori is by looking at
the agreements themselves. Agreements that commit belligerents to renounce the use of force to settle disputes, or that restore diplomatic relations, or formally end a state of war can be considered peace agreements,
while other agreements are only truces. By this definition the Korean armistice, all of the Middle East cease-fires except the Israeli-Egyptian
agreements after 1975, the initial cease-fire in the Falklands, and most
others are truces. The Israeli-Egyptian agreements reached in 1975 and
1979 are peace agreements, as are the 1965 and 1971 agreements between
India and Pakistan since they include statements renouncing the use of
force. By this definition the Soviets and Hungary reached peace in 1957
when they signed an agreement on Soviet troops stationed in Hungary,
and China and India reached peace in 1993.

Using this distinction, we can see that peace agreements are indeed
more likely to last than cease-fires, and cease-fires are more likely to last
than wars that end with no agreement (the omitted category in the statistical analysis), but that the differences are not statistically significant (see
table 6.4, column 1). No-agreement cases tend to be quite stable, but this
is because these are relatively easy cases where one side has decisively
beaten the other. Most agreements that renounce the use of force or restore diplomatic relations have lasted, though those between India and
Pakistan have not.

This formal or legalistic definition of peace may carry some weight.
The rhetoric of committing to settle disputes peacefully can be politically
costly, and formal diplomatic relations are not meaningless. Imagine for
example the difference it would make if Syria and Israel recognized each
other and formally ended their state of war, even if they did not settle the
issues of the Golan and Palestinian statehood. This formal distinction
between types of agreements is not irrelevant, but neither does it have a
very strong or robust effect on the duration of peace.

Another way, more subjective but probably more meaningful, to separate peace agreements from mere cease-fires is to examine whether belligerents reached a political settlement on the issues over which they fought

TABLE 6.4
Political Settlement

	Weibull Hazard Ratios (robust standard errors)		
Cease-fire agreement	0.594 (0.583)		
peace agreement	0.280 (0.301)		
Political settlement			
Unilateral		0.000*** (0.000)	1.317 (2.005)
Agreed		0.000*** (0.000)	0.000*** (0.000)
Tie	31.605*** (7.901)	18.891*** (8.942)	21.425*** (9.393)
Cost of war	0.514*** (0.090)	0.519*** (0.093)	0.545*** (0.094)
History of conflict	3.048*** (0.829)	2.492*** (0.570)	2.729 *** (0.558)
Existence at stake	5.505*** (2.751)	4.734*** (2.138)	3.893*** (1.619)
Contiguous	2.147 (1.061)	1.969* (0.713)	3.399*** (1.001)
Change in relative capabilities	2.752*** (0.526)	2.249*** (0.536)	
P	0.744* (0.124)	0.721* (0.136)	0.738* (0.116)
N	770	770	48
No. of subjects	48	48	
Log likelihood	−47.160	−46.394	−50.440

Notes: Time-constant data are used in the rightmost column. Cases clustered by conflict.
* Statistically significant at the .10 level.
** Statistically significant at the .05 level.
*** Statistically significant at the .01 level.

the war. Political issues might be settled unilaterally by force (de facto settlement) or through an explicit agreement (de jure). Most wars in the last half-century have ended with no settlement. Its other problems aside, war is a surprisingly ineffective means of settling disputes. In only nine wars have the issues over which the war was fought been settled unilaterally by a clear victor: the Russo-Hungarian war, China's territorial issue with India, Vietnam (North vs. South), Bangladesh (though Kashmir's status was not settled), the second round of fighting between Turkey and Cyprus, Uganda and Tanzania, the Falklands, and the second part of the Azeri-Armenian war. In very few has an explicit agreement been reached: Israel and Egypt settled their political issues in the process leading up to the 1979 peace agreement; Iraq formally conceded the territorial issue in Kuwait when it surrendered in 1991; to secure its flank, Iraq also settled its territorial issue with Iran on the Shatt al-Arab waterway in an agreement a few years after the end of the Iran-Iraq War. In a handful of other cases, former belligerents eventually laid their dispute to rest long after the fighting was over. El Salvador and Honduras accepted the International Court of Justice's ruling on their disputed border in 1992, for example, and Israel and Jordan reached peace in 1994.[89]

Unilateral settlement tends to be very stable (table 6.4, column 2). But note that there is a risk of tautology here. If these unilaterally settled conflicts had been contested by force (i.e., in another war) we would not consider them settled. Moreover, India and Pakistan fought yet again in 1999 despite India's unilateral settlement of their previous war (though their settlement in 1971 was limited to Bangladeshi secession, not Kashmir). This failure is not captured in the time-varying analyses because it occurs after the point of censoring in that version of the data. When a time-constant model is used with data on resumption of war to 2000 (column 3), the hazard of unilaterally settled wars is statistically indistinguishable from those with no settlement at all. The hazard ratio is actually greater than 1.0, so if anything, imposed settlements are less stable than no-settlement cases.[90]

Not surprisingly, de jure settlement of the issues leads to very durable peace (column 2). In the last 50 years at least, war has not resumed between any states that reached an explicit peace agreement settling the political issues over which they fought.[91] Political agreement on the fundamental issues leads to stable peace. But political agreement is of course extremely difficult to come by. In the vast majority of cases, even if one side has beaten the other clearly, the fundamental issues they fought over

---

[89] The Soviets and Hungary reached a formal settlement of sorts with their Treaty of Friendship, Cooperation and Mutual Assistance in 1967. The United States and Vietnam began making peace in the late 1980s, a process that culminated in the signing of a trade agreement normalizing relations in July 2000.

[90] These findings support those of Hensel 1994 that disputes ending in negotiated compromise are least likely to recur.

[91] The United States and Iraq provide an exception now that war has resumed in the Gulf because Iraq's renunciation of its claim to Kuwait in 1991 fits my definition of political settlement.

remain contested. The issues that caused war remain unsettled after five rounds of fighting between Israel and Syria. Kashmir is still contested after four wars between India and Pakistan; China and Vietnam fought twice without settling their border dispute. A major war and almost half a century have not settled the Korean conflict.

So while an explicit agreement on the political issues is the best way to secure peace, this advice is not particularly useful for most belligerents. When the underlying issues remain disputed, it is the other mechanisms examined in this study that can be used to maintain peace.

CONCLUSION

What lessons can we draw from the cease-fires of the last half-century? The foregoing analysis tells us what works and what does not work to maintain peace in the aftermath of war. Withdrawal from territory captured in war does not guarantee stable peace, but failure to withdraw is quite likely to bring on another round of fighting, and withdrawal beyond the status quo ante sends a strong signal of commitment to peace. Demilitarized zones have been an effective way to separate forces so as to increase the cost of an attack and prevent skirmishes that might escalate to full-scale war. Demilitarization of contested areas as a way of skirting sovereignty issues can produce dangerous power vacuums, however. Arms control may help bolster buffer zones, providing additional protection from attack or minimizing the risk of military tension, but arms control is not in general an effective tool for maintaining peace. Concrete measures to prevent involuntary defection by rogue groups can be effective, but often the problem is "voluntary" or deliberate use of allegedly rogue groups to subvert peace. Belligerents have not devised effective ways to deal with this problem. Simply stating that both sides are responsible for attacks originating from their territory has not been helpful.

Outsiders interested in bolstering peace can affect its prospects by providing explicit guarantees of the peace. However, while lower levels of involvement, such as mediation of the initial cease-fire, may help states stop fighting, they do not translate into effective guarantees of the peace. Peacekeeping does in fact help keep peace; peace is more likely to last when the international community deploys monitors or troops. But the credibility of peacekeeping missions is fragile. Once it has been undermined by renewed fighting, keeping a mission in place provides no benefit. Interestingly, it is not the credibility of peacekeeping as a whole that is damaged by failure, but of particular missions. Sending a new mission can help even when an old one has failed. UNDOF does not seem to have been affected by the failure of UNTSO, for example.

Confidence-building measures may provide some positive effect by reducing the possibility for military tension, but we do not have enough information to judge their effectiveness rigorously. Ongoing negotiations through a mediator do not provide much in the way of a communication channel for dispute resolution (although selection effects may be at work here), but joint commissions made up of the belligerents themselves are an effective way to manage disputes. Cooperation with such commissions also provides an important signal of intent to keep the peace. Specific agreements are more likely to last than vague ones. In particular, demarcation of the cease-fire line appears to be important for preventing "salami tactics." Formal agreements also fare somewhat better than tacit ones, but this difference is not large. The norm against aggression applies almost as strongly to tacit cease-fires as to formal and explicit ones. It is quite clear, however, that international reactions play an important role in decisions about war and peace.

In short, arms control, third-party mediation, and statements of responsibility for hostile acts do not help maintain peace. Confidence-building measures, formalizing an agreement, and withdrawal of forces to the pre-war lines may help, but the evidence is not clear-cut. The most effective mechanisms for maintaining peace in the aftermath of war are withdrawal beyond the status quo ante, demilitarized zones, explicit third-party guarantees, peacekeeping, joint commissions for dispute resolution, specification of the cease-fire terms, and the invocation of international audience costs. Each of these measures helps contribute to more durable peace.

CONCLUSION

THE MOTIVATION FOR THIS BOOK is a normative and practical question: are some war-torn areas simply doomed to repeated conflict and warfare, or can something be done to improve the chances for peace? The answer I come to is essentially optimistic. Between deadly enemies, peace is hard to maintain, but there are things that combatants and the international community can do to improve its chances. Peace is precarious, but it is possible.

The job of building a durable peace is more difficult after some wars than others, but when it is most difficult, states tend to invest more in efforts to bolster peace. And these efforts work. Concrete measures implemented as part of a cease-fire agreement contribute to more durable peace. Mechanisms such as demilitarized zones, dispute resolution commissions, peacekeeping, and external guarantees help combatants alter the incentives to break the cease-fire, reduce uncertainty about each other's actions and intentions, and help prevent or manage accidents that could lead back to war.

This book began with an empirical question, why does peace sometimes last and sometimes fall apart? We have learned that the prospects for peace are dimmer when war ends in a military draw than when one side wins a decisive victory. Peace is more difficult between enemies with a history of conflict, particularly those whose struggle began at or before independence. It is harder to achieve when one or both sides feel that their existence is threatened. It is more difficult between neighbors. Shifts in the relative military capabilities of states may upset a fragile peace, but it is unclear whether these shifts cause war or war causes the shifts. Maintaining peace is easier after very long and costly wars. The high cost of fighting gives states an incentive to avoid another war.

We have also learned that some factors we might have thought were important predictors of recurrent war do not have large or significant effects. These negative findings are as important as the positive ones. Peace is no harder or easier to maintain between evenly matched military powers than between states with a large discrepancy in power. Relative power is the variable many analysts would look to first to answer international relations questions, but it does not help us answer ours. The democratic peace is the closest thing we have to a law in the field of international relations, but democracy is not particularly helpful in explaining why some wars repeat and others do not. Because democracies do not tend to fight each other, there are few if any cease-fires between democracies. But the Kargil war between India and Pakistan suggests that among deadly enemies, achieving joint democracy does not necessarily ensure lasting peace. Interestingly, while we might expect states with a historic enemy to be most likely to become aggressive during the process either of democratizing or becoming more autocratic, regime change on the part of one ex-combatant does not seem to make peace more likely to fall apart. Nor does the number of states involved in a war affect the prospects for peace. The multilateral wars in the Middle East have resumed repeatedly, but other multilateral wars have been followed by durable peace. Calculations of states' utility for war based on capabilities and alliance data are no help in predicting when peace will break down.

To gauge the baseline prospects for peace, therefore, the most important things to know are the cost of war, the decisiveness of military victory, the belligerents' prior history, whether the conflict threatens one side's existence, whether the belligerents are contiguous, and perhaps how their relative capabilities are changing over time. Knowing something about these factors begins to answer our basic question about why peace lasts or falls apart, but it also helps us answer an important question about when states undertake efforts to strengthen peace. We have to be able to answer this question to know whether these efforts work. For if states only implement strong measures to keep peace when peace would be easy to keep in any case, then we cannot conclude that those measures have a strong empirical effect. Their relationship to lasting peace might well be spurious. But we have seen that, if anything, just the opposite is true. Stronger agreements, implementing more serious efforts to keep peace, are reached not in the easy cases but when peace is most precarious.

The strength of the measures belligerents implement as part of their cease-fire agreements is not fully determined by the underlying prospects for peace. Other factors (such as concerns over sovereignty, the personal experience of statesmen and mediators, or the state of the art of peace practices) shape agreements to some extent. This helps explain why states do not always "get it right"—why they do not always implement exactly the measures needed to prevent another war. But to the extent that there is a relationship between the degree of difficulty of the case and the agreements belligerents reach, it suggests that agreements are a functional response to the obstacles to peace. The counterargument that strong agreements are epiphenomenal, reached only when peace would last in any case, does not hold water.

Measures to alter incentives by raising the cost of breaking a cease-fire, to clear up uncertainty about belligerents' actions and intentions, or to reduce the possibility of accidents or spirals are implemented because they are expected to make peace more stable. This is the first systematic study of whether these measures work. We have learned that, in general, they do.

Peace lasts longer when stronger agreements are in place, all else equal. By looking at cease-fires that fall apart quickly, those that last longer but eventually fail, and those that have lasted to date, and by taking the baseline prospects for peace into account, we can show systematically that there are things states can do to improve the chances for peace. This conclusion is supported by quantitative and qualitative evidence, large-N and small. It holds across the full universe of interstate wars in the post–World War II period, both statistically and in a survey of cases, and in a much more detailed and nuanced look at the India-Pakistan and Israel-Syria experiences.

While some students of international relations might be surprised to learn that states can institute measures to overcome the obstacles to peace, practitioners probably know this already. For them, it is the lessons of the final chapter of the book that are the most important. By breaking agreement strength into its component parts and examining the effects of each measure systematically, we can evaluate what works and what does not work to maintain peace. We have learned that withdrawal to the status quo ante does not necessarily ensure peace, though holding onto territory captured in war can provide incentive for another. Withdrawing from territory held even before the war sends an important signal and makes peace very stable. We learned that demilitarized zones make peace last longer, but that we should be wary of creating power vacuums in disputed territory. Arms control measures have been less effective and can even create unstable power discrepancies in some cases. We learned that concrete efforts to deal with involuntary defection by rogue groups can be useful, but that statements that each side is responsible for hostile acts from its territory do not effectively counter the deliberate use of irregular forces to carry out aggression. We have learned that joint commissions for dispute resolution help states keep peace, and that specific agreements are more stable than weaker ones.

Outsiders interested in maintaining peace can improve its chances by providing an explicitly stated guarantee of the cease-fire, and by sending international monitors or troops as peacekeepers. But outsiders should be aware that simply being involved in mediation and negotiation does not convey a clear commitment to upholding peace. And peacekeeping is easily discredited. Leaving a peacekeeping mission in place after war has broken out anew does nothing to bolster the prospects for peace. The international community has a strong effect on belligerents' decisions about war and peace. States worry about international audience costs. This has the unintended consequence of making the problem of covert aggression through allegedly rogue forces worse, but it also means that the international community has a powerful tool for making peace more stable. During the Cold War, this tool was not used to full effect. Superpowers sometimes turned a blind eye to provocations by client states, and a hamstrung UN worried about maintaining impartiality, often to the point of ignoring evidence about aggression. In the post–Cold War world, the leverage of international reactions has even greater potential.

In short, we have learned that peace is harder maintain in some cases than in others, but that states can and do implement measures to overcome the obstacles to peace. Among deadly enemies, maintaining peace requires cooperation. It does not come automatically, but neither is it impossible. By raising the cost of attack, by reducing uncertainty about actions and intentions, and by preventing and managing accidents, belligerents and the international community can help make peace last.

The most important lessons from this study are the practical ones about how states can better foster durable peace. But this research also has implications for debates and literatures within academia. By drawing on both realist and institutionalist ideas about cooperation, it moves beyond the often stagnant debate about the prospects for cooperation. It shows the importance of taking the degree of difficulty into account when assessing the impact of institutions and international agreements (that is, of taking seriously arguments about epiphenomenality and spuriousness). It also shows some of the ways in which institutions matter empirically. Agreements affect state behavior, but only because through them states implement concrete measures to tie their hands, to signal their intentions, and to deal with accidents.

This research also speaks to the fundamental question posed by the literature on "enduring rivalries," that is, why some conflicts and rivalries endure and others pass by fleetingly. Part of the answer has to do with characteristics of the situation between the belligerents at the time of a cease-fire, and part has to do with the agreements states put in place at the end of war. This research also sheds light on the other end of the enduring rivalry life span. Deliberate efforts to maintain cease-fires can help to break cycles of repeated warfare that plague enduring rivals. Even the intractable conflicts between Israel and Syria and between India and Pakistan can be managed to reduce the likelihood of war. This study helps answer why some rivalries endure and others do not. Another promising avenue for research that would speak to how rivalries end would entail expanding the dependent variable by comparing wars followed by pacific relations, wars followed by disputes that do not escalate to full-scale war, and wars that are repeated. This would allow a distinction between cases where a rivalry persists but is managed peacefully, and those where the rivalry itself abates.

There are important related questions that this study does not address. It is not a study of how states move from relationships of enmity to friendship. It deliberately limits itself to cases where war is a likely event, not to cases in which war eventually becomes unthinkable. But that process of transformation to truly stable peace is the logical next step. The measures studied here might be able to set states down that road by breaking the cycle of violence and allowing peace to settle in, but they are not likely to help states get beyond that first stage. Some might argue that by allowing states to go on living with their differences, these measures make more fundamental peace less likely. There may be some truth to that, although it is hard to imagine states ever moving to amicable relations if they cannot prevent war from recurring.

Nor is this a study of how to maintain peace in the aftermath of civil war. The same general strategies that help states from fighting again should help parties in a civil war to ensure peace. And some of the specific mechanisms discussed here are likely to work just as well between parties to a civil war. Dispute resolution procedures, formal and specific agreements, and measures to deal with potential rogue factions or extremists are all likely to help in the aftermath of civil war just as they do after interstate war. Third-party guarantees of the peace have already been shown to be very important in intrastate conflicts.[1] Other measures might need some modification. In the last decade or so, the UN has adapted peacekeeping to the civil war context, adding functions such as police and election monitoring to its traditional roles. We do not yet have a good understanding of how effective peacekeeping has been in this context, however. As with studies of interstate peacekeeping, work on peacekeeping in civil wars has tended to look only at peacekeeping cases and has not compared those with nonpeacekeeping cases.[2] Still other measures are inappropriate for the civil war context. Unless an intrastate war ends in the partition of the country, demilitarized zones cannot be used to keep belligerents apart, except perhaps temporarily.

The most important difference between maintaining peace after civil and interstate wars is that in the latter, belligerents have the luxury of leaving the fundamental political issues unsettled. It is extremely rare for civil wars to end with a cease-fire that does not at least de facto settle the underlying issue.[3] States can continue to exist with territorial or policy disputes unsettled, but it is difficult for countries torn by civil war to go about their business with issues of secession or of who will run the country still up in the air. Combatants in civil wars cannot retreat to opposite sides of a border and agree to live with their differences; such a territorial split would itself constitute a political settlement.[4] Civil wars almost always end either with an imposed settlement by the victor, or by a compromise settlement on power sharing or regional autonomy or independence.

[1] Walter 1997, 2001.

[2] For one exception, see Doyle and Sambanis 2000.

[3] One notable exception was the ill-fated peace in Chechnya in 1996 putting off a settlement for five years.

[4] For an argument that this fact makes impartial intervention impossible, see Betts 1994.

Whether imposed or negotiated, these settlements may not always last. But the issue of maintaining peace in the absence of some sort of political settlement does not generally arise in the context of civil wars. Measures to maintain peace are therefore likely to be tied to the settlement reached in ways that do not apply in our study of interstate cease-fires.

Lessons from this study certainly cannot be applied to civil conflicts without concern for the differences between the two types of war. But the general strategies of changing incentives, reducing uncertainty, and managing accidents are likely to apply in both contexts. Moreover, the framework of analysis used here, in particular the importance of examining the baseline prospects and their relationship to the measures employed to keep peace, provides a template for a similar study of the durability of peace after civil war.

That states can implement measures to make the resumption of war less likely raises the question of whether they could do more to prevent war in the first place. If mechanisms such as demilitarized zones, peacekeeping, or joint commissions for dispute resolution can help maintain peace after war has been fought, could they do so beforehand? Obviously we cannot answer that question definitively without a much wider study, but at least in theory, the measures discussed in this book should be able to be used preventively. The challenge in using these mechanisms is likely to be in convincing states to implement them. It is normal and therefore politically acceptable to take measures to ensure peace in the immediate aftermath of war, but before war has broken out it could be politically difficult for states to give up territory along their borders to create a buffer zone, or to allow their sovereignty to be infringed by international peacekeepers. Some of the mechanisms discussed here have been used to try to prevent war in the first place, most notably arms control and confidence-building measures, both of which likely played a role in helping to prevent a hot war between the United States and the Soviet Union during the Cold War. Assessing the empirical effects of such measures to prevent war in the first place is difficult because the counterfactual is difficult to establish. Nonetheless, the possibility of using measures to alter incentives, reduce uncertainty, and manage accidents to pull states back from the brink of war is certainly worth further empirical exploration.

Whether they help states avoid war to begin with or not, the measures investigated in this study are important tools of peace. They help even the most deadly of enemies to avoid an incessant cycle of violence. The conclusions of this study warrant optimism. Peace is difficult to maintain in the aftermath of war, and a realistic assessment of the prospects for peace is necessary. But there is something that can be done to help maintain peace, even between bitter foes. States can and do institute measures to foster peace that lasts. Maintaining peace requires work, but it is possible.

CEASE-FIRES (1946–1998) AND THE RESUMPTION OF WAR

War	Between		Cease-Fire (follow-up agreement)	War Resumes
Palestine 1	Israel	Iraq	18 Jul 1948	15 Oct 1948
Palestine 1	Israel	Egypt	18 Jul 1948	15 Oct 1948
Palestine 1	Israel	Syria	18 Jul 1948	15 Oct 1948
Palestine 1	Israel	Lebanon	18 Jul 1948	15 Oct 1948
Palestine 1	Israel	Jordan	18 Jul 1948	15 Oct 1948
Palestine 2	Israel	Iraq	31 Oct 1948	06 Oct 1973
Palestine 2	Israel	Egypt	07 Jan 1949	29 Oct 1956
Palestine 2	Israel	Syria	31 Oct 1948	05 Jun 1967
Palestine 2	Israel	Lebanon	31 Oct 1948	11 Apr 1982
Palestine 2	Israel	Jordan	31 Oct 1948	05 Jun 1967
Kashmir 1	India	Pakistan	01 Jan 1949	05 Aug 1965
Korean	U.S.	China	27 Jul 1953	
Korean	U.S.	No. Korea	27 Jul 1953	
Korean	So. Korea	China	27 Jul 1953	
Korean	So. Korea	No. Korea	27 Jul 1953	
Russo-Hungarian	U.S.S.R.	Hungary	14 Nov 1956	
Follow-up agreement			(27 May 1957)	
Follow-up agreement			(07 Sep 1967)	
Sinai	U.K.	Egypt	06 Nov 1956	
Sinai	France	Egypt	06 Nov 1956	
Sinai	Israel	Egypt	06 Nov 1956	05 Jun 1967
Sino-Indian	China	India	22 Nov 1962	
Follow-up agreement			(07 Sep 1993)	
Follow-up agreement			(26 Nov 1996)	
Vietnam	No. Vietnam	U.S.	27 Jan 1973	
Vietnam	No. Vietnam	So. Vietnam	30 Apr 1975 [a]	
Kashmir 2	Pakistan	India	23 Sep 1965	03 Dec 1971
Six-Day	Israel	Egypt	10 Jun 1967	06 Mar 1969
Six-Day	Israel	Syria	10 Jun 1967	06 Oct 1973
Six-Day	Israel	Jordan	10 Jun 1967	10 Oct 1973
War of Attrition	Israel	Egypt	07 Aug 1970	06 Oct 1973

(cont'd)

War	Between		Cease-Fire (follow-up agreement)	War Resumes
Football	El Salvador	Honduras	18 Jul 1969	
Follow-up agreement			(09 Aug 1976)	
Follow-up agreement			(30 Oct 1980)	
Bangladesh	India	Pakistan	17 Dec 1971	
Follow-up agreement			(06 Apr 1991)	26 May 1999[b]
Yom Kippur	Israel	Egypt	24 Oct 1973	
Follow-up agreement			(01 Sep 1975)	
Follow-up agreement			(26 Mar 1979)	
Yom Kippur	Israel	Syria	24 Oct 1973	05 Jun 1982
Yom Kippur	Israel	Jordan	24 Oct 1973	
Follow-up agreement			(26 Oct 1994)	
Turco-Cypriot 1	Turkey	Cyprus	29 Jul 1974	14 Aug 1974
Turco-Cypriot 2	Turkey	Cyprus	16 Aug 1974	
Ethiopian-Somalian	Cuba	Somalia	14 Mar 1978	
Ethiopian-Somalian	Ethiopia	Somalia	14 Mar 1978	
Follow-up agreement			(03 Apr 1988)	
Ugandan-Tanzanian	Tanzania	Uganda	12 Apr 1979	
Ugandan-Tanzanian	Tanzania	Libya	12 Apr 1979	
Sino-Vietnamese 1	China	Vietnam	10 Mar 1979	05 Jan 1987
Iran-Iraq	Iran	Iraq	20 Aug 1988	
Follow-up agreement			(06 Jan 1991)	
Falklands	U.K.	Argentina	20 Jun 1982	
Follow-up agreement			(19 Oct 1989)	
Lebanon	Israel	Syria	05 Sep 1982	
Sino-Vietnamese 2	China	Vietnam	06 Feb 1987	
Follow-up agreement			(10 Nov 1991)	
Follow-up agreement			(19 Oct 1993)	
Gulf War	U.S.	Iraq	11 Apr 1991	[c]
Gulf War	Saudi Arabia	Iraq	11 Apr 1991	
Gulf War	Kuwait	Iraq	11 Apr 1991	
Azeri-Armenian 1	Armenia	Azerbaijan	21 Mar 1992	11 Apr 1992
Azeri-Armenian 2	Armenia	Azerbaijan	12 May 1994	

[a] Censored immediately.
[b] Occurs after time varying data are censored.
[c] War resumes in March 2003, after these data are censored.

CEASE-FIRES DATA SET

Situational Variables

Variable	Values	Sources and Notes
Military tie	0 = military victory 1 = Tie	Stam 1996 and COW
Imposed	0 = tie or victory short of imposed 1 = lopsided military outcome	Stam 1996, COW, MID Coded 1 if tie = 0 and MID "settlement" = imposed
Cost of war	Natural log of both states, battle deaths	COW and Clodfelter 1992
Duration of war	Duration of fighting (in months)	COW dates
Multilateral war	0 = bilateral war 1 = multilateral war	
History of conflict	Prewar MID disputes / years both states part of the interstate system	MID Coded 1 for wars at independence
Territorial issues	0 = not territorial 1 = territorial	MID "revision type"
Stakes	1 = influence 2 = political system 3 = territorial integrity 4 = grave damage 5 = existence	Highest "gravity of value threat- ened" in dyad. Brecher and Wilkenfeld's International Crisis Behavior data (ICB2). See Gelpi 1997.
Contiguity	0 = not contiguous 1 = contiguous by land, or < 150 miles by sea	
U.S. belligerent	0 = U.S. did not fight in the war 1 = U.S. fought in the war	Coded 1 for all dyads in wars in- volving the U.S.
Arab-Israeli	0 = not an Arab-Israeli war 1 = dyad includes Israel and an Arab state	
Preponderance of power	$|cap\_1\text{-}cap\_2|/(cap\_1+cap\_2)$	COW capabilities index: state's share of the system's total population, urban popu- lation, iron and steel produc- tion, energy consumption, military manpower and mili- tary expenditures, averaged

(cont'd)

Situational Variables

Variable	Values	Sources and Notes
Change in relative capabilities	$\|((cap\_1\text{-}lagcap\_1)/lagcap\_1) - ((cap\_2\text{-}lagcap\_2)/lagcap\_2)\|$[a]	Lagcap is capability index from previous year
Lagged change	d_relcap from previous year	
Expected utility		
Diamond	0 = equilibrium outcome not demand 1 = equilibrium demand	Bueno de Mesquita and Lalman's "international interaction game" and Bennett and Stam's EUGene
War	0 = equilibrium not war 1 = equilibrium outcome war	
Monadic democracy	0 = neither side a democracy 1 = one side a democracy	Democracy if Polity III "dem" score = 6 or higher
Joint democracy	0 = one or both not a democracy 1 = both sides democracies	
Polity change	$\|dem1\text{-}lagdem1\| + \|dem2\text{-}lagdem2\|$	Polity III
Democratization	0 = neither side newly a democracy 1 = one side newly a democracy	Newly a democracy if "dem" in previous year, now ≥ 6

[a] Following Werner 1999, 923 n. 7.

(*cont'd*)

Situational Variables		
Variable	*Values*	*Sources and Notes*

Agreement Variables

Variable	Values	Sources and Notes
Withdrawal	0 = none 1 = partial 2 = to status quo ante 3 = beyond status quo ante	Includes unilateral withdrawals, but not withdrawals from partial DMZs
Demilitarized zones	0 = none 1 = partial (not along full cease-fire line, or < 2 km) 2 = full demilitarized zone, at least 2 km	
Arms control	0 = none 1 = arms embargo; standfast; limits near cease-fire line; prohibition on specific weapons	
Internal control	0 = none 1 = stated responsibility for actions from own territory 2 = concrete measures to control forces	
Third-party involvement	0 = none 1 = mediate cease-fire, restraint, patron etc. 2 = explicit or well-understood guarantee of peace	Does not include UN mediation
Peacekeeping	0 = none 1 = monitoring (unarmed military observers) 2 = peacekeeping forces (armed)	Includes UN, other regional organization, and ad hoc peacekeeping missions
Previous peacekeeping	0 = new for this war 1 = present from earlier conflict	
Confidence-building measures	0 = none 1 = information exchange; hot line; on-site or aerial verification	
Dispute resolution	0 = none 1 = ongoing third-party mediation 2 = joint commission of belligerents	Does not include peacekeepers providing dispute resolution
Specificity	= number of paragraphs in agreement text	

(cont'd)

Situational Variables

Variable	Values	Sources and Notes
Formalism	0 = no declared cease-fire 1 = unilaterally declared, tacitly accepted 2 = tacit or informal acceptance of proposal 3 = formal acceptance of cease-fire proposal 4 = formal bilateral or multilateral agreement	
Formal agreement (dummy)	= 1 if formal > 2	
Agreement strength (subjective)	0 = no agreement 1 = very weak (very few minor provisions) 2 = weak (some mechanisms) 3 = moderate (many minor or some major mechanisms) 4 = strong (many substantial mechanisms)	
Index of strength (objective)	formal_dum + with_sqa + dmz_dum + ac_dum + (pk/2) + (ext_inv/2) + (detail/3) + (internal/2) + info_dum + (disp_res/2)	—dum variables are dummies —sqa is status quo ante
Cease-fire/Peace-agreement	0 = no agreement (war fizzles or ends unilaterally) 1 = cease-fire or armistice 2 = renunciation of use of force, restoration of diplomatic relations, or full-fledged peace treaty	
Political settlement	0 = no settlement 1 = unilateral settlement (de facto) 2 = settlement by agreement (de jure)	

[a] Following Werner 1999, 923 n. 7.

REFERENCES

Abbott, Kenneth W., Robert O. Keohane, Andrew Moravcsik, Anne-Marie Slaughter, and Duncan Snidal. 2000. The Concept of Legalization. *International Organization* 54 (3): 401–19.

Abbott, Kenneth W., and Duncan Snidal. 2000. Hard and Soft Law in International Governance. *International Organization* 54 (3): 421–56.

Akerlof, George. 1970. The Market for Lemons: Quality Uncertainty and the Market Mechanism. *Quarterly Journal of Economics* 84 (3): 488–500.

Allcock, John B. 1992. *Border and Territorial Disputes*. 3d ed. Harlow, U.K.: Longman Group.

Anderson, Thomas. 1981. *The War of the Dispossessed: Honduras and El Salvador, 1969*. Lincoln: University of Nebraska Press.

Aron, Raymond. 1966. *Peace and War*. Garden City, N.Y.: Doubleday.

Avi-Ran, Reuven. 1991. *The Syrian Involvement in Lebanon since 1975*. Boulder: Westview.

Axelrod, Robert. 1984. *The Evolution of Cooperation*: Basic Books.

Azcarate, Pablo de. 1966. *Mission in Palestine*. Washington, D.C.: Middle East Institute.

Bailey, Sydney D. 1982. *How Wars End: The United Nations and the Termination of Armed Conflict, 1946–1964*. Vol. 2. Oxford: Clarendon Press.

———. 1990. *Four Arab-Israeli Wars and the Peace Process*. London: Macmillan.

Bajpai, Kanti P. 1996. Conflict, Cooperation, and CSBMs with Pakistan and China: A View from New Delhi. In *Mending Fences: Confidence- and Security-Building Measures in South Asia*, edited by S. Ganguly and T. Greenwood. Boulder: Westview.

Baldwin, David A., ed. 1993. *Neorealism and Neoliberalism*. New York: Columbia University Press.

Barnett, Michael. 1998. *Dialogues in Arab Politics : Negotiations in Regional Order*. New York: Columbia University Press.

Bar-Yaacov, N. 1967. *The Israel-Syrian Armistice: Problems of Implementation, 1949–1966*. Jerusalem: Magnes Press, Hebrew University.

Bennett, D. Scott, and Allan C. Stam. 2000a. EUGene: Expected Utility Generation and Data Management Program. Available at <www.eugenesoftware.org>.

———. 2000b. A Universal Test of an Expected Utility Theory of War. *International Studies Quarterly* 44 (3): 451–80.

Bercovitch, Jacob, and Robert Jackson. 1997. *International Conflict: A Chronological Encyclopedia of Conflicts and Their Management, 1945–1995*. Washington, D.C.: Congressional Quarterly Press.

Betts, Richard. 1994. The Delusions of Impartial Intervention. *Foreign Affairs* 73 (3): 20–33.

Blainey, Geoffrey. 1973. *The Causes of War*. New York: Free Press.

Blinkenberg, Lars. 1972. *India-Pakistan: The History of Unsolved Conflicts.* Munksgaard, Denmark: Dansk Udenrigspolitisk Institut.

Box-Steffensmeier, Janet M., and Bradford S. Jones. 1997. Time Is of the Essence: Event History Models in Political Science. *American Journal of Political Science* 41 (4): 1414–61.

Brecher, Michael. 1984. International Crises and Protracted Conflicts. *International Interactions* 11 (3–4): 237–97.

Brecher, Michael, and Jonathan Wilkenfeld. 1989. *Crisis, Conflict, and Stability.* Vol. 3. Oxford: Pergamon Press.

———. 1992. International Crisis Behavior Project, 1918–1988. Distributed by Inter-university Consortium for Political and Social Science, ICPSR no. 9286.

Brecher, Michael, Jonathan Wilkenfeld, and Sheila Moser. 1988. *Crises in the Twentieth Century: Handbook of International Crises.* Oxford: Pergamon Press.

Bremer, Stuart A. 1992. Dangerous Dyads: Conditions Affecting the Likelihood of Interstate War, 1816–1965. *Journal of Conflict Resolution* 36 (2): 309–41.

Brines, Russell. 1968. *The Indo-Pakistani Conflict.* London: Pall Mall Press.

Brogan, Patrick. 1992. *World Conflicts: Why and Where They Are Happening.* London: Bloomsbury.

Brown, Michael E., Sean M. Lynn-Jones, and Steven E. Miller, eds. 1997. *Debating the Democratic Peace.* International Security Reader. Cambridge: MIT Press.

Bueno de Mesquita, Bruce, and David Lalman. 1992. *War and Reason.* New Haven: Yale University Press.

Bull, Odd. 1976. *War and Peace in the Middle East: The Experiences and Views of a U.N. Observer.* London: Leo Cooper.

Butterworth, Robert Lyle. 1976. *Managing Interstate Conflict, 1945–1974: Data with Synopses.* Pittsburgh: University Center for International Studies.

Chayes, Abram, and Antonia Handler Chayes. 1995. *The New Sovereignty: Compliance with International Regulatory Agreements.* Cambridge: Harvard University Press.

Claude, Inis. 1962. *Power and International Relations.* New York: Random House.

Clodfelter, Michael. 1992. *Warfare and Armed Conflict: A Statistical Reference.* Vol. 2. Jefferson, N.C.: McFarland.

Coase, R. H. 1988. *The Firm, the Market, and the Law.* Chicago: University of Chicago Press.

Croft, Stuart. 1996. *Strategies of Arms Control.* Manchester: Manchester University Press.

Das, Durga. 1969. *India: From Curzon to Nehru and After.* New York: John Day.

Dawson, Pauline. 1994. *The Peacekeepers of Kashmir.* London: Hurst.

Diehl, Paul F. 1991. Geography and War: A Review and Assessment of the Empirical Literature. *International Interactions* 17 (1): 11–27.

———. 1993. *International Peacekeeping.* Baltimore: Johns Hopkins University Press.

Downs, George W., and David M Rocke. 1995. *Optimal Imperfection? Domestic Uncertainty and Institutions in International Relations*. Princeton: Princeton University Press.

Doyle, Michael W. 1995. *UN Peacekeeping in Cambodia: UNTAC's Civil Mandate*. International Peace Academy Occasional Papers. Boulder: Lynne Rienner.

Doyle, Michael W., and Nicholas Sambanis. 2000. International Peacebuilding: A Theoretical and Quantitative Analysis. *American Political Science Review* 94 (4): 779–802.

Dubey, Amitabh. 2002. Domestic Institutions and the Duration of Civil War Settlements. Paper presented at Annual Meeting of the International Studies Association, March 24–27, New Orleans.

Durch, William J., ed. 1993. *The Evolution of UN Peacekeeping*. New York: St. Martin's Press.

———, ed. 1996. *UN Peacekeeping, American Politics, and the Uncivil Wars of the 1990s*. New York: St. Martin's Press.

Evron, Yair. 1987. *War and Intervention in Lebanon: The Israeli-Syrian Deterrence Dialogue*. Baltimore: Johns Hopkins University Press.

Farrell, Joseph, and Matthew Rabin. 1996. Cheap Talk. *Journal of Economic Perspectives* 10 (3): 103–18.

Fazal, Tanisha M. 2001. Born to Lose and Doomed to Survive: State Death and Survival in the International System. Ph.D. diss., Political Science, Stanford University.

Fearon, James D. 1994. Domestic Political Audiences and the Escalation of International Disputes. *American Political Science Review* 88 (3): 577–92.

———. 1995. Rationalist Explanations for War. *International Organization* 49 (3): 379–414.

———. 1997. Signaling Foreign Policy Interests. *Journal of Conflict Resolution* 41 (1): 68–90.

Fearon, James D., and David D. Laitin. 1996. Explaining Interethnic Cooperation. *American Political Science Review* 90 (4): 715–35.

Fetherston, A. B. 1994. *Towards a Theory of United Nations Peacekeeping*. New York: St. Martin's Press.

Fortna, Virginia Page. 2002. Does Peacekeeping Keep Peace? And If So, How? Paper presented at Workshop on Peacekeeping and Politics, Columbia University, October 18.

Fox, William, ed. 1970. *How Wars End*. The Annals, vol. 392. Philadelphia: American Academy of Political and Social Science.

Ganguly, Sumit. 1986. *The Origins of War in South Asia: Indo-Pakistani Conflicts since 1947*. Boulder: Westview Press.

———. 2001. *Conflict Unending: India-Pakistan Tensions since 1947*. New York: Columbia University Press.

Garthoff, Raymond L. 1994. *Detente and Confrontation: American Soviet Relations from Nixon to Reagan*. Rev. ed. Washington, D.C.: Brookings Institution.

Gartner, Scott Sigmund, and Randolph M. Siverson. 1996. War Expansion and War Outcomes. *Journal of Conflict Resolution* 40 (1): 4–15.

Gartzke, Erik. 1999. War Is in the Error Term. *International Organization* 53 (3): 567–87.

Gelpi, Christopher. 1997. Crime and Punishment: The Role of Norms in Crisis Bargaining. *American Political Science Review* 91 (2): 339–60.

George, Alexander, and Richard Smoke. 1974. *Deterrence in American Foreign Policy.* New York: Columbia University Press.

Ghali, Mona. 1993a. United Nations Disengagement Observer Force. In *The Evolution of UN Peacekeeping,* edited by W. J. Durch. New York: St. Martin's.

———. 1993b. United Nations Emergency Force I. In *The Evolution of UN Peacekeeping,* edited by W. J. Durch. New York: St. Martin's Press.

Gilpin, Robert. 1981. *War and Change in World Politics.* Cambridge: Cambridge University Press.

Goemans, H. E. 2000. *War and Punishment: The Causes of War Termination and the First World War.* Princeton: Princeton University Press.

Goertz, Gary, and Paul F. Diehl. 1992. The Empirical Importance of Enduring Rivalries. *International Interactions* 18 (2): 151–63.

———. 1993. Enduring Rivalries: Theoretical Constructs and Empirical Patterns. *International Studies Quarterly* 37 (2): 147–71.

Goldstein, Erik. 1992. *Wars and Peace Treaties, 1816–1991.* London: Routledge.

Gray, Colin S. 1992. *House of Cards: Why Arms Control Must Fail.* Ithaca: Cornell University Press.

Greene, William H. 1993. *Econometric Analysis.* New York: Macmillan.

Grieco, Joseph. 1988. Anarchy and the Limits of Cooperation: A Realist Critique of the Newest Liberal Institutionalism. *International Organization* 42 (4): 485–507.

Groseclose, Tim, and Nolan McCarty. 2001. The Politics of Blame: Bargaining before an Audience. *American Journal of Political Science* 45 (1): 100–119.

Gupta, Sisir. 1966. *Kashmir: A Study in India-Pakistan Relations.* New Delhi: Asia Publishing House.

Hampson, Fen Osler. 1996. *Nurturing Peace: Why Peace Settlements Succeed or Fail.* Washington, D.C.: United States Institute of Peace Press.

Hensel, Paul R. 1994. One Thing Leads to Another: Recurrent Militarized Disputes in Latin America, 1816–1986. *Journal of Peace Research* 31 (3): 281–97.

———. 1996. The Evolution of Interstate Rivalry. Ph.D. diss., University of Illinois.

———. 2000. Territory: Theory and Evidence on Geography and Conflict. In *What Do We Know about War?* edited by J. A. Vasquez. Lanham, Md.: Rowman and Littlefield.

Herzog, Chaim. 1984. *The Arab-Israeli Wars: War and Peace in the Middle East from the War of Independence to Lebanon.* London: Arms and Armour Press.

Hoffmann, Steven A. 1990. *India and the China Crisis.* Berkeley and Los Angeles: University of California Press.

Holst, Johan Jørgen, and Karen Alette Melander. 1977. European Security and Confidence-Building Measures. *Survival* 19 (4).

Holsti, Kalevi J. 1991. *Peace and War: Armed Conflicts and International Order, 1648–1989.* Cambridge: Cambridge University Press.

Howard, Lise Morjé. 2001. Learning to Keep the Peace? United Nations Multidimensional Peacekeeping in Civil Wars. Ph.D. diss., Political Science, University of California, Berkeley.

Huth, Paul K. 2000. Territory: Why Are Territorial Disputes between States a Central Cause of International Conflict? In *What Do We Know About War?* edited by J. A. Vasquez. Lanham, Md.: Rowman and Littlefield.

Iklé, Fred. 1991. *Every War Must End*. Rev. ed. New York: Columbia University Press.

Jackson, Robert. 1975. *South Asia Crisis: India, Pakistan, and Bangla Desh, a Political and Historical Analysis of the 1971 War*. New York: Praeger.

Jaggers, Keith, and Ted Robert Gurr. 1996. Polity III: Regime Type and Political Authority, 1800–1994. Distributed by Inter-university Consortium for Political and Social Science, ICPSR no. 6695.

Jervis, Robert. 1978. Cooperation under the Security Dilemma. *World Politics* 30 (2): 167–86.

———. 1983. Security Regimes. In *International Regimes*, edited by S. D. Krasner. Ithaca: Cornell University Press.

———. 1997. *System Effects: Complexity in Political and Social Life*. Princeton: Princeton University Press.

———. 1999. Realism, Neoliberalism, and Cooperation. *International Security* 24 (1): 42–63.

Jones, Daniel M., Stuart A. Bremer, and J. David Singer. 1996. Militarized Interstate Disputes, 1816–1992: Rationale, Coding Rules, and Empirical Patterns. *Conflict Management and Peace Science* 15 (2): 163–213.

Kacowicz, Arie, M., Yaacov Bar-Siman-Tov, Ole Elgström, and Magnus Jerneck, eds. 2000. *Stable Peace among Nations*. Lanham, Md.: Rowman and Littlefield.

Kecskemeti, Paul. 1964. *Strategic Surrender: The Politics of Victory and Defeat*. New York: Atheneum.

———. 1970. Political Rationality in Ending War. In *How Wars End*, edited by W.T.R. Fox. The Annals, vol. 392. Philadelphia: American Academy of Political and Social Science.

Kegley, Charles W., and Gregory Raymond. 1999. *How Nations Make Peace*. New York: St. Martin's Press.

Keohane, Robert O. 1984. *After Hegemony: Cooperation and Discord in the World Political Economy*. Princeton: Princeton University Press.

———. 1989. *International Institutions and State Power*. Boulder: Westview.

———. 1994. The Problem of Commitment in United States Foreign Policy. Paper presented at Yale University, September 29.

Khouri, Fred J. 1963. Friction and Conflict on the Israeli-Syrian Front. *Middle East Journal* 17 (1–2): 14–34.

———. 1985. *The Arab-Israeli Dilemma*. 3d ed. Syracuse: Syracuse University Press.

King, Charles. 2001. The Benefits of Ethnic War: Understanding Eurasia's Unrecognized States. *World Politics* 53 (4): 524–52.

Kinsolving, Lucien Lee. 1967. The Israeli-Syrian Demilitarized Zones: The UN Security Council Record. Master's thesis, International Relations, American University.

Kissinger, Henry. 1982. *Years of Upheaval*. Boston: Little, Brown.

Klingberg, Frank. 1966. Predicting the Termination of War. *Journal of Conflict Resolution* 10 (2): 129–71.

Korbel, Joseph. 1954. *Danger in Kashmir.* Princeton: Princeton University Press.

Koremenos, Barbara. 2001. Loosening the Ties That Bind: A Learning Model of Agreement Flexibility. *International Organization* 55 (2): 289–325.

Koremenos, Barbara, Charles Lipson, and Duncan Snidal. 2001. Rational Designs: Explaining the Form of International Institutions. Special issue of *International Organization* 55 (4).

Kozhemiakin, Alexander. 1994. Outcomes of War and the Durability of Peace Settlements. Unpublished paper.

Krepon, Michael, et al. 1993. *A Handbook on Confidence-Building Measures for Regional Security.* Washington, D.C.: Henry L. Stimson Center.

Krepon, Michael, and Amit Sevak, eds. 1995. *Crisis Prevention, Confidence Building, and Reconciliation in South Asia.* New York: St. Martin's Press.

Kydd, Andrew. 1997. Sheep in Sheep's Clothing: Why Security Seekers Do Not Fight Each Other. *Security Studies* 7 (1): 114–54.

Lakhanpal, P. L. 1965. *Essential Documents and Notes on Kashmir Dispute.* 2d ed. Delhi: International Books.

Lamb, Alastair. 1966. *The Kashmir Problem.* New York: Praeger.

———. 1991. *Kashmir: A Disputed Legacy, 1846–1990.* Hertingfordbury: Roxford Books.

Lefebvre, Jeffrey A. 1991. *Arms for the Horn: US Security Policy in Ethiopia and Somalia, 1953–1991.* Pittsburgh: University of Pittsburgh Press.

Legro, Jeffrey W. 1995. *Cooperation under Fire: Anglo-German Restraint during World War II.* Ithaca: Cornell University Press.

Levy, Jack. 1987. Declining Power and the Preventive Motivation for War. *World Politics* 40 (1): 82–107.

———. 1989. The Causes of War: A Review of Theories and Evidence. In *Behavior, Society, and Nuclear War,* edited by P. Tetlock et al. Oxford: Oxford University Press.

Levy, Jack S., and T. Clifton Morgan. 1986. The War Weariness Hypothesis: An Empirical Test. *American Journal of Political Science* 30 (1): 26–49.

Licklider, Roy. 1995. The Consequences of Negotiated Settlements in Civil Wars, 1945–1993. *American Political Science Review* 89 (3): 681–87.

Lipson, Charles. 1991. Why Are Some International Agreements Informal? *International Organization* 45 (4): 495–538.

Lowi, Theodore J. 1969. *The End of Liberalism.* New York: Norton.

Lundmark, Thomas. 2001. Verbose Contracts. *American Journal of Comparative Law* 49 (121).

Mackinlay, John. 1989. *The Peacekeepers: An Assessment of Peacekeeping Operations at the Arab-Israeli Interface.* London: Unwin Hyman.

Makinda, Samuel M. 1992. Security in the Horn of Africa. *Adelphi Papers* 269.

Mansfield, Edward, and Jack Snyder. 1995. Democratization and the Danger of War. *International Security* 20 (1): 5–38.

Ma'oz, Moshe. 1995. *Syria and Israel: From War to Peacemaking.* Oxford: Clarendon Press.

Maoz, Zeev. 1984. Peace by Empire? Conflict Outcomes and International Stability, 1816–1976. *Journal of Peace Research* 21 (3): 227–41.

———. 2001. Comments on the MID 2.1 Dataset and Its Transformation to Dyadic MID Data DYADMID1.1. Tel Aviv University.

Maoz, Zeev, and Bruce Russett. 1993. Normative and Structural Causes of Democratic Peace: 1946–1986. *American Political Science Review* 87 (3): 624–38.

Martin, Lisa. 1992. Interests, Power, and Multilateralism. *International Organization* 46 (4): 766–92.

———. 1993. Credibility, Costs, and Institutions: Cooperation on Economic Sanctions. *World Politics* 45 (3): 406–32.

Martz, Mary Jeanne Reid. 1978. *The Central American Soccer War: Historical Patterns and Internal Dynamics of OAS Settlement Procedures.* Athens: Ohio University Center for International Studies.

Mearsheimer, John J. 1994–95. The False Promise of International Institutions. *International Security* 19 (3): 5–49.

Merryman, John Henry. 1969. *The Civil Law Tradition: An Introduction to the Legal Systems of Western Europe and Latin America.* Stanford: Stanford University Press.

Miall, Hugh. 1992. *The Peacemakers: Peaceful Settlement of Disputes since 1945.* Basingstoke: Macmillan.

Morgan, Patrick. 1977. *Deterrence: A Conceptual Analysis.* Beverly Hills: Sage.

Morrow, James. 1999. The Strategic Setting of Choices: Signaling, Commitment, and Negotiation in International Politics. In *Strategic Choice and International Relations,* edited by D. Lake and R. Powell. Princeton: Princeton University Press.

Mueller, John E. 1989. *Retreat from Doomsday: The Obsolescence of Major War.* New York: Basic Books.

North, Douglass C. 1990. *Institutions, Institutional Change, and Economic Performance.* Cambridge: Cambridge University Press.

Olson, Mancur. 1965. *The Logic of Collective Action.* Cambridge: Harvard University Press.

Oren, Nissan. 1982. Prudence in Victory. In *Termination of Wars,* edited by N. Oren. Jerusalem: Magnes Press, Hebrew University.

Organski, A.F.K. 1968. *World Politics.* 2d ed. New York: Knopf.

Ovendale, Ritchie. 1984. *The Origins of the Arab-Israel Wars,* edited by H. Hearder. London: Longman.

Oye, Kenneth A. 1986a. Explaining Cooperation under Anarchy: Hypotheses and Strategies. In *Cooperation under Anarchy,* edited by K. A. Oye. Princeton: Princeton University Press.

———, ed. 1986b. *Cooperation under Anarchy.* Princeton: Princeton University Press.

Pelcovits, Nathan A. 1984. *Peacekeeping on Arab-Israeli Fronts: Lessons from the Sinai and Lebanon.* SAIS Papers in International Affairs. Boulder: Westview.

———. 1993. *The Long Armistice: UN Peacekeeping and the Arab-Israeli Conflict, 1948–1960.* Boulder: Westview.

Peretz, Don. 1996. *The Arab-Israeli Dispute.* New York: Facts on File.

Pillar, Paul. 1983. *Negotiating Peace: War Termination as a Bargaining Process.* Princeton: Princeton University Press.

Pogany, Istvan. 1987. *The Arab League and Peacekeeping in the Lebanon*. New York: St. Martin's Press.

Powell, Robert. 1991. Absolute and Relative Gains in International Relations Theory. *American Political Science Review* 85 (4): 1303–20.

Putnam, Robert. 1988. Diplomacy and Domestic Politics: The Logic of Two-Level Games. *International Organization* 42 (3): 427–60.

Randle, Robert F. 1973. *The Origins of Peace*. New York: Free Press.

Reiter, Dan. 1995. Exploding the Powder Keg Myth: Preemptive Wars Almost Never Happen. *International Security* 20 (2): 5–34.

Rikhye, Indar Jit. 1984. *The Theory and Practice of Peacekeeping*. London: Hurst.

Rosen, Steven. 1972. War Power and the Willingness to Suffer. In *Peace, War, and Numbers*, edited by B. M. Russett. Beverly Hills: Sage.

Russett, Bruce. 1993. *Grasping the Democratic Peace*. Princeton: Princeton University Press.

Ryan, Stephen. 1998. The Theory of Conflict Resolution and the Practice of Peacekeeping. In *A Future for Peacekeeping?* edited by E. Moxon-Browne. New York: St. Martin's Press.

Schelling, Thomas C. 1966. *Arms and Influence*. New Haven: Yale University Press.

Schelling, Thomas C., and Morton H. Halperin. 1961. *Strategy and Arms Control*. New York: Twentieth Century Fund.

Schiff, Zeev. 1984. Dealing with Syria. *Foreign Policy* 55:92–112.

Schiff, Zeev, and Ehud Ya'ari. 1984. *Israel's Lebanon War*. Edited and translated by Ina Friedman. London: Counterpoint.

Schoffield, Victoria. 1996. *Kashmir in the Crossfire*. London: Tauris.

Schweller, Randall L. 1996. Neorealism's Status-Quo Bias: What Security Dilemma? *Security Studies* 5 (3): 90–121.

Setear, John K. 1996. An Iterative Perspective on Treaties: A Synthesis of International Relations Theory and International Law. *Harvard International Law Journal* 37 (1): 139–229.

Shalev, Aryeh. 1994. *Israel and Syria: Peace and Security on the Golan*. Boulder: Westview Press.

Shebtai, Roseanne. 1990. Bunche at Rhodes: Diplomatic Negotiator. In *Ralph Bunche: The Man and His Times*, edited by B. Rivlin. New York: Holmes and Meier.

Signorino, Curt S., and Jeffrey M. Ritter. 1999. Tau-B or Not Tau-B: Measuring the Similarity of Foreign Policy Positions. *International Studies Quarterly* 43 (1): 115–44.

Sivard, Ruth Leger. 1993. *World Military and Social Expenditures 1993*. Washington, D.C.: World Priorities.

Slaughter, Anne-Marie. 1995. A Theory of International Law and International Relations. Paper presented at Seminar in Law and International Relations, Harvard University, February 7.

Small, Melvin, and J. David Singer. 1982. *Resort to Arms: International and Civil Wars, 1816–1980*. Beverly Hills: Sage.

Smith, Alastair, and Allan C. Stam. 2001. Issues and the Nature of War. Paper presented at Annual Meeting of the American Political Science Association, San Francisco, August 30–September 2.

Snidal, Duncan. 1991. Relative Gains and the Pattern of International Cooperation. *American Political Science Review* 85 (3): 701–26.

Snyder, Glenn. 1965. The Balance of Power and the Balance of Terror. In *The Balance of Power*, edited by P. Seabury. San Francisco: Chandler.

Snyder, Jack L. 1991. *Myths of Empire: Domestic Politics and International Ambition*. Ithaca: Cornell University Press.

Stedman, Stephen John. 1991. *Peacemaking in Civil War: International Mediation in Zimbabwe, 1974–1980*. Boulder: Lynne Rienner.

Stinnett, Douglas M., and Paul F. Diehl. 2001. The Path(s) to Rivalry: Behavioral and Structural Explanations of Rivalry Development. *Journal of Politics* 63 (3): 717–40.

Stockholm International Peace Research Institute (SIPRI). 1994–2000. *SIPRI Yearbook: Armaments, Disarmament, and International Security*. Oxford: Oxford University Press.

Tepperman, Jonathan D. 2002. Truth and Consequences. *Foreign Affairs* 81 (3): 128–45.

Thakur, Ramesh. 1987. *International Peacekeeping in Lebanon: United Nations Authority and Multinational Force*. Special Studies in Peace, Conflict, and Conflict Resolution. Boulder: Westview.

Tillema, Herbert K. 1991. *International Armed Conflict since 1945: A Bibliographic Handbook of Wars and Military Interventions*. Boulder: Westview Press.

Towle, Philip. 1997. *Enforced Disarmament: From the Napoleonic Campaigns to the Gulf War*. Oxford: Clarendon Press.

United Nations. 1996. *The Blue Helmets: A Review of United Nations Peacekeeping*. 3d ed. New York: United Nations.

United Nations Commission for India and Pakistan (UNCIP). 1949. Kashmir Papers: Reports of the United Nations Commission for India and Pakistan, June 1948–December 1949. New Delhi: Government of India, Ministries of External Affairs.

Urquhart, Brian. 1972. *Hammarskjold*. New York: Norton.

Valentino, Benjamin. 2002. *Final Solutions: Genocide and Mass Killing in the Twentieth Century*. Ithaca: Cornell University Press.

Vasquez, John A. 1993. *The War Puzzle*. Cambridge: Cambridge University Press.

———. 1995. Why Do Neighbors Fight? Proximity, Interaction, or Territoriality. *Journal of Peace Research* 32 (3): 277–93.

———, ed. 2000. *What Do We Know about War?* Lanham, Md.: Rowman and Littlefield.

Wainhouse, David W. 1966. *International Peace Observation*. Baltimore: Johns Hopkins Press.

———. 1973. *International Peacekeeping at the Crossroads*. Baltimore: Johns Hopkins University Press.

Wallander, Celeste. 1999. *Mortal Friends, Best Enemies: German-Russian Cooperation after the Cold War*. Ithaca: Cornell University Press.

Walter, Barbara. 1994. The Resolution of Civil Wars: Why Negotiations Fail. Ph.D. diss., University of Chicago.

Walter, Barbara. 1997. The Critical Barrier to Civil War Settlement. *International Organization* 51 (3): 335–64.

———. 2001. *Committing to Peace: The Successful Settlement of Civil Wars.* Princeton: Princeton University Press.

Waltz, Kenneth N. 1979. *Theory of International Politics.* Reading, Mass.: Addison-Wesley.

Weinberger, Naomi Joy. 1986. *Syrian Intervention in Lebanon: The 1975–76 Civil War.* New York: Oxford University Press.

Wendt, Alexander. 1992. Anarchy Is What States Make of It: The Social Construction of Power Politics. *International Organization* 46 (2): 391–425.

Werner, Suzanne. 1997. The Possibility of Recurrent Conflict: A Decision to End the Peace. Paper presented at Annual Meeting of the American Political Science Association, Washington, D.C.

———. 1999. The Precarious Nature of Peace: Resolving the Issues, Enforcing the Settlement, and Renegotiating the Terms. *American Journal of Political Science* 43 (3): 912–34.

Williamson, Oliver E. 1985. *The Economic Institutions of Capitalism.* New York: Free Press.

Wirsing, Robert G. 1994. *India, Pakistan, and the Kashmir Dispute.* New York: St. Martin's Press.

Wolfers, Arnold. 1962. *Discord and Collaboration: Essays on International Politics.* Baltimore: Johns Hopkins University Press.

Zartman, I. William. 1989. *Ripe for Resolution: Conflict and Intervention in Africa.* New York: Oxford University Press.

———, ed. 1995. *Elusive Peace: Negotiating an End to Civil Wars.* Washington, D.C.: Brookings Institution.

UNITED NATIONS SECURITY COUNCIL DOCUMENTS

United Nations. Security Council Document S/1453, February 6, 1950. Letter dated February 3, 1950, from General McNaughton, Permanent Representative of Canada to the United Nations, to the President of the Security Council Communicating His Report on the India-Pakistan Question.

United Nations. Security Council Document S/1791, September 15, 1950. Letter dated September 15, 1950, from the United Nations Representative for India and Pakistan to the President of the Security Council Transmitting His Report.

United Nations. Security Council Document S/2375, October 15, 1951. Letter dated October 15, 1951, from Dr. Frank P. Graham, United Nations Representative for India and Pakistan, to the Secretary-General Transmitting His Report to the Security Council.

United Nations. Security Council Document S/6651, September 3, 1965. Report by the Secretary-General on the Current Situation in Kashmir with Particular Reference to the Cease-Fire Agreement, the Cease-Fire Line and the Functioning of UNMOGIP.

United Nations. Security Council Document S/6683, September 16, 1965. Preliminary Report by the Secretary-General on His Visits to the Government of India and Pakistan.

United Nations. Security Council Document S/6710 and addenda, September 25, 1965–January 28, 1966. Report by the Secretary-General on Observance of the Cease-Fire under Security Council Resolution 211 of 20 September 1965.

United Nations. Security Council Document S/6719 and addenda, October 27, 1965–February 26, 1966. Report by the Secretary-General on Compliance with the Withdrawal Provisions of Security Council Resolution 211 of 20 September 1965.

United Nations. Security Council Document S/10410, December 3, 1971. Report of the Secretary General. (India-Pakistan).

United Nations. Security Council Document S/11302 and addenda, May 29–July 9, 1974. Report of the Secretary General. (Israel-Syria).

UNITED NATIONS RESOLUTIONS

United Nations. General Assembly Resolution 181 (II), November 29, 1947 (Partition of Palestine).

United Nations. Security Council Resolution 54, July 15, 1948 (The Palestine Question).

United Nations. Security Council Resolution 211, September 20, 1965 (The India-Pakistan Question).

United Nations. Security Council Resolutions 233–36, June 6–11, 1967 (The Situation in the Middle East).

United Nations. Security Council Resolution 242, November 22, 1967 (The Situation in the Middle East).

United Nations Commission for India and Pakistan. Resolution S/995, August 13, 1948.

United Nations Commission for India and Pakistan. Resolution S/1196, January 5, 1949.

INDEX

abdullah, Sheikh Mohammed, 58–59n.43, 61, 65n.62

accidents: as cause of war, 3, 16–20, 35, 104, 113; prevention and control of, 13, 23–24, 31, 37, 150–51, 158, 165–66, 173, 175, 180, 209, 211–12, 214, 216

aggression, 13, 15–17, 21–24, 141, 177n.4, 181, 184–85, 190, 200–202, 205, 210, 213–14. *See also* incentives to attack

agreement strength: effect on durability of peace, 29, 151–72; endogeneity of, 4, 9–10, 29–38, 40–41, 57, 74, 114–50, 169, 212, 214; measurement of, 50–52, 153, 221–22

Aksai Chin, 60, 62n.50

American exceptionalism. *See* United States

Amin, Idi, 15n.13, 54–55, 89

anarchy, consequences of, 7, 12, 19, 21

Arab-Israeli conflict, 67–74, 93–94, 105, 122, 177, 184, 191, 206, 212; in data set, 47, 57, 122, 123n.11, 125n.14, 169, 171n.35, 174n.1, 219. *See also* Egypt; Israel; Palestine war; Sinai war; Six-Day war; War of Attrition; Yom Kippur war

Arab-Israeli war, first. *See* Palestine war

Argentina. *See* Falklands war

Armenia. *See* Azeri-Armenian war

arms control, 108, 149n.88; effect on durability of peace, 9, 21, 23, 25, 158, 163n.22, 165, 174, 181–83, 194, 209–10, 213, 216; endogeneity of, 31n.55, 122, 126, 128, 136–37, 139, 147; measurement of, 49, 51, 220

arms race, 65, 70, 108–109, 183

Asad, Hafez al-, 71–72, 143, 165n.29, 185

Auchinleck, Army Supreme Commander (India and Pakistan), 59n.46

audience costs, 21–23, 27–28, 174, 199–205, 210, 213

autocorrelation, 47

Awami League, 64

Ayub Khan, Mohammad, 62–64, 91n.48, 140, 161, 200n.66, 201

Azad Kashmir forces, 23n.39, 26, 59, 61, 63, 139, 160, 184, 191, 201

Azeri-Armenian war, 41n.2, 46–47, 95, 121, 151–54, 158, 186, 195, 199, 208, 218

balance of power. *See* capabilities, relative military

Balfour Declaration, 67n.70

Bangladesh war, 48n.23, 60, 64–65, 87–89, 96, 104, 121, 135, 153, 159, 161, 178, 189, 201, 208, 218. *See also* India and Pakistan

Barre, Siad, 159

baseline prospects for peace, 2, 5, 10, 35–37, 40, 74, 76–113, 175, 179; and agreement strength, 31–35, 40, 114–52

Beirut, siege and evacuation of, 73, 142–44, 146–47, 166–67, 178, 188, 193, 199

Belgium, 46n.13, 163

Ben-Gurion, David, 14n.8, 101n.82

Bernadotte, Count Folke, 68, 146, 184, 186, 195, 203

Bhutto, Benazir, 66

Bhutto, Zulfikar Ali, 64–65, 136n.33, 201

bias, 39–42, 46, 49, 116, 130–32, 134, 148, 171n.37, 193n.55

Biqa' Valley, 102, 142–43, 147, 181n.19, 188, 199

Brass Tacks military exercises, 66, 162

Britain. *See* United Kingdom

buffer zones. *See* demilitarized zones

Bull, General Odd, 148

Bunche, Ralph, 195

Cambodia, 15n.13, 45n.12, 155

Camp David. *See* Israel-Egypt peace agreement

Canada, 11, 46n.13, 158n.7, 188

capabilities, relative military: effect on agreement strength, 117–18, 120, 123n.12, 124–26, 128–30; effect on durability of peace, 2, 5, 8, 35, 76, 82–85, 86, 105, 107, 112–13, 211; measurement of, 52–53, 123nn.10, 219

236 • Index

238 • Index

hazard ratios, interpretation of, 85, 167, 174
history of conflict: effect on agreement strength, 117–18, 120, 122–26, 128–30; effect on durability of peace, 2, 3n.3, 5, 8, 35, 76, 80, 84, 86, 94–98, 105, 107, 112–13, 152, 168, 170, 176, 187, 196, 207, 211–12; measurement of, 52–53, 74, 219
Honduras and El Salvador: in 1906 Central American war, 87. See also Football war
Hungary, 158n.7, 188; and Russia (see Russo-Hungarian war)
Hyderabad, 58

incentives to attack, 3, 13–15, 19, 35, 37; changing the, 21–22, 24, 31, 37, 150–51, 158, 165, 173, 175, 209–12, 212, 214, 216
India: and China (see Sino-Indian war)
— and Pakistan, 12, 60, 74–75, 104, 110, 117, 150, 177, 179, 190, 209, 214; case study of, 6, 8, 41, 56–58; 1947–1948 background to conflict, 58–59, 94–95, 100, 184; 1948–1949 first Kashmir war, 14, 26, 59–63, 76, 87, 91, 96, 121–22, 217; 1949–1965 cease-fire, 14, 26, 61–63, 95–96, 101, 135, 139, 151, 153–54, 160, 162, 177–78, 180, 183, 190, 194, 198, 200–202; 1965 second Kashmir war, 17–18, 23n.39, 40, 63, 87, 91, 96, 101, 108–9, 120–22, 154, 161, 184, 191, 217; 1965–1971 cease-fire, 63, 87, 109, 135–37, 139, 153, 159, 161–62, 175, 177–80, 182, 186, 191, 194–95, 198, 200–202, 206; 1971 Bangladesh war, 17, 23n.39, 48n.22, 64–65, 87, 89, 91, 96, 106, 108–9, 121, 141, 161, 184, 218; 1971–1999 cease-fire, 43, 135–37, 140, 150, 153, 158–60, 162, 178–79, 189, 194, 200, 206, 208; 1999 Kargil war, 18, 43, 48, 66–67, 88, 92, 96–97, 101, 109, 111–12, 135n.30, 162, 194, 201, 203, 208, 212
Indonesia, 188
Indus Waters Treaty, 100, 108n.100
information and war, 14–15, 16n.20, 29–30, 44, 171–72. See also uncertainty about intentions and capabilities
institutionalism, 2, 3n.3, 7, 18, 32n.59, 118–19, 214

intentions and agreement strength, 33–35, 197
internal control: mechanisms for, 4, 24; effect on durability of peace, 26, 156–57, 174, 176, 183–85, 209–10, 213, 215; endogeneity of, 126, 129, 136, 139, 163; measurement of, 49, 51, 220. See also involuntary defection; irregular forces
international community, 5, 23n.39, 31, 33, 66–68, 70, 75, 101, 114, 128, 134, 146, 161, 172, 184–85, 189–90, 200–205, 209–11, 213. See also audience costs; mediation; peacekeeping; third-party guarantee
International Court of Justice, 28n.52, 157, 208
international law, 21
involuntary defection, 13, 17–20, 24, 26, 139, 184–85, 213. See also accidents; internal control; irregular forces
Iran, in Azeri-Armenian war, 151, 185–86; and Iraq (see Iran-Iraq war)
Iran-Iraq war, 50–52, 89, 91, 98–99, 105, 121–22, 154, 158, 186, 194, 200, 208, 218
Iraq: and Iran (see Iran-Iraq war); in Palestine war, 68, 103, 121, 153; in Gulf War, 89–90, 114n.1, 128, 152–54, 182, 194n.56, 218 (see also Gulf War); resumption of war with United States, xiii, 44, 48n.22, 153–54nn. 158n.8, 218
Irgun, 184
irregular forces, 18, 20, 26, 104–105, 157, 163, 213; deliberate use of, 18, 23n.39, 68, 102, 139, 162, 184–85, 201–202, 209, 213. See also Azad Kashmir forces; fedayeen; internal control; mujahedin; Mukti Bahini; Pathaun forces
Israel, 93, 98, 103n.89, 120–22, 129
— and Egypt (see Egypt, and Israel)
— and Jordan, 1, 47, 52, 68–69, 74, 93, 98, 121, 145, 153–55, 158, 184–85, 192, 197, 208, 217–18
— and Lebanon, 154, 184, 218
— recognition of, 71, 142–43, 145, 147, 167, 205–6
— and Syria, 12, 69, 74–75, 93, 105, 110, 117, 150, 185, 194, 209, 214; case study of, 6, 8, 41, 56; 1948 background, 67–68, 94, 97, 101; 1948–1949 first Arab-Israeli war, 14, 21, 68–70, 97–98, 178, 218 (see also Palestine war); 1949–1967

cease-fire and armistice, 57, 70, 88, 142, 144–45, 147–48, 153–55, 163, 178, 180, 198; 1967 Six-Day war, 1, 53, 17, 70–71, 75, 92–94, 98, 102, 105, 108, 121, 165, 198, 218; 1967–1973 cease-fire, 57, 71, 102, 142–45, 148, 150, 153, 155, 178–79, 181, 192; 1973 Yom Kippur war, 20, 39, 71–72, 75, 92, 101–102, 108, 153, 178, 181, 198, 218; 1973–1982 cease-fire and disengagement agreement, 19n.28, 42, 57, 72, 142–45, 147–48, 153, 155, 158, 165–66, 178–79, 181–82, 185, 188, 192, 198, 200, 205n.87; 1982 Lebanon war, 42, 48n.22, 72–73, 92, 98–99, 102, 108, 121, 143, 145n.69, 147–48, 153, 158, 166–67, 178–79, 181, 188, 199, 205, 218; 1982–present, 43, 73, 155, 179
— and United Nations, 41, 145–46, 204. *See also* Arab-Israeli conflict; Sinai war, United Nations
Israel-Syria Military Armistice Commission (ISMAC), 70, 97, 143, 145, 163–64, 197
issues at stake *See* existence, threat to; stakes of conflict; territorial conflict

Japan, 5n.5
Jinnah, Mohammed Ali, 59n.47
joint commissions. *See* dispute resolution procedures
Jordan and Israel. *See* Israel, and Jordan
Junagadh, 58

Karabakh, 47n.16, 158. *See also* Azeri-Armenian war
Karachi Agreement, 61, 135, 160–61, 200, 202. *See also* India and Pakistan, 1949–1965 cease-fire
Kargil, 60, 66–67, 109, 111, 201, 203. *See also* India, and Pakistan, 1999 Kargil war
Kashmir, 12, 14, 39, 41, 48n.23, 58–67, 88, 91, 95–96, 98, 100–101, 104, 108, 135–37, 160, 162, 184, 208; separatist conflict in, 65–66, 141n.57, 162. *See also* India, and Pakistan
Kennedy, John F., 101
Khan, Liaquat Ali, 59
Khan, Mohammad Ayub, 62–64, 91n.48, 140, 161, 200n.66, 201
Khan, Zafrullah, 140n.51, 200
Kissinger, Henry, 72, 145n.68, 165, 188

Korbel, Josef, 104n.51, 160, 200
Korean war, 1, 9, 12, 46, 53, 87n.35, 89–90, 93, 103, 120–22, 127–29, 132–33, 156, 209, 217; armistice, 1, 29, 43, 49n.28, 50, 55, 151, 153–54, 156, 158, 181, 194–95, 200, 206
Kosygin, Alexei, 64, 186
Kuwait, 52, 122, 153, 208, 218. *See also* Gulf War

large-N qualitative research (*see* research methods
Lebanon, 68, 74, 102, 115n.2, 121, 146, 153–54, 184–85, 217; Israel and Syria in, 72–73, 142–43, 145n.69, 166. *See also* Israel, and Syria, 1982 Lebanon war
Libya, 46n.14, 54–55, 93, 103n.89, 121, 154, 218. *See also* Uganda-Tanzania war
line of control (Kashmir), 65–66, 141n.57, 162, 178, 201, 203
logistic regression, 45, 123, 127n.15

Maharaja of Kashmir, 58–59, 67, 95
Makarios, Archbishop, 110, 190
Malvinas war. *See* Falklands war
Managua, Act of, 156
Maoz/EUGene data set, 53–54, 85–87, 99, 107
Marambio, Brig.Gen. Tulio, 195
Maronites, 72–73. *See also* Lebanon
mediation, 14, 23, 28, 49, 129, 148, 167, 185–88, 195–96, 199, 209–10, 221. *See also* dispute resolution
Meir, Golda, 72n.85, 88, 204
Middle East. *See* Arab-Israeli conflict
military outcome. *See* decisiveness of victory
misperception, 16n.20, 23, 93
mistrust, 3, 11–12, 16. *See also* fear of attack; uncertainty about intentions and capabilities
monitoring, 2, 9, 22–24, 26, 32, 128, 156–57, 185, 187, 189–93 (*see also* peacekeeping); in India-Pakistan conflict, 40, 136, 140–41, 202 (*see also* UNCIP, UNIPOM, UNMOGIP); in Arab-Israeli conflict, 70, 143, 148, 154 (*see also* MFO, MNF I, UNDOF, UNEF, UNTSO)
Mountbatten, Governor General, 59n.45, 95
mujahedin, 63, 160–61. *See also* irregular forces

Somalia, and Ethiopia. *See* Cuba; Ethiopia-Somalia war

South Asia. *See* India-Pakistan conflict

sovereignty, 75, 138, 141, 143, 145, 147–49, 164, 180, 183, 190, 197–98, 212, 216

Soviet Union, 188; in Arab-Israeli conflict, 70–73, 92, 94, 101–102, 109, 146, 164–66, 184n.30, 186, 205; and Hungary (*see* Russo-Hungarian war); in India-Pakistan conflict, 63, 108–109, 141, 186; and United States (*see* Cold War; superpowers)

specificity: effect on durability of peace, 4, 22, 28, 164, 174, 196, 198–99, 210, 215; endogeneity of, 126, 129–30, 143–44; measurement of, 49, 51, 221

spuriousness. *See* agreement strength, endogeneity of

stability/instability paradox, 92n.52

Stag Hunt, 15, 19n.28

stakes of conflict: effect on agreement strength, 117–18, 120, 128–29; effect on durability of peace, 2, 5, 8, 76, 81, 84, 99–103, 112–13; measurement of, 52–53, 54n.36, 219. *See also* existence, threat to

Stern Gang, 184

strategies for maintaining peace, 13, 20–24. *See also* accidents; incentives to attack; uncertainty about intentions and capabilities

superpowers, 41, 92, 101–2, 108–9, 137n.38, 146, 156, 183, 186, 202, 213, 216. *See also* Cold War

surprise attack, 21, 71–72, 181, 190

Sweden, 55, 129n.20

Switzerland, 55, 129n.20

Sykes-Picot Treaty, 67n.70

Syria and Egypt. *See* Egypt, and Syria; United Arab Republic

Syria and Israel. *See* Israel, and Syria

Tanzania and Uganda. *See* Libya; Uganda-Tanzania war

Tashkent, Declaration of, 64, 109, 135, 137, 140–41, 161, 178, 180, 191, 200, 202. *See also* India, and Pakistan, 1965–1971 cease-fire

Ter-Petrossian, Levon, 47n.16

territorial conflict, 100n.81, 157, 177–80; effect on agreement strength, 117–18,

120, 124–26, 128–30, 144, 147; effect on durability of peace, 9, 81–82, 86, 98–99, 103, 107, 112–13, 167, 169; measurement of, 53, 219

terrorism, 66n.66, 67, 163, 184–85

Thant, U, 71n.80, 191, 192n.51, 200n.65, 202

third-party guarantee: effect on durability of peace, 2–3, 5, 9, 21, 27, 167, 174, 185, 187–88, 209–11, 213, 215; endogeneity of, 125–26, 129, 138, 146–47; measurement of, 49, 51, 221

threat. *See* stakes of conflict

tie. *See* decisiveness of victory

time-varying covariates, 47–48, 85, 208

troop withdrawal, 61, 64, 66, 73, 96n.66; effect on durability of peace, 2, 21, 23, 25, 34n.64, 151, 157–60, 167, 173–79, 209–10, 213; endogeneity of, 75, 118, 125–26, 128, 136–37, 139, 142–44, 147; measurement of, 49, 50, 220

Turco-Cypriot war, 23n.4,1 46, 53, 89, 94, 105, 110, 120–22, 153, 156–57, 190, 195, 198, 208, 218

Uganda-Tanzania war, 15n.13, 50, 54–55, 89–90, 93, 99, 103n.89, 120–21, 123, 153–54, 158, 175, 189, 199, 208, 218

uncertainty about intentions and capabilities: as cause of war, 15–16, 35, 93; reducing, 3–4, 22–24, 150–51, 165, 173, 211–12, 214, 216

unitary actors, 11. *See also* internal control; involuntary defection; irregular forces

United Arab Republic, 70, 93. *See also* Egypt, and Syria

United Kingdom, 134n.24, 188; in Arab-Israeli conflict, 14, 67–68, 97, 163; and Argentina (*see* Falklands war); in India-Pakistan conflict, 62, 95–96, 138, 186; in Sinai war, 70, 93, 103, 121, 129, 153, 157, 164, 200, 217; in Turco-Cypriot conflict, 46, 190

United Nations, 25, 185, 205, 213; and Arab-Israeli conflict, 1, 14, 67, 71, 88, 109, 144–46, 154, 163–65, 178, 180, 186; and India-Pakistan conflict, 61, 63, 135–36, 140–41, 154, 160–61, 195, 200, 202; peacekeeping, 26, 40, 115n.2,

GPSR Authorized Representative: Easy Access System Europe - Mustamäe tee
50, 10621 Tallinn, Estonia, gpsr.requests@easproject.com

9 780691 115122